Silvester O

The Good News of Luke's Year

NEW REVISED EDITION

the columba press

This new revised edition, first published in 2000 by
the columba press
55A Spruce Avenue, Stillorgan Industrial Park, Blackrock, Co Dublin
Reprinted 2004

Cover by Bill Bolger
Origination by The Columba Press
Printed in Ireland by Colour Books Ltd, Dublin

ISBN 1 85607 312 2

Contents

Introduction

Since twelve years is a long time in the shelf-life of any product, it is time to give a fresh focus and new presentation to this book of reflections on the Sunday Gospels of Cycle C in the Roman Lectionary.

The changes in Ireland since its first publication in 1988 have been dramatic. The social mood then was very depressing, the economy in serious trouble, unemployment very high, with massive emigration of talented young people resulting in great loss to local communities. These factors have been dramatically reversed by a buoyant economy and the amazing turn about with shortage of people to fill the labour market.

Thanks be to God, the gun and bomb are no longer part of the daily news in Northern Ireland. On the world scale, the Iron Curtain has disappeared, Communist dictatorships have been replaced with scarcely a shot fired, while in South Africa, apartheid has gone from the statute books. Who could have anticipated such rapid changes twelve years ago?

Much has happened in the life of the church. Our composure has been shaken to the roots by the sexual scandals which have been exposed in the last decade of the twentieth century. Who can tell what the next ten years will bring? But of one thing we can be sure: the word of God will not pass away nor lose its relevance. In fact, a period of rapid change is all the more reason for building on the solid rock of God's word, unchanging yet always new.

It is good to report that there has been a notable increase in the number of people taking scripture as the source of prayer, alone and in groups. Particularly heartening is the growth of groups who meet every week to ponder prayerfully on the gospel texts of the Sunday liturgy. I have taken account of the comments of people who have used my reflections on the three cycles of Sunday gospels. Many have told me that they appreciate getting two reflections each week, the first in the style of a commentary on the text, and the other availing of a variety of approaches.

In this new edition I have omitted the Introduction and Good News sections each Sunday and incorporated whatever was of value there into the reflections. Almost one-third of the reflections have been newly written, some to take account of the changes since my first writing, others in the interests of clarity of thought.

Recalling the introduction to the original edition, my own love affair with the gospels goes back to my days in Shanbally National School, Co Cork, where my parents were the teachers. My mother, still happily with us, introduced us to the great stories about God and prepared us for First Communion. After four years in her room we graduated to my father's classroom for a further four years. He possessed a special talent for drawing us into the living atmosphere behind a song, a history lesson or a gospel story, so that each event was newly alive in our telling of it. He always wanted us to retell the stories in our own way and encouraged us to search patiently for the appropriate word to express what we thought. Imaginative reflection on the gospel began for me in the Primary School. To those great parents and wonderful teachers I dedicate this book.

For all who read these pages, I pray that they will be led to the experience of the disciples on the road to Emmaus: 'Did not our hearts burn within us as he talked to us on the road and explained the scriptures to us?' (Lk 24:32)

Silvester O'Flynn OFM Cap
Ard Mhuire,
Easter 2000

First Sunday of Advent

Luke 21: 25-28, 34-36

Jesus said to his disciples: 'There will be signs in the sun and moon and stars; on earth nations in agony, bewildered by the clamour of the ocean and its waves; men dying of fear as they await what menaces the world, for the powers of heaven will be shaken. And then they will see the Son of Man coming in a cloud with power and great glory. When these things begin to take place, stand erect, hold your heads high, because your liberation is near at hand.'

'Watch yourselves, or your hearts will be coarsened with debauchery and drunkenness and the cares of life, and that day will be sprung on you suddenly, like a trap. For it will come down on every living man on the face of the earth. Stay awake, praying at all times for the strength to survive all that is going to happen, and to stand with confidence before the Son of Man.'

First Reflection

The Coming of Christ

Advent is a season of preparation for the coming of Christ. We look back in memory to the first coming of Christ at Christmas and we prepare for his second coming at the end of time. As Advent advances towards Christmas the liturgy will lead our thoughts to people like Isaiah, John the Baptist, Mary and Joseph who were involved in God's plan of preparation. The focus of the first week of Advent is not on Christmas but on the final coming of the Lord at the end of time.

It might seem odd to begin the year with thoughts of the end of life. But this is like consulting a map to check our destination before we start the journey.

The gospel of the day is in that style of writing known as apocalyptic, which means the revelation of divine secrets. We do not exactly know how the physical universe and life on earth came to be. Nor do we know if or how life will cease on earth. Faced with the secrets of God's mind, the biblical writers painted highly imaginative pictures of physical destruction and accompanying terror all around. We read of signs in sun, moon and stars and of fear paralysing people. Perhaps people who have lived through war or the victims of violent abuse will recognise the feelings. It is quite possible that Luke had in mind the stories then circulating of the destruction of the temple in Jerusalem and of the annihilation of Pompeii after the eruption of Mount Vesuvius.

What is most significant about the Good News of Luke is the optimism of his message. Agony and terror are replaced by hope and glory. For the Christian believer the emphasis is not on the physical life which is ending but on the new life which is about to begin. Science fiction films seek the sensational in pictures of cataclysmic destruction and the terror of people in the face of alien powers.

To think about the end of the world as we know it need not be frightening or morbid. It is merely being realistic. To imagine that any of us is going to stay here forever is to live a lie.

Our Christian faith anticipates the ending here as a beginning elsewhere. With Christ on our side who can be against us? In daily contact with him we pray for the strength to survive in faith. He gives us the confidence to look forward to the day of liberation. With deepening wonder we tingle with the excitement of one day knowing the power and glory of the Lord.

Spend time savouring these great messages of hope.

Stand erect.

Hold your heads high.

Your liberation is near at hand.

Stand with confidence before the Son of Man.

Lord Jesus, we ask for a faith that will survive and grow.

We ask for hope that stands firm under trial and testing.

We ask for that love which drives out all fear.

Maranatha, come, Lord Jesus, come.

Second Reflection
Advent Wakefulness

'Stay awake, praying at all times'. What can this 'praying at all times' mean? Saying prayers twenty-four hours of the day? Hardly that. If the ideal is something going on all the time, then surely it must be understood as God's doing more than ours. Prayer is not simply the initiative we take in articulating a relationship with God – be it in petition, thankfulness, praise or whatever. Prayer is much more the result of God's initiative to-wards us: and our part is to respond to him, waiting on him with watchful eye and open ear. Then it is not so much a matter of prayers as prayerfulness. In fact, prayers can be the enemy of prayerfulness: if we talk too much and never listen: or if saying prayers causes such a smug complacency at having the job done that we never get to the depths of thirsting for God.

Advent emphasises prayer as an alert waiting on God. He who once came in the flesh and will come again as liberating Judge, comes every day into our lives in many ways. The prayerful soul is attentive to his coming. In a sense, all of life is an Advent. The celebration of the season draws attention to what is going on all the time – that God is coming to us. Advent is then the vigil of waiting for the Lord while waiting with the Lord.

We wait with the Lord if we live with attentive minds and prayerful hearts. Prayerfulness is the art of seeing and hearing the constant signs and sounds of God's love in our lives. Those who mastered this sensitivity were saints. In the words of T.S. Eliot:

'But to apprehend
the point of intersection of the timeless
with time, is an occupation for the saint.' (*The Dry Salvages*)

But for the most of us there is only the 'unattended moment'. To use a modern image: God is like a great radio station broad-casting to us on many wavelengths. Wherever you are, as you read these words, the air is carrying the broadcast of dozens of radio stations, but the sounds, mercifully, are on a frequency too high for the ear, unaided, to hear. But switch on a radio receiver, turn the tuning dial, and you will pick up a plethora of sounds.

Radio God broadcasts daily on many wavelengths ... through our experiences of life, scripture, nature, people we meet, things we hear, our favourite symbols and so on. But we can all too easily settle for a lifestyle in which we rarely if ever switch on our receivers, rarely make the effort to tune in to the waveband where the eternal God intersects our road of hours and days.

Obviously, if we listen to every and any station except Radio God, then prayer will not even begin for us. The very least we must do is to create space in our time and in our minds for God. And then learn which is the wavelength on which we can best listen to him. It will be difficult for us to be prayerful if we allow our receiving set become damaged – if the sensitivity of the tuner is 'coarsened with debauchery, drunkenness and the cares of life.' These sensual gratifications only draw a veil over the huge abyss in the heart which can be filled by God alone. The experience of St Augustine taught him that the heart is made for God and will know no rest until it comes to rest in him.

The first Sunday of Advent directs our attention to God's return to us and our return to God. We have come from God's creative hand: we wait in hope for his coming as liberating Judge of the world. As our journey began from him and will end with him, it makes perfect sense that life between the beginning and the end should be attentive to him… in prayerfulness. Advent is the vigil of waiting for the Lord while waiting with him.

Second Sunday of Advent

Luke 3: 1-6

In the fifteenth year of Tiberius Caesar's reign, when Pontius Pilate was governor of Judaea, Herod tetrarch of Galilee, his brother Philip tetrarch of the lands of Ituraea and Trachonitis, Lysanias tetrarch of Abilene, during the pontificate of Annas and Caiaphas, the word of God came to John son of Zechariah, in the wilderness. He went through the whole Jordan district proclaiming a baptism of repentance for the forgiveness of sins, as it is written in the book of the sayings of the prophet Isaiah: A voice cries in the wilderness:

Prepare a way for the Lord,
make his paths straight.
Every valley will be filled in,
every mountain and hill be laid low,
winding ways will be straightened
and rough roads made smooth.
And all mankind shall see the salvation of God.

First Reflection
The Wilderness

The good news is that the word of God came to John in the wilderness. This inspired a campaign of repentance to prepare a way for the Lord. This is the first of two Sundays which focus on the mission of the Baptist.

Luke takes us on a geographical tour. The imperial capital was Rome and the religious centre of the Jewish world was Jerusalem. But it was far away from these centres of power that the story begins It was in the wilderness that the word of God came to John. In the wilderness life can survive only with difficulty. Its wildness suggests untamed predators in search of prey.

At that time the Jews were in a political wilderness because their land was divided under the various rulers named by Luke. There was a religious wilderness because of the controversy over the replacement of the high priest Annas with his son-in-law, Caiaphas. And there was a prophetic wilderness because so many years had passed since they last had an outstanding preacher of God's word to inspire the people with vision and hope. Into this wilderness came the word of God to John.

Today, Advent is the season to face whatever wilderness of life we must face and to discern the presence of God's healing word there. The wilderness of life is met

- in the barren times when failure and frustration defy our efforts:
- when the very energy for effort has dried up:
- when the sandstorms of fear obscure the light of God's help:
- where a mirage dances tantalisingly before the imagination in the illusions which tempt us away from the way of truth:
- where the shadows conceal wolves on the prowl for unsuspecting prey, as blind drives and tyrannical compulsions grapple with our resolution.

Unless we honestly face the darker sides of our lives we will not recognise our need of a Saviour.

Who can celebrate Advent? Only those who know their need of a Saviour. Unless you have experienced your weakness and your need of the healing hand of God, you will never appreciate his coming.

How wonderful is God in his ways ... that the story of the coming of the Saviour began ... when the word of God ... came to John ... in the wilderness,

Into my wilderness, come, Lord Jesus, come.

Second Reflection
Advent Examination of Conscience

John, having received the word, proclaimed the urgent need of repentance for the forgiveness of sin. A man with a sense of the dramatic, he led his followers to a symbolic washing in the Jordan. He borrowed his words from the prophet who urged the people to prepare for the journey back from exile to Jerusalem.

The proper celebration of Advent calls for a return to the way of the Lord through a searching confession. The imagery of Isaiah can guide my examination of conscience.

I have paths to straighten wherever my heart has deviated from loving God: whenever I have acted as if God's all-seeing eye had turned away from me: or whenever I allowed anger or resentment blind my remembrance of the way of charity.

The valleys to be filled in are the times when I wandered from the sense of God's presence: or when enthusiasm for God's work was low.

The mountains to be laid low are the obstacles which I imagine to be insurmountable because I have forgotten to trust in God: or the hills to be levelled can be areas of pride where, because I am good at something, I look down on others in judgement.

The winding ways are the delaying tactics I employ on the journey of my soul back to God ... the delays, the postponements and procrastinations ... 'tomorrow, Lord.'

The rough ways to be made smooth are the jagged edges of my personality which irritate others or make me rub them up the wrong way – my insensitivities, my lack of generosity, my unwillingness to compromise, my dominance of others in subtle ways.

The rough ways can be the work of a tongue which is an agent of malice or mockery.

The Lord waits for my return. I will celebrate when I hear the voice of his pardon in my wilderness: and when I see a healing hand raised over me to trace the sign of his cross of salvation.

Third Sunday of Advent

Luke 3: 10-18

When all the people asked John, 'What must we do?' he answered, 'If anyone has two tunics he must share with the man who has none, and the one with something to eat must do the same.' There were tax collectors too who came for baptism, and these said to him, 'Master, what must we do?' He said to them, 'Exact no more than your rate.' Some soldiers asked him in their turn, 'What must we do ?' He said to them, 'No intimidation! No extortion! Be content with your pay!'

A feeling of expectancy had grown among the people, who were beginning to think that John might be the Christ, so John declared before them all, 'I baptise you with the water, but someone is coming, someone who is more powerful than I am, and I am not fit to undo the strap of his sandals; he will baptise you with the Holy Spirit and fire. His winnowing fan is in his hand to clear his threshing-floor and to gather the wheat into his barn; but the chaff he will burn in a fire that will never go out.' As well as this, there were many other things he said to exhort the people and to announce the Good News to them.

First Reflection
Unlikely Listeners

Advent is the story of a God who comes. God is life ... and his creative power must sustain us or we perish. God is light ... and light must shine. God is love ... and love of its very nature must reach out. Who, then, can stop God from coming? It is the mystery of our freedom that we can.

One common mistake is the conviction that we must first prove worthy of God's love by the perfection of our efforts. We wrongly imagine that we will some day advance from the petty squabbles and tatty agitation of the familiar world and then, in that pure, anaesthetised dwelling, we shall have a home worthy of God! But that is like the little boy who thought he was not ready to go to school until he could read and write like his older brothers and sisters.

It is easy to forget that when God came to us in Jesus he was content with a cave as maternity unit and the animals' feeding trough for a cradle. Mary knew that all she had to offer was the virginal womb of her nothingness. If we had the planning of Christmas would we have arranged things along God's lines? Or would we have opted for the best of everything?

The preaching of John the Baptist was good news for many who were given no hope by the religious institutions of the day. The word of God which he proclaimed stirred up in people a surprising willingness to amend their ways. There were many unlikely faces turning towards John. They were excited by the glimpse of a God who would reach out to us in our sinfulness. One did not need to be perfect to come to him. And so, they came willingly, tax collectors and soldiers, hardly foremost in the ranks of piety at the time. A feeling of expectancy had grown among them.

But those who congratulated themselves on their religious observance were not ready to hear. They did not know their need of a Saviour. They had no need of Advent, or so they thought.

Our classical mistake makes us imagine that our meeting with God will take place in the Great-out-there, the land of perfection. Some day I will be ready to meet you, God. The way of incarnation is God telling us that he wants to meet us in the Little-in-here ... in our draughty caves and smelly feeding troughs ... in our wounds of the past and fears of the future ... in our sins and failures, our regrets and frustrations. God is not waiting on the richness of our perfection. Who do we think we are that we might ever be worthy of God?

All God wants of you in Advent is that you would let God be the One who comes ... the God of life, the God of light and the God of love. What God seeks out is our cave and empty trough in the poverty and neediness of our lives.

O God of life ... come to the wintry branches where our lives bear no fruit, where our efforts have failed, where our courage has faltered, where the sap of energy has died. We are poor and we need a Saviour. Come, Lord Jesus, come.

O God of light, come to the dark depths where we live with obscure fears and untamed forces. We are poor and we need a Saviour. Come, Lord Jesus, come.

O God of love, desiring to reach into our hearts, come to the unredeemed areas where we block your love ... where we know jealousy, lust, impatience, pride, anger and bitterness. We are poor and we need a Saviour. Come, Lord Jesus, come.

Second Reflection
Someone is Coming

'What must we do?' The sinners who came to John discovered a new energy in their lives and a willingness to do something about improving. His message touched the winter of their lives with a glimpse of spring ... 'Someone is coming' And the sap of energy began to race through their veins.

The celebration of Advent-Christmas is intimately related to the return of the sun after the winter solstice. From my desk I look through the window over our precious vegetable garden, now in the sleep of mid-winter. The hard grip of frost is breaking down the upturned sods into a fine tilth. The scattered compost, in losing its former composition, is returning a rich, tacky substance to the earth. Spring sowing will be in more fertile soil, thanks to winter. I have learned to love the contribution of winter's night-sleep to spring's morning-energy. The thought of the first crocus peeping through the grass, like the flickering of the eyelids of mother earth makes the sleep of winter loveable. That's the glimpse of future that we call hope. Someone is coming ... Someone more powerful. As fire is a more powerful element of change than the water in which John stood. Fire to warm the bones, to light the night, to melt and purify and change things. Fire to boil and bake and cook. Fire to draw people together and flames to tickle the imagination. Or fire to threaten destruction, to consume the rubbish and empty chaff of life. John's message of life was a mixture of fear and hope. Fear that a dire sentence would fall unless people amended their ways. And hope that something could be done about conversion. Fear on its own would have paralysed initiative.

It was the glimpse of future which generated the energy to ask, 'What must we do?'

O God, may I always know you as Someone-is-Coming. May I experience my loneliness as a space for your company, my darkness as the stretching of my sight to your vastness, my coldness as the need for your warmth, my inertia as the sleep which restores energy, my winter as an enriching season before spring's excitement.

Take me and use me, Lord, to be someone-coming for others. Make me caring towards those who are neglected, sensitive towards all who are hurt. Use me as good news for those who only know the sadness of sin, as the spark of joy for those who are down and depressed.

How beautiful upon the mountains are the feet of one who brings good news. Grant me beautiful feet, Lord.

Fourth Sunday of Advent

Luke 1: 39-44

Mary set out at that time and went as quickly as she could to a town in the hill country of Judah. She went into Zachariah's house and greeted Elizabeth. Now as soon as Elizabeth heard Mary's greeting, the child leapt in her womb and Elizabeth was filled with the Holy Spirit. She gave a loud cry and said, 'Of all women you are the most blessed, and blessed is the fruit of your womb. Why should I be honoured with a visit from the mother of my Lord? For the moment your greeting reached my ears, the child in my womb leapt for joy. Yes, blessed is she who believed that the promise made her by the Lord would be fulfilled.'

First Reflection

A Blessed Day

There is an old tradition that the evangelist Luke was a portrait painter. Whatever the truth of that claim, he certainly had a marvellous ability to paint a picture in words. The events surrounding the births of John the Baptist and Jesus are picture-stories painted onto two separate panels.

Luke liked the theme of a journey. The great story he was telling was about God's journey into our lives to take us back from exile to our heavenly home. There would be important journeys to Bethlehem and to the temple in Jerusalem. And in the life of Jesus he would resolutely journey to his destiny in Jerusalem. But today's story is about Mary's journey.

Mary had been informed by the angel of Elizabeth's pregnancy. It is easy to understand how she was moved with compassion for her aged cousin, who was surely in need of young, helpful hands.

But there was a deeper, personal motive which lent haste to Mary's steps in that countryside of hills. The deep, interior experience of God which came to her at the Angel's annunciation was something she needed to share with another.

How often have we seen that a deep, inner experience

changes one's entire perspective, creating an urgent need to travel. The familiar world of everyday experience is no longer large enough to contain the experience. Abraham, the first person to receive divine revelation, immediately set out on a journey from his father's house and country.

Elizabeth had been offered to Mary as a sign that nothing is impossible to God. It was not as if Mary needed to verify the sign. No, her inner need was to share with somebody who might understand the great mystery which had begun to grow in her virginal womb. It was an immense joy to Mary when she saw that Elizabeth too had been gifted by the Holy Spirit.

Luke catches the mood of their meeting as a joyous celebration of God's work. That beautiful word 'blessed', which tells of God's giving, is heard three times.

'Of all women you are the most blessed': this celebrates what God has done in his election of Mary.

'Blessed is the fruit of your womb': in this second blessing Elizabeth celebrates how the grace bestowed upon Mary will be a divine fruitfulness for all of us.

'Yes, blessed is she who believed that the promise made her by the Lord would be fulfilled.' The third blessing is about the free and total co-operation of Mary with God. Her personal greatness lay in the depth of her faith and the totality of her obedience. Later in the gospel we will hear Jesus praise her faith and obedience: 'Blessed is she who heard the word of God and put it into practice.' (Lk 8:21)

She was chosen by God to be the personal way of God's journey into our lives to embrace us in his healing and uplifting hands. Saint Francis encouraged devotion to Mary because she received the Lord of majesty and gave him to us for our brother. The heights of divine majesty reach down to our poor, broken condition. And in becoming human, the Son of God becomes our brother, our lover, our healer and redeemer. Mary, in her free co-operation with God, is central in that story.

Elizabeth discerned the blessedness of that day when Mary came to visit her. Even the unborn babe in her womb was caught up in the joy that God was visiting our world to become our brother.

The story of the visitation is a joy for us too. For the blessed fruit of Mary's womb is to be our Lord and Saviour.

Second Reflection

Leaping for joy

'The child in my womb leapt for joy'.

St Luke had a great sense of the joy which comes with receiving the good news. The gift of God which is received interiorly wells up into praising and blessing, glorifying and magnifying, rejoicing and leaping in celebratory dance.

True joy of spirit is one of the surest signs of a life attuned to God's loving presence. Among the fruits of the Spirit's indwelling, St Paul listed joy in second place, immediately after love.

A first effect of joy is the desire to share the experience with others. But talk of joy, if it is not carried into practical action, will be offensive to those who do not have the necessities of life, or who do not know what love is, or who walk in the darkness of unbelief. Times of celebration such as Christmas put an extra strain on the lonely and depressed who become more aware of what they are missing. The historical pilgrimage of Christian joy has motivated believers to enrich the world with countless ministries of service and caring. The beauty of it all is the way that the joy which is shared comes back with interest.

Those who share out of their joy know from experience that it is in giving that we receive.

A second operation of joy is a new way of seeing things. The soul that is attuned to God's presence is introduced to the beauty of the world. Joy in the Lord opens our eyes to the thrilling beauty of God to be seen along the everyday road to life. The glory and mystery of God is reflected in nature's adornment and the rhythm of seasons. The simple parables of Jesus express how his mind saw the mysteries of heaven reflected in the ordinary things of earth. Joy opens the eye to the uniqueness of the commonplace, to the goodness and quiet heroism of people, to the honest satisfaction of labour. And the pleasures of life and gratification of the senses are returned in thanks to God. In this joyful vision of beauty the Giver is appreciated behind every gift.

A third area of joy is in believing.

To believe ... *credere* ... *cor dare* ... is to give your heart to what is revealed of God. The joy of believing means that one knows in the heart that God so loved the world that he gave his only Son... that Jesus, having loved those who were his in the world, loved us to the end in a worldwide embrace. To believe is to know in the heart the sustaining, healing and forgiving love of God in the sacraments.

Believing is knowing intimacy with God whose Spirit is given to us.

True joy is in the ocean depth of the soul. It's equanimity is preserved beneath the agitations and storms on the daily surface of life.

True joy withstands the test of suffering whereas superficial bonhomie will evaporate. In fact, joy in the Lord often grows with suffering because it is a purifying process. The more that self-gratification is taken away, the more space there is for God to be our joy.

'The deeper that sorrow carves into your being, the more joy you can contain. Is not the cup that holds your wine the very cup that was burned in the potter's oven. And is not the lute that soothes your spirit the very wood that was hollowed with knives.' (Kahlil Gibran: *The Prophet*)

It was in prison that St Paul came to recognise the joy of his faith. His letter to the Philippians bears testimony to his joy in the midst of suffering. There is only one source of this joy – the conviction that the Lord is very near. 'I want you to be happy, always happy in the Lord... the Lord is very near.' (Phil 4:4-5)

The Lord is near ... that's the reason for Advent joy. Let your soul leap for joy. Let your whole countenance announce the good news to the world.

Christmas Day

Luke 2: 1-20

Now at this time Caesar Augustus issued a decree for a census of the whole world to be taken. This census – the first – took place while Quirinius was governor of Syria, and everyone went to his own town to be registered. So Joseph set out from the town of Nazareth in Galilee and travelled up to Judaea, to the town of David called Bethlehem, since he was of David's House and line, in order to be registered together with Mary, his betrothed, who was with child. While they were there the time came for her to have her child, and she gave birth to a son, her first-born. She wrapped him in swaddling clothes, and laid him in a manger because there was no room for them at the inn.

In the countryside close by there were shepherds who lived in the fields and took it in turn to watch their flocks during the night. The angel of the Lord appeared to them and the glory of the Lord shone round them. They were terrified, but the angel said, 'Do not be afraid. Listen, I bring you news of great joy, a joy to be shared by the whole people. Today in the town of David a saviour has been born to you; he is Christ the Lord. And here is a sign for you: you will find a baby wrapped in swaddling clothes and lying in a manger.' And suddenly with the angel there was a great throng of the heavenly host, praising God and singing:

'Glory to God in the highest heaven,

and peace to men who enjoy his favour'.

Now when the angels had gone from them into heaven, the shepherds said to one another, 'Let us go to Bethlehem and see this thing that has happened which the Lord has made known to us'. So they hurried away and found Mary and Joseph, and the baby lying in the manger. When they saw the child they repeated what they had been told about him, and everyone who heard it was astonished at what the shepherds had to say. As for Mary, she treasured all these things and pondered them in her heart. And the shepherds went back glorifying and praising God for all they had heard and seen; it was exactly as they had been told.

First Reflection

Meetings

It was a night of meetings. On that night a meeting of heaven and earth, between God and humanity, took place such as never before or since. From the most important man in the world, Caesar Augustus, came a decree which touched on the lives of two unimportant people in a remote backwash, Joseph and Mary. Rome, capital of the political world, was linked with humble Bethlehem, the little house of bread. In a glorious reversal of roles the time would come when Rome would realise how blessed for her was that meeting. In the countryside closeby there were shepherds who lived in the fields. In a religion which highly regarded laws of hygiene, these field-dwellers were held in low esteem. But the vastness of heaven entered their field and the glory of God shone in their night. Their natural terror was assuaged by words of peace and joy.

The silence of night erupted into a heavenly chorus celebrating the glory of God and the blessing of peace. The shepherds were directed to Bethlehem. There in the memory of David, the shepherd who became king, they found the King who became Shepherd. He who would describe his role as a shepherd in search of lost sheep, was introduced on the stage of the world by shepherds.

All these circumstances of the event are part of the flavour of Luke's story. When God stepped into the story of humanity, the people who were caught up in the event were the poor and religiously despised, the little people of the world ... those who were empty enough to receive, silent enough to listen and open enough to wonder. But there was no room for them at the inn which was too full, too noisy and too closed to the wonder of the skies.

Luke as a writer had the gift of entering into the feelings and inner reactions of people. The initial reaction of the shepherds was terror. We will always be terrified of meeting God if we keep thinking that we must be worthy of meeting him. The angel had to urge them to let go of their terror. Only then did the wonder of the night begin to enter into their souls. They spoke of their wonder and everybody who heard them was astonished. Only those who know the littleness of their own fields can be open to the wonder of greater realities. Mary, the littlest of all, treasured these things and pondered them in her heart. She knew that the full wonder could not be absorbed all at once. The

shepherds meanwhile took up the song of the angels and responded to all that they had experienced by glorifying and
praising God.

It was a night of meetings, when the vastness of heaven met
the confined fields of earth, when the richness of heaven invaded
the poverty of cave and manger, when the glorious chorus of angels filled the silence of night. It was the night which brought in
the day of glorifying and praising God.

Second Reflection
The Compassion of God

The Second Mass of Christmas Day uses the words of Paul to
Titus: 'When the kindness and love of God our saviour for
mankind were revealed, it was not because he was concerned
with any righteous actions we might have done ourselves; it was
for no reason except his own compassion that he saved us.'

People needed a saviour and healer but could never have
merited or deserved what happened at Christmas. The coming
of the Son of God into our human condition was an act of divine
kindness and love. St Paul wrote of compassion to express God's
initiative when his love for us made him move towards us.
Compassion means that God in Jesus would wear our human
skin, walk in our shoes, look out at the world through our eyes,
enjoy love or suffer rejection with our hearts. He would live in
our kind of living, celebrate in our joys, weep in our tears, suffer
in our humiliations and give thanks in our accomplishments. He
would feel with our emotions, think with our thoughts, fear in
our forebodings and stand up in our courage.

He was born in our infancy, grew in our childhood, advanced in our maturing and died in our dying. In compassion he
reached down to us ... wherever in human life we are. Now we
know for sure that there is no hiding from God even though in
the ignorance of sin we might think we have lost him, in the
blindness of self-importance we might try to go it alone, or in the
anger of pride we might fancy that we have rebelled against
him. In compassion he reached down to us ... wherever in life
we might be ... so as to touch our skin and heal our leprosy and
raise us up. He raised us up to a life far beyond any human expectation or merit. 'To all who did accept him he gave power to
become children of God.' (Jn 1:11)

In his compassion God shared in human life so that we might
share in God's life. An ancient liturgical antiphon marvels at this

wonderful exchange in which we become sharers in the divinity of him who humbled himself to take on our humanity.

All we need in order to receive the compassion of God at Christmas is a cave and a feeding trough or manger. We have a cave of emptiness when we acknowledge our sinfulness and recognise our need of a saviour. The manger is there in the heart that hungers for God's presence, thirsts for his will and desires his beauty.

The first cave and manger were at Bethlehem, which means the house of bread. Each Eucharist is a new house of bread, a new Bethlehem, a new meeting with God, who reaches down in compassion to us to raise us up.

The Holy Family
(Sunday within the octave of Christmas)

Luke 2: 41-52
Every year his parents used to go to Jerusalem for the feast of the
Passover. When he was twelve years old, they went up for the feast as
usual. When they were on their way home after the feast, the boy Jesus
stayed behind in Jerusalem without his parents knowing it. They as-
sumed he was with the caravan, and it was only after a day's journey
that they went to look for him among their relations and acquaintances.
When they failed to find him they went back to Jerusalem looking for
him everywhere.

Three days later, they found him in the Temple, sitting among the
doctors, listening to them, and asking them questions; and all those
who heard him were astounded at his intelligence and his replies. They
were overcome when they saw him, and his mother said to him, 'My
child, why have you done this to us? See how worried your father and I
have been, looking for you.' 'Why were you looking for me?' he replied.
'Did you not know that I must be busy with my Father's affairs?' But
they did not understand what he meant.

He then went down with them and came to Nazareth and lived
under their authority. His mother stored all these things in her heart.
And Jesus increased in wisdom, in stature, and in favour with God and
men.

First Reflection
Hidden in the Family
Jesus lived the hidden life at Nazareth for thirty years before
he taught and worked in the public eye for three years. For every
year in public life he spent ten years in homely life. Surely in that
silence there is a great message from God about the importance
of family relationships and everyday work.

The hands that would minister healing and comfort were not
too proud to be soiled in weeding the garden or notched by chisel
and splinter. The Son of the Eternal Father was happy to be
known as the son of Joseph and Mary. The Word who is the perfect image and expression of the Father had to mature in human

relationships as son, as brother-cousin, as neighbour and as the lad down the road. We are left to speculate on whether he was good at the games the local children played, did he have favourite hobbies, how did his teachers find him or did ever a girl cast a hopeful eye in his direction. Jesus advanced in wisdom, he grew in physical stature and matured in favourable relationships with God and people.

The family was the greatest school of his life. In the family school the principal subject is People. One learns to live off people, for people and with people. Living off people means learning to depend on others. Trust in others is the first great lesson in the family school and the pupil who fares badly at this subject will have serious emotional problems all through life. In learning to trust people we learn something of our relationship with the Father on whose continuing act of creation we totally depend. It is noteworthy that in the prayer of Jesus his favourite word for God is Abba, the family name for father. His prayer language must have developed from his experience of dependence and trust in the family home at Nazareth.

Living for people is our way of returning the contribution. The person who in childhood received, now in growing learns to share and give. Jesus developed into a man whose ideal was to serve rather than to be served and to give his very life for others. He became the man for others.

Living with people demands the harmony of being able to receive and to give, each at the proper time. This double movement, to and fro, is an expression of the Holy Spirit who is the unifying love between the giving of the Father and the returning of the Son.

The dynamics of family life prepare us for entering into the eternal movements of the inner life of God. Just as the submission of Jesus to the human authority of Joseph and Mary prepared him for submission to the final demands of the Father.

Second Reflection
Lost and Found

Luke's episode in Jerusalem when Jesus was twelve is a bridge between the growing years and the public life, a link between the subjection of Jesus to family authority and his later submission to the demands of the Father's will.

At the age of twelve a Jewish boy attained *bar mitzvah*, which meant becoming a son of the Law. He, towards whom the Law was a pointer, was now celebrating his becoming a full son of that Law. The family celebrated the event by making pilgrimage to Jerusalem for the Passover. Luke narrates the story as a minor statement of a major theme which he will later develop. The public career of Jesus was to become a journey to Jerusalem, and his arrival there would be again at the time of the Passover. There he would encounter the experts in the Law with the important difference that their astonishment in the boyhood episode was to become a rejection in the adult encounter. In each story Jesus is lost from sight, as it were, for some days. The way that his parents were overcome upon finding him on the third day anticipates the stunning news of his resurrection on the third day. The boy Jesus explained that he must be busy with his Father's affairs. The same sense of necessity was expressed by the risen Christ to the men on the road: 'Was it not ordained that the Christ should suffer and so enter into his glory?' (Lk 24:26).

At twelve, Jesus was no longer child and not yet fully adult. He is at a stage of losing and finding, of leaving and entering, of letting go and making commitment. The temple incident offered a glimpse of what must develop. Childhood relationships must be let go if adult responsibility is to be undertaken. The intimacy of the family circle must expand to the strangeness of the larger community. The subjection of the child to human parents must give way to the greater authority of the heavenly Father. Later he would echo that theme in his teaching: one must let go of life in order to find it: bread must be broken before it can be shared: Jesus had to die in the flesh before he was raised in the Spirit.

Having glimpsed the future, Jesus went back to Nazareth and family. He waited on the call, increasing in wisdom, in stature and in favour with God and people.

Second Sunday after Christmas

John 1: 1-18

In the beginning was the Word: the Word was with God and the Word was God. He was with God in the beginning. Through him all things came to be, not one thing had its being but through him. All that came to be had life in him and that life was the light of men, a light that shines in the dark, a light that darkness could not overpower.

A man came, sent by God. His name was John. He came as a witness, as a witness to speak for the light, so that everyone might believe through him. He was not the light, only a witness to speak for the light.

The Word was the true light that enlightens all men: and he was coming into the world. He was in the world that had its being through him, and the world did not know him. He came to his own domain and his own people did not accept him. But to all who did accept him he gave power to become children of God, to all who believe in the name of him who was born not out of human stock or urge of the flesh or will of man but of God himself. The Word was made flesh, he lived among us, and we saw his glory, the glory that is his as the only Son of the Father, full of grace and truth.

John appears as his witness. He proclaims: 'This is the one of whom I said: He who comes after me ranks before me because he existed before me.'

Indeed, from his fullness we have, all of us, received – yes, grace in return for grace, since, though the Law was given through Moses, grace and truth have come through Jesus Christ. No one has ever seen God: it is the only Son who is nearest to the Father's heart, who has made him known.

First Reflection
The Word was made flesh

To believe with John that the historical, flesh-and-blood Jesus of Nazareth was truly God demands the mind to accept some extraordinary conclusions. The timeless steps into the laws of time. The infinite, unlimited, comes into the restrictions of the finite. The creator accepts the condition of creature. The ocean fits into our bucket … the sky is caught in a puddle … the sun is seen through a pinhole

Christian spirituality has always felt the tension of two opposing pulls in the soul's response to God. In the one direction is the statement that God is too great for the human mind to understand: hence, to us his light is blinding darkness: and the way to him is through 'unknowing' or unlearning all rational ways of thought. In the other direction is the statement that in Jesus the Word was made flesh: that God has spoken to us in a language we can understand, the language of the human life of Jesus. He called himself the light of the world and intended his followers to walk in his light. Hence, knowing Jesus offers the way, the truth and the light of life.

To know Jesus is truly to know God. John holds both polarities together in saying that while no one has ever seen God, yet the only Son, enfleshed, has made him known. God is greater than all yet closer to us than we are to ourselves. God is beyond the ages yet he supports every single moment of time.

God is sublime, distant beyond our imagination, yet not a hair from your head falls without his knowing it. We are caught in the magnificent tension between his majestic power and his intimate care. God the unknowable is made known in Jesus in an enfleshed word that we can understand up to the fullness of our limitations. 'He lived among us, and we saw his glory, the glory that is his as the only Son of the Father, full of grace and truth.' The ocean fits into our bucket.

Second Reflection
He pitched his tent among us

Since the incarnation of the Son of God there is a new depth of sacredness in all things. In putting on human flesh the Son of God has touched everything on earth. The flesh he wore, the bones and juices of his body were made up of the same chemical elements as the everyday things before our eyes.

So deeply was the reality of the incarnation impressed upon the mind of Francis of Assisi that he understood Jesus as the Brother of all things. He addressed all created things as brother and sister because first there had been Brother Christ. He was drawn into a special reverence for those creatures which were associated with Christ in any way by the Scriptures. Lambs, rocks, wood, worms and light were special reminders of Jesus for him because of their mention in the sacred texts.

The highly developed mystical sensitivity of Francis can be a pointer for everybody towards the sacredness of creation which has been touched, entered and put on by the Son of God. Yet his enfleshed dwelling among us was transitory. John says that he 'pitched his tent' among us. The image of the tent dweller suggests one who is moving on, not settling down or staying put in the one place. The Lord in his enfleshed life was a pilgrim moving through this world.

His journey was from the Father, down into human life at its lowest depths, and then back from there in triumphant return to the Father. Being a pilgrim he had nowhere permanent to lay his head and was not in the least interested in amassing earthly riches. So, although he was clad in the flesh, yet he made an option for the things of the spirit over those of the flesh.

Francis may have been the mystic brother of all created things, but being first a faithful follower of Jesus, he did not settle for the beauty of the world but hurried beyond it to Beauty itself. His biographer remarked that to him all things were good. Yet they pointed beyond, crying, 'He who made us is best.' Since the incarnation there is a new depth of holiness to all things. Yet they are transitory and part of the pilgrimage of life. The fullness of reality is reached in joining Jesus in his return to the Father.

Feast of the Epiphany

Matthew 2: 1-12

After Jesus had been born at Bethlehem in Judaea during the reign of King Herod, some wise men came to Jerusalem from the east. 'Where is the infant king of the Jews?' they asked. 'We saw his star as it rose and have come to do him homage.' When King Herod heard this he was perturbed, and so was the whole of Jerusalem. He called together all the chief priests and the scribes of the people, and inquired of them where the Christ was to be born. 'At Bethlehem in Judaea,' the told him 'for this is what the prophet wrote: 'And you, Bethlehem, in the land of Judah, you are by no means least among the leaders of Judah, for out of you will come a leader who will shepherd my people Israel.'

Then Herod summoned the wise men to see him privately. He asked them the exact date on which the star had appeared, and sent them on to Bethlehem. 'Go and find out all about the child,' he said 'and when you have found him, let me know, so that I too may go and do him homage.' Having listened to what the king had to say, they set out. And there in front of them was the star they had seen rising; it went forward and halted over the place where the child was. The sight of the star filled them with delight, and going into the house they saw the child with his mother Mary, and falling to their knees they did him homage. Then, opening their treasures, they offered him gifts of gold and frankincense and myrrh. But they were warned in a dream not to go back to Herod, and returned to their own country by a different way.

First Reflection
An imaginative story

Matthew's story is the product of a rich imagination expanding on the wider dimensions of Christmas. He expects the reader to go beyond the factual details of the scene at Bethlehem in order to draw out its message for all times and places. He invites us to step out into the world of stars and astrologers, and to move into the inner world of memory and dreams. The Jewish past is evoked by subtle allusion and the future is suggested by symbolic gifts.

Inner meanings are more important in this story than the outer details of history and astronomy. There is no need to search for the identity or background of the wise men. They represent all people who make an honest search for the truths of life.

Nor need we consult the history of astronomy to verify the appearance of some large star or conjunction of lights. The star they followed is called 'his star', for it was popularly believed that a new star appeared at the birth of any great future leader. This star represents the light of God which is sent to everybody on their pilgrimage of life. Though stars may be distant lights and pale in comparison with the sun or moon, yet they were always the great direction finders for those who navigated the seas. God will never fail to send us the star of guidance through the darkness of night and the stormy seas of life.

The wise men found, however, that the light of nature could only lead them so far. They needed the divine wisdom which was stored in the Jewish revelation to enable them to complete their journey. The light of revelation directed them towards Bethlehem and confirmed their hopes of a new leader and shepherd.

The behaviour of Herod, who was perturbed and paranoid, recalled the memory of Egypt at the time when Moses was born. Matthew is anxious that his readers would begin to see the parallel between Jesus and Moses, who led his people out of slavery and delivered to them the law of the covenant.

The wise men travelled forward until the light halted over the place where the child was. They happily entered the house and, falling on their knees, they paid homage. At the time when Matthew was writing the Gentile people were flocking into the house of the church whereas the Jews remained where they were and refused to follow the light of Christ to journey forward.

The wise men offered their gifts of gold, frankincense and myrrh. Matthew may have intended us to see these as part of the stock-in-trade of the magi, the magic-men of natural religion. But now these are offered as gifts to the babe at Bethlehem in recognition of his unique lordship. Christian commentators have delighted in seeing these gifts as symbolic expressions of Jesus' future destiny. Gold represents his kingship: incense expresses his priestly role: and the myrrh of anointing anticipates his redeeming death.

The wise men were warned in a dream not to go back to Herod but to return to their own country by another way. Dreams are often used in the bible as a source of God's guidance as they offer a more total vision, in the light of which an alternative course of action can be seen.

Matthew's story is accompanied in the liturgy with two readings and a psalm which together proclaim the coming of all nations to the Lord. Today, however, we are witnessing the movement in reverse, with people drifting away from the house of the church. Ironically many are going back to the very things that the wise men left behind them.

Stars have again become the substitute gods for those who believe that the likes of Taurus or Gemini control their lives and destinies.

Gold stands for the materialism which chokes the spiritual sensitivity and capacity for God in so many people. The frankincense represents the incense that is burnt to create the atmosphere of meditation which is cultivated by those who prefer some oriental vagueness to the clarity of the Christian revelation. And the myrrh of bodily embalming represents that excessive cult of the body which neglects the calls of the spirit. Obviously, development of meditation and deep respect for the body, which is the temple of the soul, are important, but they should not be ends in themselves, growing into substitute religions. The Epiphany is the recognition of Jesus Christ alone as the leader and shepherd of all people. He is the divine king, the eternal priest and the anointed redeemer

Second Reflection
An invitation to believe

The Epiphany is a celebration of faith. The feast celebrates how the divinity of Jesus was manifested in a very special way in the story of the Magi, at his baptism in the Jordan, and at the wedding feast at Cana.

Those who were drawn by God to see beyond the scope of the eyes of the flesh became believers. Faith is the gift of being able to move beyond the external sign to the One towards whom the sign points. John concludes the Cana story with the statement: 'He let his glory be seen, and his disciples believed in him.'

In Matthew's story the wise men represent the believer: Herod stands for the unbeliever.

The wise men observed the star and heard the word. They let themselves be led forward unto where the star halted. There they went into the house. Their travels were but the expression of the inner journey they were making through imagination, intuition, memory and association of ideas. This journey eventually entered into faith and adoration.

The gifts they offered were symbolic. It is interesting that the word 'symbolic' comes from the Greek for the movement of things together towards unification. And the opposite movement is 'diabolic', literally the tearing of things apart.

An educational system which is heavily weighted towards scientific, left-brain functioning teaches people to control things by analysis and separation of parts. Divide and conquer. If the corresponding right-brain function which sees totality and relationships is neglected, then the system must be literally diabolical. Is it any wonder then that many people today find it hard to believe? Or that sexual behaviour can be separated or divorced from faithful love? Or that far more of the world's money is spent on keeping enemies apart and stockpiling weapons of destruction than on facilitating brotherhood and feeding the hungry.

Herod is the unbeliever in the story. No signs could move him to journey towards that house of faith. He remained where he was, in the outside world of facts concerning exact dates and location. His vision of kingdom could not see beyond the possibility of a threat to his own position. He was perturbed. Even a tiny infant was a threat to be removed at the most horrific cost.

The diabolical mind cannot let go of control, or embrace in love, or bow in homage. It separates the details, tears asunder... tore the child from mother's breast and killed. To kill is the ultimate diabolical act.

The act of faith must employ the imagination and intuitive powers of the brain to make the leap beyond the details which are immediately accessible to the outer senses. Only then does one move from the parts to the whole, from the footprints to the One who made them. Matthew's story is an invitation to journey with the flickering light of the rising star and the wisdom of scripture and to enter into the house of faith.

The Baptism of the Lord
(Sunday after Epiphany)

Luke 3: 15-16. 21-22

A feeling of expectancy had grown among the people, who were beginning to think that John might be the Christ, so John declared before them all, 'I baptise you with water, but someone is coming, someone who is more powerful than I am, and I am not fit to undo the strap of his sandals; He will baptise you with the Holy Spirit and fire.'

Now when all the people had been baptised and while Jesus after his own baptism was at prayer, heaven opened and the Holy Spirit descended on him in bodily shape, like a dove. And a voice came from heaven, 'You are my Son, the Beloved; my favour rests on you.'

First Reflection
The Life of Baptism

Baptism comes from a Greek word for having a bath or a good wash. Some form of ceremony with water is an obvious symbol for washing off the dirt of past misbehaviour as one seeks to enter a renewed state of life. John the Baptist urged people to repent of their sinful ways and to manifest their new commitment by undergoing a ceremonial washing in the waters of the Jordan river.

Water is a symbol rich with many layers of meaning. We use it for washing off dirt, so expressing the washing away of guilt. Water is a force of death but also of life. The waters of the flood brought destruction and death. But as a life giving force, no form of life can survive without water.

John's ceremonial washing stirred up a messianic expectancy among the people. But he was quick to point beyond himself to the one coming after him, whose baptism would be more than a washing but would be invested with the Holy Spirit and the fire of divine life.

Unlike Matthew and Mark, Luke tells us nothing of the actual baptism of Jesus by John: he merely notes that it happened. His interest is more in the divine manifestation that happened afterwards.

We notice that Luke says that Jesus was at prayer. The prayers of Advent were that God would tear open the heavens and come to us. In answer to that plea, heaven opened and the divine presence was manifested in two ways: in the appearance of the Holy Spirit in bodily or visible shape as a dove; and in the voice of the Father. Scripture always respects the majesty of the Father whom no mortal person has ever seen or can see.

Luke is the evangelist of the Holy Spirit and of prayer. He has already told of the coming of the Holy Spirit to Mary, Elizabeth, Zechariah and Simeon. At the beginning of the Acts he will describe a dramatic scene at the coming of the Holy Spirit upon the apostles at Pentecost. In all of these cases people received divine power from on high.

At the descent of the Spirit upon Jesus his divine identity is proclaimed. He is the beloved Son of God the Father.

John the Baptist promised that Jesus would give them a baptism with the Holy Spirit and fire. At the end of his mission on earth the Risen Lord sent out the disciples to all nations instructing them to baptise people in the name of the Father and of the Son and of the Holy Spirit.

'In the name of' is a formula to express the presence and power of the person invoked. In the new life symbolised by the water of baptism a person is lifted up into a new relationship with the three divine persons.

In the water of baptism a person enters into the death of Jesus in the cleansing of original sin and of sins committed before baptism. Saint Paul understood immersion into baptismal water as entering into the tomb with the Lord. Then, coming out of the water and being clad in the white garment denoted sharing in the life of the Risen Lord emerging from the tomb. The name Christian may originally have been used as a sort of nickname, but happily it is the proper name for somebody who now shares in the life of Jesus Christ and is a member of his living body on earth.

Adopted into divine life in Christ, we are taught by him to call on God as our Father. Saint Paul wrote of the Holy Spirit moving the soul to pray in the outreach of a child to 'Abba, Father'.

The Holy Spirit is the fire of divine life in the Christian soul. The person who is in daily converse with the Spirit and who co-operates with grace grows with the fruits of love, joy, peace, harmonious relationships with others and gentle inner strength.

The feast of the Baptism of the Lord is a day for Christians to celebrate our adoption into divine life in the sacrament of our baptism. Let us hear the Father say to us in the depth of our heart: 'You are my beloved child: rejoice in the favours I bestow on you.'

Second Reflection
Like a dove

They say that a picture paints a thousand words. A symbol opens up rich possibilities which the analytical mind, for all its labour, cannot make available. The dove invites the mind to make connections, to remember, to savour the atmosphere.

Birds frequently flit across the pages of Scripture. Jesus pointed to the providential feeding of the birds when he wanted to warn against excessive anxiety about the morrow. Life is so precious in God's eyes that the humble sparrow, sold so cheaply in the market, is not forgotten in his sight.

The pilgrim psalmist arriving at the temple noticed the sparrow and swallow nesting in the eaves of the sacred building and yearned for their privilege of dwelling in the house of the Lord all their days.

The freedom of the bird is envied by one weighed down under the fatigue of worry and care. How one would escape from the pressure, fly like a bird to its mountain!

The great bird of the mountain is the eagle. The little eaglet learning to fly has to venture out some day from a lofty eyrie. As the young wings quickly tire, the little one seems sure to crash helplessly to the rocks beneath. But the watchful parent swoops underneath and carries it up on outstretched wings. Such is God's care for us when a complete collapse seems imminent. 'Like an eagle watching its nest, hovering over its young, he spreads out his wings to hold him, he supports him on his pinions.' (Deut 32:11)

The dove descending on Jesus at the Jordan recalls the picture of God's spirit hovering over the primeval waters in the story of creation. These were the waters of new life. The flood in the days of Noah brought the waters of destruction. But when peace with God is restored, the messenger with the good news is a dove bearing the olive branch.

Luke would write of the power of the Spirit as the dynamic energy of the mission of Jesus and later of the apostolate of the church. Power on its own can lead to pride and domination. So it

is balanced by the remembrance of the dove as the gentle messenger of peace and reconciliation.

Come then, my love, my lovely one come.

My dove, hiding in the clefts of the rock, in the coverts of the
cliff,

show me your face, let me hear your voice;

for your voice is sweet and your face is beautiful.

(Song of Songs 2:14)

First Sunday of Lent

Luke 4: 1-13

Filled with the Holy Spirit, Jesus left the Jordan and was led by the Spirit through the wilderness, being tempted there by the devil for forty days. During that time he ate nothing and at the end he was hungry. Then the devil said to him, 'If you are the Son of God, tell this stone to turn into a loaf'. But Jesus replied, 'Scripture says: Man does not live on bread alone.'

Then leading him to a height, the devil showed him in a moment of time all the Kingdoms of the world and said to him, 'I will give you all this power and the glory of these Kingdoms, for it has been committed to me and I give it to anyone I choose. Worship me, then, and it shall all be yours.' But Jesus answered him, 'Scripture says: You must worship the Lord your God, and serve him alone.'

Then he led him to Jerusalem and made him stand on the parapet of the Temple. 'If you are the Son of God,' he said to him, 'throw yourself down from here, for scripture says: He will put his angels in charge of you to guard you, and again: They will hold you up on their hands in case you hurt your foot against a stone.' But Jesus answered him, 'It has been said: You must not put the Lord your God to the test.'

Having exhausted all these ways of tempting him, the devil left him, to return at the appointed time.

First Reflection
A Taste of Things to Come

Lent is our time of forty days when the Spirit leads us to look honestly at ourselves, at our weak points, at where we are likely to be tested and to do something about it.

God's testing is a way of clarifying our goals and strengthening our resolve.

In the threefold testing of Jesus he eliminated three forms of ministry which might have compromised his mission. He will not buy people with free bread. He will not seek power by compromising his principles with evil. Nor will he fascinate people by sensational stunts.

40

The three temptations anticipate the areas of accusation and conflict that Jesus would have to face. As Luke was writing he was aware that the persecuted Christians of his day were being drawn into these same conflicts and pressures.

The first conflict is about bread. Meals and the idea of sharing at table feature very prominently in Luke' writing. It is said that in this gospel Jesus is either at a table, going to a table or coming from a table. One remembers the banquet for the return of the prodigal son, the meals to which Jesus was invited or the meal with Martha and Mary. The mission of Jesus is an anticipation of the final messianic banquet. It became a matter of complaint that he welcomed sinners and ate with them (Lk 15:3). And he was accused of being 'a glutton and a drunkard, a friend of tax collectors and sinners' (7:34). Since Jesus clearly enjoyed meals, it is all the more significant that he fasted from food before commencing his mission. In so doing he was entering into solidarity with the people of every age who are deprived of a fair share of the bountiful fruits of the earth.

Luke notes the link between this first temptation and the trial of Jesus by remarking that the devil left him to return at the appointed time. It was at the feast of Unleavened Bread that Satan made his return and entered into Judas to tempt him to break from table-fellowship with Jesus.

Luke wrote for a community of Christians who were living out the conflict of Jesus in their own lives. Bread should have been the expression of sharing at the Christian assembly, but sometimes it represented the distinction between the haves and the have-nots. Furthermore, in the growing decadence of the Empire, the Roman policy was to supply bread and circus entertainment to divert any unrest or rebellious spirits. The Christian message challenged this system which belittled the human spirit: Human beings live not on bread alone. There is more to life than entertainment.

The second temptation sees Jesus turning away from the lure of political power and the attraction of fame. He rejected the personal gratification of having power, because he wished to return all homage to the Father. Rather than be the recipient of the services and flattery normally attached to power, he chose to serve. When the people wanted to take him away to make him king he made a hasty getaway. Later, at the trial of Jesus, his words were diabolically twisted to form the accusation that he had incited people to revolt, that he was opposed to the payment of taxes and that he claimed to be a king.

At the time of Luke's writing people were liable to prosecution for refusing to worship the Emperor as a divinity. Christians would draw strength from the reply of Jesus: 'You must do homage to the Lord your God, him alone must you serve.'

The third temptation challenged the relationship of Jesus with the Father: 'If you are the Son of God, throw yourself down.' Later this is echoed in the trial before the Sanhedrin: 'If you are the Christ, tell us.'

Many of Luke's contemporaries were faced with the prospect of death if they would not deny their relationship with Jesus Christ. There would be no divine intervention to stop the sword or quench the burning pyre. Only an unfaithful, adulterous people would demand a sign. Staunch and loyal faith would not put God to the test.

The testing of Jesus, then, clarified the nature of his mission. The temptations anticipated the accusations of his trial. And the strategy and victory of the Lord would provide guidance and hope for Christians of all ages in their conflict with opposition.

Second Reflection
Hungry, Powerless and Tested

Jesus in the wilderness was hungry. He entered into the lot of all the people who never get enough of food for life, or whose life is a constant struggle to provide bread for the table. How can hunger ever be good? When it opens up the mind to the thought that there is more to life than the satisfaction of our appetites: that we do not live on bread alone. Fasting and the firm control of our appetites can express a resolute option for the spirit over the body. Society today is suffering from many forms of illness because of the failure to discipline appetites. Sick economic policies leave half of the world short of food while the other half overproduces but will not share sufficiently. Over-indulgence in tobacco, alcohol or rich food is at the root of many ailments, not to mention the abuse of mind and body with drugs. Licentious living has seriously undermined family stability and is now threatening society with a plague as bad as anything in history. If we sow in the gale we will reap in the whirlwind. When appetite is allowed to become a tyrannical monster then the rich potential of the human spirit is stifled. The answer of Jesus must be heard again: Man does not live on bread alone.

Jesus resisted the temptation to seek power and personal

glory. He entered into the poverty of the oppressed, the exploited and victimised. How can powerlessness ever be good? When it keeps a person from the pride that would attribute to oneself what should be returned to God. When it saves a person from the arrogance that would oppress others. Power is always hard to handle properly. It quickly becomes a voracious monster that never has enough: and it becomes paranoid in building fences or in making the first strike. We live in a world where the national budgets for military spending are vastly out of proportion with what is spent on education and the arts.

The lust for power can now call upon destructive weapons of potential too horrible to imagine. Rarely is power, whether as superior weaponry or financial muscle, understood as a challenge to serve. Jesus rejected the way of power and self-glorification. He chose to worship God and to serve him alone.

Jesus was challenged on his religious identity and was tested in his fundamental confidence in the Father. He entered into solidarity with all who journey towards the Jerusalem of their destiny more through the dim regions of faith than under the light of constant signs from God. How can the testing of faith and the challenging of trust be good? God may have to strip away the false images of the divine which are really the projection of our own desires. We are tempted to reverse the original order by creating God in our own image and likeness. We will use God: but will not be used by him. And 'to use God is to kill him' (Eckhart). God must be taken on his terms. Otherwise religion is warped around the projection of our own desires. Then one can wage war and kill in the name of religion: a religious veneer lends respectability to doubtful government and shady business: religious self-righteousness underpins racism and bigotry: cold legalism buries charity: or fanatical moralism drives people to morbid guilt and insanity. Sometimes prayer itself is preached on the level of primitive superstition. Jesus refused to put God to the test. He refused to lay down the conditions for God. He accepted in obedience whatever the Father would send him.

Jesus sat with the hungry, struggled with the powerless and walked the road of testing towards Jerusalem. If we travel with him in the energy of self-discipline, strengthened by prayer and guided by the light of Scripture, then we will share in his victory.

Second Sunday of Lent

Luke 9: 28-36

Jesus took with him Peter and John and James and went up the mountain to pray. As he prayed, the aspect of his face was changed and his clothing became brilliant as lightning. Suddenly there were two men there talking to him; they were Moses and Elijah appearing in glory, and they were speaking of his passing which he was to accomplish in Jerusalem. Peter and his companions were heavy with sleep, but they kept awake and saw his glory and the two men standing with him. As these were leaving him, Peter said to Jesus, 'Master, it is wonderful for us to be here; so let us make three tents, one for you, one for Moses and one for Elijah'. – He did not know what he was saying. As he spoke, a cloud came and covered them with shadow; and when they went into the cloud the disciples were afraid, And a voice came from the cloud saying, 'This is my Son, the Chosen One. Listen to him.' And after the voice had spoken, Jesus was found alone. The disciples kept silence and, at that time, told no one what they had seen.

First Reflection
With him on the holy mountain

Mountains are wonderful places. The mountain offers perspective. Every step higher brings a wider view of the world below. The shapes of farm and forest emerge: the contours of coastline: how the winding roads and meandering rivers make connection between places. The fantastic hewing of rocks tells of thousands of years of weathering. The mountain range belongs to the story of a million years. The wider sense of place and expanded sense of time invite the mind to a new perspective on life and its directions.

Peter, James and John were like pygmies taken from the dark tangled rainforest of everyday life and up the mountain of distant viewing. The unaccustomed brightness of spirit hurt their eyes of flesh. Their sense of time acquired a new distance. That moment linked up with the glories of the past in law and prophet, represented by Moses and Elijah. The future too was hinted when they heard tell of the passing of Jesus in Jerusalem. The moment of light was given towards their strengthening for the days ahead. These three, Peter, James and John would be with Jesus in the darkness of the agony in the garden. And they more than any of the others would be associated with the agonies of the church in the first century. Peter would need strength in memory to be the rock to support the others. James, the first of the apostles to face martyrdom, would draw from his hope for the transfiguration of our bodies. John would survive long after the others and inspire the deep meditation on the incarnation which is the fourth gospel. The day of light and sureness was given them for the years ahead: a homing point in memory. Peter wanted to capture the moment and hold on to it in a tent of meeting. But one tent, nor three, could not confine that meeting of God and humankind which was in Jesus. Christian memory alone would sustain the moment in every time and every place. One of the sacred writers emphasises the strength of faith rooted in the memory of Peter. 'It was not any cleverly invented myths that we were repeating when we brought you the knowledge of the power and the coming of our Lord Jesus Christ; we had seen his majesty for ourselves ... we were with him on the holy mountain.' (2 Pet 1:16-18)

Lent represents the pilgrimage of life. Sometimes our days are with the Lord in the barren wilderness of conflict. Sometimes he draws us to the mountain of prayer and to the experience of light, perspective, distance, connections and sureness. When God grants the moment of insight it is given towards future strengthening. The day on the mountain is to be treasured. Some find great support from keeping a journal of life's blessings. When God reveals his light and presence we must do all we can to receive the moment, to be aware of it and to own it. We should proclaim God's gift in praise and gratitude. Like Mary, the great contemplative, we must treasure the moment and ponder on it, storing it up in memory.

Second Reflection
Heavy with Sleep
Peter, James and John, poor wretches, always having trouble staying awake with the Lord! They were 'heavy with sleep' on the mountain of light. Later, on another hillside, when Jesus reached out for companionship, he found them 'sleeping for

sheer grief.' Energy is strange, where it comes from, how it is charged, how it evaporates. It is a sure indicator of one's inner life. When we speak of somebody being 'psyched up' we recognise that there is more to energy than physical well-being. And that physical exhaustion is not the only cause of fatigue. Football coaches know that nothing replaces motivation for lifting tired muscles. Fatigue may be due to exhaustion that is primarily physical or mental or emotional.

Enthusiasm is shown in signs of energy: interest in the eyes, light on the face, strength in the voice and forward bodily gestures. Fatigue and heaviness of spirit are shown in listlessness, boredom of mind and slothfulness in action. The original meaning of enthusiasm is living-in-God ... to be 'engodded.' Being devoid of enthusiasm must mean lacking this sense of living-in God. Spiritual writers of the middle ages pictured the sinner as bent over, looking at his feet, unable to see the world of God. Penance was understood as the process of raising up the eyes and widening the vision to the truth, beauty and goodness of God in the world. Slothfulness is the opposite of being enthusiastic. Sloth is traditionally listed as one of the seven deadly roots of sinfulness. Indeed some commentators have fancifully interpreted the original sin as sloth, on the grounds that Adam and Eve abdicated their reasoning powers and let the tempter do the thinking. The fact that one still exists is hardly sufficient proof that one is alive. T.S. Eliot wrote of the women of Canterbury in Beckett's day 'living and partly living,' going through the seasons and motions of life but trying to avoid the implications of reality ... 'not wishing anything to happen.' Jesus faced life from the bleakest wilderness to the most glorious mountain. He came that we might have life and have it to the full. And the glory of God is most clearly reflected on the face of a person who is fully alive. 'God's glory is in living people and full life for people is in the vision of God.' (St Irenaeus)

The light on the face of a saint comes from seeing God in life, even in the ugly things of life. The bent-over sinner is all in shadow and darkness. The bored faces and drooping shoulders of many people today bear witness to the emptiness of a materialistic culture. And there are many creatures of the night who sleep through the hours of daylight, afraid it seems of the light.

Energy is generated by vision and purpose. Sloth and fatigue are due to the unavailability of energy. Either there is a serious leakage from the reservoir of energy because it is being diverted to some other purpose, hidden perhaps, or the energy charge cannot sustain itself without an outside stimulant. There are times when the reason for darkness and heaviness of heart is nothing more than physical exhaustion or illness. Or the reason may be the over-extension of one's emotional capacities, known as 'burnout.' And there are times when dryness and aridity are part of God's dealing with soul: in which case the help of a wise soulfriend is invaluable. It is an important part of one's self-knowledge to recognise the situations and experiences that generate one's energy: and to monitor the occasions when leakage of energy is manifested in such conditions as lethargy, paralysing fear, blanket anxiety, self-doubting, paranoia, inability to concentrate and irritability. One can cover up the condition by long hours in bed, diversionary activity or the use of alcohol or other chemicals. But the time comes when it is better to face the root of the problem.

Three fishermen, capable of sustained physical energy through long nights of rowing and net-hauling, in different circumstances found themselves 'heavy with sleep' and 'sleeping for sheer grief.' Sometimes our life of prayer must be in meeting the Lord through openness with a competent spiritual director who can help us to understand what our tiredness means.

Third Sunday of Lent

Luke 13: 1-9

It was just about this time that some people arrived and told him about the Galileans whose blood Pilate had mingled with that of their sacrifices. At this he said to them, 'Do you suppose these Galileans who suffered like that were greater sinners than any other Galileans? They were not, I tell you. No; but unless you repent you will all perish as they did. Or those eighteen on whom the tower at Siloam fell and killed them? Do you suppose that they were more guilty than all the other people living in Jerusalem? They were not, I tell you. No; but unless you repent you will all perish as they did.'

He told this parable: 'A man had a fig tree planted in his vineyard, and he came looking for fruit on it but found none. He said to the man who looked after the vineyard, "Look here, for three years now I have been coming to look for fruit on this fig tree and finding none. Cut it down: why should it be taking up the ground?" "Sir," the man replied, "leave it one more year and give me time to dig round it and manure it: it may bear fruit next year; if not, then you can cut it down."'

First Reflection
Repentance and Mercy

Lent continues with an encouragement to repent and to improve life. There is a warning that the sinful life is on the road to destruction. However, the Lord then relates a parable of tender encouragement, comparing the sinful life to the fruitless tree which is given yet one more chance to improve.

The teaching is set in the wake of two recent tragedies which had set minds judging and tongues wagging. With the simple certainty typical of the fundamentalist, some were saying that the death of these people, at the hand of Pilate or under the collapsed tower, showed that they were sinners being punished by God. Mind you, this sort of judgemental minds has not gone away.

Jesus corrects them and warns that the consciences they ought to examine are their own. 'Unless you repent, you will be the ones who perish.' When I point a finger towards another in condemnation there are three fingers pointing back at myself.

The God of unconditional love, whom Jesus represents, is not in the business of punishing. The fact is that sin carries its own inbuilt punishment in many ways. Sinful behaviour alienates a person from God and so destroys the peace and joy of a loving relationship with God. On the social level, sin disrupts the harmony of relationships. It festers in anger, bitterness, hurt, prejudice and a hundred other negative ways.

Sin is so negative that it needs no God to punish it for it bears the seeds of self-destruction and unhappiness. Even the ultimate punishment of hell is self-inflicted. 'Everybody who does wrong hates the light and avoids it to prevent his actions from being shown up' (Jn 3:20). Those who are so hardened in evil that they will not accept God's love turn forever from the light. Light brings life to the healthy eye but it hurts the sore eye. The light of God draws the virtuous soul towards greater life but it is painful to the soul sick with sin.

How beautiful is the compassion of the Lord who follows the warning to repent with the parable of encouragement. The gardener in the story wants to give yet another chance to the fruitless tree. The judgmental mind wants to cut it down, get rid of it once and for all. No mercy. It had its chance and failed to take it.

This parable reveals God as the One who will always give another chance. Digging suggests the humiliation and painful side of repentance. Without analysing the manure too much, we can say that it represents the help that is forthcoming once the process of repentance begins.

God is not vindictive, not in the business of storing up punishment. Personal sufferings or tragic accidents should not be construed as punishments struck from heaven. God, in mercy, prefers to see the return of the sinner and, like the patient gardener, will help the one who repents. The perfect balance is achieved between the demands of justice and the pleadings of mercy ... between warning and encouragement.

It is beautifully expressed by the psalmist:

Mercy and faithfulness have met, justice and peace have embraced.

Faithfulness shall spring from the earth and justice look down from heaven.

Second Reflection
The Patience of Christ

A number of Jesus' stories are about gardening, farming,

things growing. The people of an earlier age were nomadic flock-people. Flock-people can live off nature: their flocks graze and move on: nothing is put back into the land. They could think strongly of a God who provides. By the time of Jesus the people had settled down and this had seen the change from the totally pastoral life to the development of horticulture and agriculture. They had learned to live more in co-operation with nature, which demanded humility and patience. Jesus could see the patient approach of God mirrored in the fields and gardens before his eyes. A farmer plants seeds and waits. Night and day, while he sleeps, when he is awake, the seed is sprouting and growing. He waits and wonders and hopes that all will go well. One farmer has a serious problem with weeds growing with the wheat. Lest the good roots be disturbed he waits until the proper time to harvest. Such is the patience of God. So it is that God makes his sun to shine and rain to fall on good and bad, honest and dishonest alike. The story of the fig tree that gets another chance, even after three years care, is a picture of the ministry of Jesus. 'Think of the patience of Christ as your opportunity to be saved.'(2 Pet 3:14) A false idea of perfection can trap one in unnecessary anxieties and fears.

There are people who are afraid to confess because they know that they are likely to fall again after confession. But who ever said that all faults would be healed instantly, that the weeds would be instantly rooted out from the wheat? The way of Jesus is patient growth.

Perfectionism makes it impossible for some people to forgive themselves. They seem to think that they have to impress God with success and faultlessness before they deserve to be loved. But love surely is free: it does not have to be deserved or earned.

All must learn from the growing of things. Plants which sprout rapidly from seed to stalk last but a short life span. The seed of a hardwood tree can take up to two years to sprout above soil. But this slow grower will develop mightily and last for hundreds of years.

Lasting growth is usually a slow and gradual process.

The patience of God as pictured in our gardens and fields is a saving thought.

A helpful verse to stay with in prayer is:
'The Lord is compassion and love,
    slow to anger and rich in mercy.' (Ps 102:8)

Fourth Sunday of Lent

Luke 15: 1-3. 11-32

The tax collectors and the sinners, meanwhile, were all seeking his company to hear what he had to say, and the Pharisees and the scribes complained. 'This man,' they said, "welcomes sinners and eats with them.' So he spoke this parable to them.

'A man had two sons. The younger said to his father, "Father let me have the share of the estate that would come to me." So the father divided the property between them. A few days later, the younger son got together everything he had and left for a distant country where he squandered his money on a life of debauchery.

'When he had spent it all, that country experienced a severe famine, and now he began to feel the pinch, so he hired himself out to one of the local inhabitants who put him on his farm to feed the pigs. And he would willingly have filled his belly with the husks the pigs were eating but no one offered him anything. Then he came to his senses and said, "How many of my father's paid servants have more food than they want, and here am I dying of hunger! I will leave this place and go to my father and say: Father, I have sinned against heaven and against you; I no longer deserve to be called your son; treat me as one of your paid servants." So he left the place and went back to his father.

'While he was still a long way off, his father saw him and was moved with pity. He ran to the boy, clasped him in his arms and kissed him tenderly. Then his son said, "Father, I have sinned against heaven and against you. I no longer deserve to be called your son." But the father said to his servants, "Quick! Bring out the best robe and put it on him; put a ring an his finger and sandals on his feet. Bring the calf we have been fattening, and kill it; we are going to have a feast, a celebration, because this son of mine was dead and has come back to life; he was lost and is found." And they began to celebrate.

'Now the elder son was out in the fields, and on his way back, as he drew near the house, he could hear music and dancing. Calling one of the servants he asked what it was all about. "Your brother has come," replied the servant, "and your father has killed the calf we had fattened because he has got him back safe and sound."

'He was angry then and refused to go in, and his father came out to

51

plead with him; but he answered his father, "Look, all these years I have slaved for you and never once disobeyed your orders, yet you never offered me so much as a kid for me to celebrate with my friends. But for this son of yours, when he comes back after swallowing up your property – he and his women – you kill the calf we had been fattening."

'The father said, "My son, you are with me always and all I have is yours. But it was only right we should celebrate and rejoice, because your brother here was dead and has come to life; he was lost and is found."'

First Reflection
The World's Greatest Story
If all of Scripture were to be destroyed with the exception of one passage, my choice to be preserved would be this story of sin and God's total forgiveness. It is the essence of salvation history. The story pictures three steps in the downward journey to the pits of sin, followed by the moment of return and three steps back to the waiting father.

The first move towards sin is in giving me an exaggerated place at the centre of affairs. 'Give me my rights.' The father's will and handing over of inheritance ought not take effect until after his death. Effectively, the son is saying to his father, 'Da, I want it now. I want you out of my way.' This is the beginning of sin when I tell God that I am now going to act in my way whether you like it or not. Back in the first pages of the bible this is the nature of the first temptation. 'This is the tree of the knowledge of good and evil. Eat this fruit and you will be like gods. You will have the freedom to make up your own commandments and morality.'

Having put me into God's place the next stage is the journey away from home and the values that home represents. A distant country, squandering the inheritance, a life of debauchery, these express the rapid deterioration of values after the first step out the door.

The third stage of sin is the famine: the famine of peace of mind; the lack of contentment and joy; the loss of self-respect and idealism; all the self-punishment inherent in sin. Feeding with the pigs, to the Jewish mind, represented the lowest of the low: utter depravity.

The turning moment comes when the lad came to his senses. He looked into the mirror of life and he did not like the reflection he saw there. Many people do not like what they see in their lives. But they do not know where to turn. They are smitten with the sorrow called remorse, literally a biting sorrow. This is the devil's sorrow, and the more it bites, the less confident one feels, and the more one is vulnerable to further temptation.

Fortunately for this sinner he remembered his father's house and the generosity that abounded there. Remembrance gave direction to his steps. Remorse was changed into repentance. Repent comes from the Latin *re-pensare*, to have a re-think. In his new thinking he makes three decisions: I will leave this place; I will go to my father; I will say 'I have sinned ... against heaven and against you.'

Honest confession is one of the greatest helps towards peace of mind. Getting in touch with the truth of one's personal story is a basic requirement in psychiatry.

In saying 'I have sinned' one accepts personal responsibility for what wrongs one has done. 'Against heaven' expresses the insult to God that is in every sin. Then the son apologises for the hurt he has caused his father. Honest confession must involve making up for the hurts or injustices done to others.

The focus of the story then switches to the father. Here is my own favourite picture of God. He is the one who throws righteousness and self-dignity aside as the old man runs to the boy, clasps him in his arms and hugs him back home. He clothes him in all the garments of full family membership. This is no partial or provisional pardon but a total acceptance into family. It is an event to be celebrated.

Many people question the need to come to the sacrament of Reconciliation. 'Why can't I tell my sins privately to God?' Of course, we must confess our sorrow privately to God. The point of the sacrament is the celebration of the victory of Jesus Christ now applied to our lives. The father might have taken in the son by the back door in a private capacity. But for such a loving man that would not be enough. His love called for the celebration and rejoicing. In the sacrament of Reconciliation the repentance of the sinner is changed into the rejoicing of the church as we celebrate the merits of the death and resurrection of the Lord applied to our lives.

Surely this is the greatest story ever told, taking us from the pits of remorse to the steps of repentance and eventually to the table of rejoicing.

Second Reflection
'Father, I have sinned against heaven and against you. '
The return of the prodigal son began when he came to his

senses and admitted in the privacy of his own mind that he had
made a fool of himself. The next step was to undo the social
harm of his living: this demanded that he go to his father and
apologise; furthermore, he felt he deserved to be degraded from
the level of sonship to that of servant. The third dimension of his
return was in his admission that he had sinned against heaven.
The sinner's return to the father is the basis of the sacrament of
penance. But many people are finding it hard to make sense out
of a sacramental practice that has become the victim of routine
ritual. In their experience of the sacrament they are left uncomfortable or even hating it. Far removed is their experience from
the celebration of family reconciliation. The courtroom model of
the sacrament has left people struggling with an unattractive
concept of God as a moralistic judge.

The story told by Jesus pictures God as a father who is generous in giving ... and even more generous in forgiving, that is, in
continuing to give to one who has wasted his inheritance and
disgraced his name. The policy of referring to the sacrament as
reconciliation reflects a significant change of emphasis.
Sometimes the problem with reconciliation is one's own failure
to grow out of a childish use of the sacrament or beyond a routine ritual which lacks spontaneity and freshness of challenge.
There may be another problem in finding a priest who knows
how to celebrate the sacrament properly.

The most serious problem is the prevailing confusion about
sin. What is 'sin against heaven'? The sense of sin is blunted by
many influences such as: the constant propaganda of secularistic thinking which worships the values of action and production, diversion and pleasure while belief in God (our first beginning and last end!) is at most tolerated although regarded as irrelevant to the decisions and pursuits of life: the utter amorality
of the husks of entertainment upon which minds are fed from
TV, video, magazines and newspapers: a shallow psychology
which explains away personal responsibility and guilt: the confusion caused by differences of opinion among theologians on
serious moral matters: the swing away from extreme moralism
which saw sin everywhere to the opposite extreme which
scarcely recognises sin at all: the swing from too much emphasis
on fear of punishment to an unbalanced view of the love of God,
giving the impression that one never has to face the light of
judgment: most importantly, the lack of prayerful relationship
with God and 'the obscuring of the notion of God's fatherhood
and dominion over human life.' (Pope John Paul II)

So, while many sources in the world say that sin is an outdated and harmful concept, the gospel stresses the need to say: 'Father, I have sinned against heaven ...' When last did you make a humble and honest confession that you had sinned? How honest is your confessing? Is it a humble admission of particular faults and shortcomings of attitude, or a vague generalisation under which you obscure more than you admit? Is your soul now in a country distant from the Father's intimacy? If so, it's time to come home. What diet of husks have you fed your mind on? Have you forgotten the delights of your Father's table? 'Taste and see that the Lord is good.'

Confession frequently turns out to be less difficult than anticipated. When the prodigal son rehearsed his speech he planned on saying something very humiliating: 'Treat me as one of your paid servants.' But the welcome he received was so warm and generous that he knew immediately that it would only insult the father to suggest that anything less than full restoration to the family would take place. So he never said the bit about becoming a paid servant. Reconciliation is principally a gift of the heavenly Father. And the son who was poor enough to beg for reconciliation is much closer to the father than the other son who never asked for anything.

In the secrecy of our own reflection we come to our senses and confess privately to God. In our honesty with others we have to reach out in words of apology and gestures of restitution. The sacrament is a moment when these private and social movements are celebrated in the light of God's giving and forgiving love.

(Many of the above ideas are taken from Pope John Paul II's letter *Reconciliatio et Paenitentia*, CTS, 1984. Further reflections on this gospel may be taken from the Twenty-Fourth Sunday of the Year.)

Fifth Sunday of Lent

John 8:1-11

Jesus went to the Mount of Olives. At daybreak he appeared in the Temple again; and as all the people came to him, he sat down and began to teach them.

The scribes and Pharisees brought a woman along who had been caught committing adultery; and making her stand there in full view of everybody, they said to Jesus, 'Master, this woman was caught in the very act of committing adultery, and Moses has ordered us in the Law to condemn women like this to death by stoning. What have you to say?' They asked him this as a test, looking for something to use against him. But Jesus bent down and started writing on the ground with his finger. As they persisted with their question, he looked up and said, 'If there is one of you who has not sinned, let him be the first to throw a stone at her'. Then he bent down and wrote on the ground again. When they heard this they went away one by one, beginning with the eldest, until Jesus was left alone with the woman, who remained standing there. He looked up and said, 'Woman, where are they? Has no one condemned you?' 'No one, sir,' she replied. 'Neither do I condemn you,' said Jesus, 'go away, and don't sin any more. '

First Reflection

Healing the past

Last Sunday's theme of sin and forgiveness continues in this story. Although it is found in John's gospel, it is a story that fits very smoothly into the themes of Luke which we have this year.

The other readings at Mass today encourage people to forget the past. Isaiah encourages people to forget the trials of the exile in Babylon and to trust in the future God has in store for them. 'No need to recall the past, no need to think about what has gone before. See, I am doing a new deed...'

Saint Paul has his eyes so firmly set on Christ Jesus that everything in his past history pales into insignificance. 'All I can say is that I forget the past and I strain ahead for what is still to come.'

But is it all that easy to forget the past? Especially for some-body who has been the victim of hurt, abuse or any injustice in the past. We cannot dictate to memory when to switch off atten-tion. If something is remembered it is there in the mind. Our op-tion is not between remembering or forgetting . If we have any option it is about how we remember, either negatively or posi-tively. Negative remembering dwells on the injustices and hurts, bringing up anger, revenge and a whole train of destruc-tive thoughts and desires. And the one who suffers most from these is the one who holds onto these memories. Positive re-membering draws from a higher power which transcends the in-justice or wrong suffered. The power which especially tran-scends all wrongs and negativity is love.

This story of Jesus and the woman opens up both negative and positive reactions. The negative energies abound in the stance of the scribes and Pharisees against the woman. Where is the partner in adultery? Why does he get no mention? The accu-sations against the woman are loud. The letter of a law which was more often honoured in the breach than in the observance was now cited in order to trap Jesus. Righteousness without mercy can be very cruel.

The righteousness that Jesus represented was directed to-wards helping and healing. Gently he turned the tables on the accusers in the classical answer: let whoever is without sin cast the first stone.

We live at a time when many hidden sins, abuses and injus-tices of the past are being exposed. Letting out the poison is nec-essary. It has brought great relief to many people. But it is im-portant for the victim to move from the past in a positive direc-tion. Staying with the injuries of the past is like picking and pok-ing at a scar, thereby preventing any healing. Our option is not about forgetting the past but about how we deal with it. Do we stay with the negative reactions or do we move positively to-wards healing and new life?

Our gospel passage shows how compassionate God is to-wards the sinner. Jesus was more eager to restore life than to de-stroy. He forgave the sinner, clothed her nakedness with dignity and restored her to the ideal of sinning no more.

What marvels the Lord worked for us!

Indeed we were glad.

Second Reflection
Their Hands

'Hands are the heart's landscape' (Karol Wojtyla). In imagination you can watch the hands of the people here revealing
their inner attitudes. See how the beckoning hands call out the
mob's support from every doorway and dark corner. Cruel
hands roughly drag the woman and throw her into the centre.
Her trembling hands vainly attempt to cover up her shame and
keep a shred of dignity. 'Master, Rabbi ...,' their hands gesturing
like a pleading advocate, though they cannot altogether mask
the hypocrisy of their appeal to him. Then fingers of criticism
stab the air like darts in the direction of the accused ... 'this
woman' ... as if she had no name ... no right to person. The
pointing fingers of condemnation then rise upright and wag
forth and back in righteous indignation ... 'adulteress!' Fingers
lock savagely and the upright hand is clenched into an angry
fist. 'She should be put to death by stoning!' Stones ... and hands
are now frantic claws that rake the ground and dig. Bulging
hands clasping the rocks of wrath are drawn and poised, waiting for the word. 'What do you say?'

How relaxed are the hands of Jesus. No pointing: no bulging
veins of frenzy: no angry clenching. There he is at the butt of a
pillar, taking the shade and playing as a child in the dust.

Was he writing their sins? Or engaging in a little act of distraction to draw attention from her embarrassment? Or just
playfully doodling a daydream?

That one relaxed hand gave her a ray of unexpected hope. A
hand not dealing a heartless death sentence. A hand of compassion, playing in the dust of creation, restoring the dead to life.
'Go away, and don't sin any more.'

Wisely did David say: 'Let us rather fall into the hand of God,
since his mercy is great, and not into the hands of men' (2 Sam
24:14). Into your hands, O Lord, I commend my spirit.

Passion Sunday

Luke 22:14 - 25:56
Because of the length of this passage, the reader is asked to take it directly from the lectionary or bible.

First Reflection
The Prayerfulness of the Passion
Luke never lets us forget that the suffering and death of Jesus were all part of a great, divine plan. As the risen Lord later brings to the attention of the disciples on the Emmaus road, 'Was it not ordained that the Christ should suffer and so enter into glory.' (Lk 24:26)

In his narration of the Passion Luke was very sensitive to this divine ordination within the human drama of plots, betrayals, suffering and death. At every stage of the story the reader is reminded of Jesus' constant relationship with the Father. The mood is always prayerful.

Luke's Passion begins in a Passover meal which gives a liturgical interpretation to all that follows. The Passover commemorated the journey of God's people out of slavery in Egypt.

Luke spent many chapters describing the journey of Jesus to Jerusalem as 'the time drew near for him to be taken up to heaven.' (9:51) When the hour came he sat to table with his disciples and said, 'I have longed to eat this passover with you before I suffer; because, I tell you, I shall not eat it again until it is fulfilled in the kingdom of God.' (22:14-16)

At the beginning of a Passover meal the head of the family recalled the story of the Exodus journey as an explanation of this meal. At the last supper Jesus gave a new meaning to the Passover ritual of breaking the bread and blessing the cup of wine: the bread is his body which will be given up in sacrificial death; and the cup of blessed wine is the blood which ratifies the new covenant.Thus, the last supper is presented to us as the meal of the new Passover, and all the subsequent events of the Passion are to be understood in the context of this new covenant with God.

From the supper room the story proceeds to the garden of olive trees. Prayer dominates Luke's description of what happened there. He understands the agony as a testing at the deepest prayer level of Jesus' total union with the Father's will. Jesus is depicted as kneeling, a strong position, not prostrate in agony. There is no mention of fear and sadness: serenity and strength mark this prayer of Jesus. He hands over everything to the Father's will. In this testing he proves to be God's faithful servant. The coming of the angel to strengthen him testifies that the Father accepts this proof of his fidelity.

The prayerful fidelity of Jesus sets the example for the disciples. At the beginning and end he exhorts them: 'Pray not to be put to the test.' It is the last petition of the Our Father. But in contrast to the strength of Jesus in prayer, the disciples are weak. The more Jesus was in anguish, the more earnest and steadfast was his prayer, even when the physical intensity produced large bloodlike drops of sweat. The disciples, however, lost all energy in their testing and they were 'sleeping for sheer grief.'

The inner serenity of Jesus is apparent during the various trials he has to face. His standing with the Father is sure for he is totally innocent of the charges trumped up against him. In his innocence Jesus speaks just the minimum with those who already have their minds made up to be rid of him. And to the curious Herod he would not speak at all.

Pilate openly admits that he can find no case against Jesus. And his innocence is finally recognised when permission is granted for his burial in a private tomb rather than in the common grave which was allotted to condemned criminals. Jesus, then, is portrayed by Luke as the innocent Servant of God, bearing the faults of others, but finally vindicated by God. Again the divine dimension of the drama is preserved by Luke.

On Calvary, Luke makes no mention of Jesus' pitiable cries of thirst and abandonment. The three utterances of Jesus which he relates are prayerful. First, he prays for the forgiveness of his persecutors. The love of Jesus is not contaminated by the injustices, hurts and mockery to which he is subjected.

Then his relationship with the repentant thief is entirely prayerful. This man begins to turn to Jesus out of a holy fear of God. He admits his own guilt while recognising the innocence of Jesus. From his lips we hear a beautiful, tender prayer: 'Jesus, remember me when you come into your kingdom.' It is the first time in the gospel that we hear somebody addressing Jesus by his name. In the brotherhood of suffering there is no need for titles such as Lord or Master, but the relationship is of person to person. To this man Jesus promises a share in the divine fruits of that day's events: 'Today, you will be with me in Paradise.'

The third utterance is the dying prayer of Jesus. In the versions of Mark and Matthew, Jesus dies painfully, in a final muscular spasm, emitting a loud cry. Luke tells us that the loud cry was a great prayer of trust: 'Father, into your hands I commit my spirit.'

The immediate reactions to the death of Jesus are prayerful. The Roman centurion gave praise to God and said, 'This was a great and good man.' And the people who saw the events went home beating their breasts, a common way of expressing the prayer of repentance.

All through the story Luke has raised our minds to the divine presence within the human drama. Jesus is innocent and sure in his standing with the Father: he is totally obedient to the Father's will: and even in the agony of human suffering he remains loving, compassionate and merciful. His words flow out from a soul that is ever in deep prayer. In a final response to his example, the people begin to turn from their sins and repent.

May we too be moved to beat our breasts and turn to God in praise as we ponder on the Passion of that 'great and good man.'

Second Reflection
Were you there?
Luke's pages teem with people. He was a person-centred writer rather than one who dealt with truth in the abstract. He was a theologian in story who proclaimed the great deeds of God through describing the actions of Jesus and the reactions of people. Luke was ever sensitive to the inner movements of mind and heart. In the Passion narrative it is important to reflect upon the various people whose paths are intertwined with the journey of Jesus to the cross.

The institution of the Eucharist is an essential part of the Passion. As the Jewish Passover meal remembered God's deeds in the Exodus and his covenant with Moses, by the time Luke was writing the Eucharist had come to be recognised as Christians' way of remembering the saving deeds of Jesus and the new covenant which was sealed by his blood.

The Eucharist represents the ideal of total love in the way that Jesus gave up his life in sacrifice for others. However, Luke is aware that the lives of Christians fall far short of that ideal. Two of the apostles, Judas and Peter, are highlighted for their behaviour represents the sins of later generations. Linked up with the betrayal of Judas is the dispute among the disciples as to which of them was to be reckoned the greatest. That sort of mentality about power and self-importance would be a betrayal of the mind of Jesus just as bad as that of Judas.

Then Jesus spoke of the denial of Peter. Although he was specially chosen and Jesus had prayed particularly for him, yet Peter would fail the testing before his recovery by the grace of God. This testing of Peter in the face of opposition prefigured the later testing of Christians in hostile conditions. The early simplicity of travelling about without purse or haversack among a supporting people would have to change as the disciples faced hostility and persecution. 'If you have no sword,' Jesus warned them, 'Sell your cloak and buy one.' It is most unlikely that Jesus was literally encouraging the use of violence. Rather, 'buying the sword' was a symbolic way of telling them to prepare for times of hostility and testing.'

Interestingly, the early ideal of utter poverty and uneducated preaching in the early days of the Franciscan movement also had to accept hard reality when the friars moved beyond the hospitable confines of Italy. Francis then accepted the need for education, books and houses.

Luke captures a beautiful moment of divine mercy for Peter. Jesus was being led down the outside stairs into the courtyard when he turned and looked straight at Peter. Words were not necessary. Peter remembered – remembered the Lord's words predicting his denial ... remembered the tumble of great days and the spiral of insights ... that morning on the lake ... the day on the mountain. He went outside and wept bitterly.

That's one of Luke's great themes – divine mercy and human repentance. On many mediaeval crucifixes the cock is depicted as a warning against pride and presumption.

I feel Luke would have little in common with those so-called 'born again' Christians who fancy they are saved and beyond sin. Some of them will not recite the Hail Mary because in it we call ourselves sinners. Nor do they like the mention of 'the poor banished children of Eve' in the Hail, Holy Queen. The church of Luke's writing was founded on the rock of Peter, vulnerable and sinful, severely tested and sifted by Satan, but strengthened in the prayer of Jesus. As a sinner, I find myself at home and with hope in that sort of church.

On the road to Calvary Jesus was helped by Simon from Cyrene who represents every follower of Jesus who lends a shoulder to anybody struggling with the crosses of life.

Large numbers followed, among them the women who sympathised with Jesus and came forward to comfort him. 'Weep for yourselves and your children,' Jesus told them, for his journey to Calvary would be repeated in the sufferings of every generation of followers. Christians came to see their own sufferings as a share in the Passion of Jesus.

Simeon had predicted that Jesus would bring about the fall and the rising of many in Israel. On Calvary the reactions of people were polarised. The two criminals represent each side. One becomes more hardened in bitterness and mockery. But the other is moved by the innocence of Jesus to turn to him in prayer. It is the first and only time in the gospel when somebody addresses him as Jesus. For only in the name of Jesus can salvation be found.

Luke gives us the reactions of people to the death of Jesus. The Centurion was moved to praise God as he recognised in Jesus 'a great and good man.' And all the people, Luke tells us, went home beating their breasts in repentance.

The well-known Negro spiritual asks: 'Were you there when they crucified my Lord?' In Luke's Passion narrative we meet with many people and their reactions to the events of the day. We are invited to put ourselves into the story and to see where we stand – with Jesus or Peter, with helpful Simon or the compassionate women, with those who mock or those who repent? Were you there? Is the story of the Passion going on around us and in us today?

Easter Sunday

John 20: 1-9

It was very early on the first day of the week and still dark, when Mary of Magdala came to the tomb. She saw that the stone had been moved away from the tomb and came running to Simon Peter and the other disciple, the one Jesus loved. 'They have taken the Lord out of the tomb,' she said, 'and we don't know where they have put him.'

So Peter set out with the other disciple to go to the tomb.

They ran together, but the other disciple, running faster than Peter, reached the tomb first; he bent down and saw the linen cloths lying on the ground, but did not go in. Simon Peter who was following now came up, went right into the tomb, saw the linen cloths on the ground and also the cloth that had been over his head; this was not with the linen cloths but rolled up in a place by itself. Then the other disciple who had reached the tomb first also went in; he saw and he believed. Till this moment they had failed to understand the teaching of scripture, that he must rise from the dead.

First Reflection
Easter Faith

Nowhere in scripture is there a description of the actual moment of the resurrection of Jesus. What we have are some texts about the discovery of the empty tomb and also some accounts of various appearances of the risen Lord. The apparition stories inspire reflection on the continuing presence of the Lord in the lives of his followers.

The empty tomb texts, one of which we read today, draw us back into the experience of the disciples on the first Easter morning with the unexpectedness of the discovery, the mental confusion, the haste and excitement, the questioning and eventual belief.

John notes that it was very early on the first day of the week: it was to be the first day of the new creation.

And it was still dark. Jesus, the light of the world, had been taken away from them by death. Gone was the light of those days of physical contact with Jesus. There was a finality about the rolling of the heavy stone across the entrance to the tomb, expressing the end of his life in the flesh.

Until then, people had experienced Jesus and the signs he worked, through what they saw and heard, or sometimes touched or even tasted. Jesus had given them signs to enable them to move beyond the physical happening to a deeper appreciation of who he was.

Yet, the step beyond physical experience did not happen for all who witnessed the signs. Some did see and believed: but others saw his signs and remained indifferent and unchanged: while still others saw what he did but only moved to plot against him. Faith cannot be without the aid of grace. 'No one can come to me unless he is drawn by the Father who sent me ... and to hear the teaching of the Father and learn from it, is to come to me.' (Jn 6:44-45)

That Easter morning Magdalen saw the empty tomb but did not venture beyond saying: 'They have taken the Lord out of the tomb.' Peter, when he saw the empty tomb and the position of the binding cloths was left like a detective amassing a dossier of facts without knowing what to do with it.

The beloved disciple made the step beyond the material evidence: 'He saw and believed.'

Belief opened their eyes to the new order of creation, a new way of understanding life. Later events would clarify that the new creation means the presence of the Lord in the community of believers through their sharing in the power of the Spirit.

When the risen Lord appeared to Magdalen he told her not to cling to him physically, for the old order had changed. The Lord did in fact invite Thomas to touch the wounds, but what he said on that occasion emphasised that the post-resurrection age is a blessed time for those who believe without the aid of physical signs.

The stone is rolled back and the tomb is empty. The body is not here: for now he is everywhere.

He is nowhere to be seen and touched because he is everywhere unseen. No where ... but now here.

Those who are drawn to the Father recognise his presence. This is the gift of faith. The risen Lord Jesus is with us now and always.

Easter is the time to celebrate in prayer the gift of faith and to renew our baptismal contract with the Lord. The liturgy of Easter Sunday affords us the opportunity of renewing our commitment.

Second Reflection
Peter Remembers

The tomb was the end of everything. All our wild dreams and great ideals ... they were all locked away with the lifeless body of Jesus. Shame had given me the pretence of courage to come out of the shadows and help them lay the body. It was unbelievably disfigured. So torn, bruised, discoloured and limp, I would not have recognised him. Raw wounds on hands and feet: a deep jagged incision in his side: his shoulders and back deeply lacerated and raw, practically stripped of skin: congealed blood matting his hair and beard with spittle and dust.

We men did the heavy lifting. The womens' gentle hands worked against time washing and cleaning and winding around the linen cloths. The linen looked so clean and smelt so fresh, it was a little consolation. His eyes were covered at last, the eyes whose look had in one brief moment given me sorrow and joy together. I did the work of two men, lifting and hauling stones that did not really need to be moved. But it relieved my shame and covered up my cowardice when I was busy. The large tombstone was the last job. I put my shoulder to it. It was round as a wheel. Too easily it fell into place, jolted for a moment and settled firm. It closed off the tomb in its fullness and opened up my heart in its emptiness.

Though I had not closed my eyes for two days I could not find sleep that night. Nor would I allow any of the others near me. Comfort was something I did not deserve. The tomb was a waking nightmare. Dark. Cold. In the dampness of earth. It was hard to imagine that Jesus was in there. Yet I had seen the body, seen the wounds and lifted that lifeless weight. I must have cried myself into oblivion and it was late on the Sabbath when I awoke. The women had got on with life and there was some food ready. We men just sat around and talked. The company eased the pain somewhat and happier memories were shared.

It was late in the night when we lay down again. Magdalen startled us with her knocking. It took me a few moments to shake the sleep from my brain. And she was so wildly incomprehensible! 'The body! The tomb! They have taken him out of the tomb! We don't know where they have put him.' I thought at first that she was having a nightmare. But she was fully dressed and had been out of doors. Eventually the message sank in.

We ran then, John and I, uphill, and I couldn't keep up with his young lungs. Sure enough, the stone was rolled back. John peered in but was staying outside. I went right in. No body! I saw the cloths. I checked if they were the same as what the women put on. And the cloth for the face was over on its own. My mind was all confused. Now, who would take the body and go to the trouble of taking off the winding cloths ! It was valuable linen.

John had come in. He was very quiet. He whispered something. I did not quite catch it at first. 'He is risen! Resurrection, remember!' I nearly passed out with shock. 'Remember Lazarus … the day in Naim, remember that girl of Jairus.' I remembered alright. Remembered that morning on the lake with the fish. Remembered waking up that day on the mountain. Remembered a hundred stunning moments. How could we have forgotten?

It was we who were in the tomb. We who were in darkness. And it wasn't a stone in front of the tomb but a deep, dark cloud of self-pity. That morning I learned a lesson I have never forgotten. There is no such thing as a tomb unless it is in yourself. There is never an end to hope. And in Jesus there is no such thing as death as we used to know it.

Second Sunday of Easter

John 20: 19-31

In the evening of that same day, the first day of the week, the doors were closed in the room where the disciples were, for fear of the Jews. Jesus came and stood among them. He said to them, 'Peace be with you,' and showed them his hands and his side. The disciples were filled with joy when they saw the Lord, and he said to them again, 'Peace be with you. As the Father sent me, so am I sending you.'

After saying this he breathed on them and said: 'Receive the Holy Spirit. For those whose sins you forgive, they are forgiven; for those whose sins you retain, they are retained.'

Thomas, called the Twin, who was one of the Twelve, was not with them when Jesus came. When the disciples said, 'We have seen the Lord,' he answered, 'Unless I see the holes that the nails made in his hands and can put my finger into the holes they made, and unless I can put my hand into his side, I refuse to believe.'

Eight days later the disciples were in the house again and Thomas was with them. The doors were closed, but Jesus came in and stood among them. 'Peace be with you,' he said. Then he spoke to Thomas, 'Put your finger here; look, here are my hands. Give me your hand; put it into my side. Doubt no longer but believe.' Thomas replied, 'My Lord and my God!' Jesus said to him, 'You believe because you can see me. Happy are those who have not seen and yet believe.'

There are many other signs that Jesus worked and the disciples saw, but they are not recorded in this book. These are recorded so that you may believe that Jesus is the Christ, the Son of God, and that believing this you may have life through his name.

First Reflection
The Lord's New Presence

Where is the risen Lord to be found? This gospel passage begins in the darkness of the Lord's absence. The doors were closed and a paralysing fear froze the energy of the apostles.

But all was changed as Jesus came to them in a new way. Peace was his greeting. And fear gave way to joy. He showed them his hands and his side as evidence of who he was.

Then he bestowed on them a double blessing from God. He commissioned them to carry on his own mission from the Father: the mission of overcoming sin and of bringing forgiveness. 'As the Father sent me, so am I sending you.'

And the second blessing was when he breathed the divine Spirit upon them. From now on the community of disciples shared in the mission of Jesus and were empowered by the same Holy Spirit who had inspired the mission of Jesus. Though Jesus was no longer present to them in his physical flesh, yet his new mode of presence called them to share in his mission and his Spirit.

Thomas was missing that day. From some other episodes in the gospel we know that he was a very cautious sort of individual. Loyal to the last: but loyal to a fault, perhaps, because he stubbornly refused to change anything. He would not believe their story. He was still searching for Jesus in the old way, the way of physical presence where he could be seen and touched. Thomas did not appreciate that Jesus in his physical flesh was confined to one small area. The risen Lord now shared his mission and power with the believing community and sent them out to every place and to all ages with his divine forgiveness to heal souls, minds and bodies.

Thomas received a personal invitation from the Lord to believe. And he responded with the highest act of faith uttered by anybody in the gospel: 'My Lord and my God.'

The Lord then extended the blessedness of faith to all who believe even without physical evidence.

The evangelist John is now ready to draw his writing to a conclusion. He tells us that his purpose was to compile a book of the great signs which Jesus had worked. A sign is something intended to direct us forward on our journey. The signs worked by Jesus were to move people beyond the physical happenings towards their spiritual meaning. And the ultimate spiritual meaning was that Jesus was the Christ, the Son of God. Whoever grows in this faith comes to share in the life of Jesus.

So, where is the risen Lord to be found?

Not in the tomb of death; nor behind the doors of life bolted in fear. Not in a physical presence, to be seen and touched, but confined to one small area.

In the new age of resurrection the Lord is now to be found in the mission of the church which has the power of God's Spirit to proclaim the kingdom, to cast out evil and to heal the broken-hearted. Today's first reading (Acts 5:11-16) is a portrait of a community totally filled with the Spirit of God.

Furthermore, in the quietness of personal prayer, the believer discovers that the Lord is present within the privacy of one's own heart. The believer 'has life through his name.'

It is one thing to say, 'The Lord rose from the dead': a statement about a past event. But it is a greater act of faith to say, 'The Lord is risen': not a statement of the past but of a living presence.

The risen Lord is in the mission of the Church. And the Lord lives in the innermost heart of all who share life in his name

Second Reflection
Touching the Wounds

Thomas was not the sort to look for signs of splendour: he sought only the wounds. And it was by the wounds of Jesus that his doubts were healed. The cross of the wounded Jesus and his resurrection in glory are inseparable in John's portrait of Jesus lifted up from the earth. Some, like Paul, were visited by the risen Lord in splendour too bright for human eyes. Others, like Thomas, have met Christ in touching his wounds. People like Mother Teresa have discovered the mission of Christ in the wounds of the poor: John Vanier in the wounds of the handicapped: Martin Luther King and Helder Camara in the wounds of discrimination and injustice. The young Francis of Assisi won a significant battle over his natural fastidiousness when he warmly embraced a leper. That was the day when he took Christ seriously and began to discover his mission.

Years later, in his last testament, he wrote of his feelings that day: 'What before seemed bitter was changed into sweetness of soul and body.' A new Francis was born out of the wounds of the leper ... for when he embraced the leper as a brother he also embraced his own wounded self and in so doing, his life embraced a mission from Christ. The first steps of a spiritual life always involve a purgation of self in our fastidiousness and fancies and fears. We can well understand how Francis thought of contact with lepers as nauseating and bitter. Or how Francis Thompson recoiled in fear when he saw that Divine Artist would have to burn the wood to charcoal before he could use it for drawing: 'Ah! must Thou char the wood ere Thou canst limn with it.'

We embrace the leper in ourselves when we accept our faults in humble confession: and there we meet the merciful Christ.

We embrace the leper in our brother and sister when we accept them in their poverty and pain, and when we accept them in their shortcomings which irritate us. And when we accept them, they minister the call of Christ to us. It is in giving that we receive. As in the mission of Father Damien among the lepers on Molokai. It was only when he could say 'we lepers' that his mission began to succeed. God asks us to submit to mysteries that puzzle us, darkness that envelopes our landscape, dry deserts to transverse, crosses that weigh us down. In the wounds of life we meet the wounded Christ. Faith awakes when we identify the Wounded One with the Lord of glory. When Thomas saw the wounds of Christ he did not recoil in nausea or object at the signs of weakness. He was drawn to a magnificent declaration of faith: 'My Lord and my God!' His search for the wounded man, Jesus, brought him to the Christ of glory. This recognition in faith of Christ's divinity is the climax of John's gospel: but observe how it is mysteriously linked with touching the wounds of Jesus. Wondrously are the words of Isaiah verified: 'Through his wounds we are healed.' (54:5)

Third Sunday of Easter

John 21: 1-19

Jesus showed himself again to the disciples. It was by the Sea of Tiberias, and it happened like this: Simon Peter, Thomas called the twin, Nathanael from Cana in Galilee, the sons of Zebedee and two more of his disciples were together. Simon Peter said, 'I'm going fishing.' They replied, 'We'll come with you.' They went out and got into the boat but caught nothing that night.

It was light by now and there stood Jesus on the shore, though the disciples did not realise that it was Jesus. Jesus called out, 'Have you caught anything, friends?' And when they answered, 'No,' he said, 'Throw the net out to starboard and you'll find something.' So they dropped the net, and there were so many fish that they could not haul it in. The disciple Jesus loved said to Peter, 'It is the Lord.' At these words 'It is the Lord', Simon Peter, who had practically nothing on, wrapped his cloak round him and jumped into the water. The other disciples came on in the boat, towing the net and the fish; they were only about a hundred yards from land.

As soon as they came ashore they saw that there was some bread there, and a charcoal fire with fish cooking on it. Jesus said, 'Bring some of the fish you have just caught'. Simon Peter went aboard and dragged the net to the shore, full of big fish, one hundred and fifty-three of them; and in spite of there being so many the net was not broken. Jesus said to them, 'Come and have breakfast.' None of the disciples was bold enough to ask, 'Who are you?'; they knew quite well it was the Lord. Jesus then stepped forward, took the bread and gave it to them, and the same with the fish. This was the third time that Jesus showed himself to the disciples after rising from the dead.

After the meal Jesus said to Simon Peter, 'Simon son of John, do you love me more than these others do?' He answered, 'Yes Lord, you know I love you.' Jesus said to him, 'Feed my lambs.'

A second time he said to him, 'Simon son of John, do you love me?' He replied, 'Yes, Lord, you know I love you.' Jesus said to him, 'Look after my sheep.' Then he said to him a third time, 'Simon son of John, do you love me?' Peter was upset that he asked him the third time, 'Do you love me?, and said, 'Lord, you know everything; you know I love you.'

Jesus said to him, 'Feed my sheep. I tell you most solemnly, when you were young you put on your own belt and walked where you liked; but when you grow old you will stretch out your hands, and somebody else will put a belt round you and take you where you would rather not go.'

In these words he indicated the kind of death by which Peter would give glory to God. After this he said, 'Follow Me.'

First Reflection
It is the Lord

The scene has changed from the claustrophobia of the locked room in Jerusalem to the open air by the Lake of Galilee. Seven of the disciples, a full number, had gone back to the old occupation as if they still did not appreciate their new mission and the Spirit they had received. Acting on their own they caught nothing.

The evangelist notes, 'It was light by now', indicating the new day of re-created humanity. But the eyes of the disciples still laboured under the dark of night and they failed to recognise that it was Jesus on the shore.

Once they followed his instructions as to where to cast the net, then their work took in a huge haul. One hundred and fifty-three fish, we are told. Commentators have offered many imaginative interpretations of the number. Some say that it is a reference to the number of species of fish then classified, indicating that the mission of the church would be to all nations. The net was not broken, a sign of unity in a community of diverse cultures and races. It took many hands to land the great catch.

It was the disciple Jesus loved who recognised Jesus: 'It is the Lord.' John likes to show that one must be lifted up in God's love before one can believe.

The focus then centres on the meal shared with the Lord on the shore. Jesus asked for some of their fish although he already had some bread and fish cooking on the fire: the mission of the church would be a combination of divine grace and human effort.

Jesus took the bread and gave it to them', actions which are clear echoes of the eucharistic offering and meal. And the evangelist, writing in Greek, was well aware that the fish had become a secret sign among the persecuted Christians because the word for fish, ICHTHUS, was made up of the first letters in Greek of Jesus Christ, Son of God, the Saviour.

Peter has a high profile in the story, corresponding to his special position in the Christian mission. He went aboard as captain and was the one who finally hauled the net to shore.

But the charcoal fire on the shore links the story with the denials of Peter, for these happened when he had gone to another charcoal fire to warm his hands against the cold of night. Three times Peter had denied his association with Jesus. Now in the new life of Easter all is undone in the healing therapy of three affirmations of his unique love for Jesus. And three times he is given a special pastoral responsibility.

Peter's future is indicated. The impetuous man who once drew a sword would mature into a perfect follower. He would let go in God's name. He would be willing to be led by another: no longer resisting, no longer compelled to fight back. In perfect discipleship he would be willing to die for the glory of God. Peter would lead the church, not in his own way, but by following Jesus ... even unto death. For as St Paul puts it: 'If we have died with him, then we shall live with him.' (2 Tim 2:11)

The whole story is a great meditation on the presence of the risen Lord in the mission of the church, in the Eucharistic breaking of the bread, and in the pastoral leadership bestowed upon Peter.

The words of the disciple whom Jesus loved gives us a prayer of faith: 'It is the Lord.'

When you have fallen back into the old ways ... when you've laboured through the darkness of night ... and the nets come in empty ... then peer through the mists with the courage that comes from knowing that you're loved. There is one who stands on the shore. It is the Lord!

Second Reflection
Peter Remembers

That charcoal fire on the shore. It stopped me on my tracks. When John had said, 'It is the Lord !' all the lost energy surged back through my veins. I grabbed my cloak, jumped overboard and waded ashore. Then I saw the charcoal fire.

He was busy cooking and did not seem to notice my hesitation so I turned back to help the lads pull the net ashore. One hundred and fifty-three. I remember counting them. Then I had run out of excuses for being busy. I hated that charcoal fire.

For once I let the others do the talking. I stayed in the background and kept avoiding his eyes. But it couldn't last. 'Simon,' I heard him say. It was always bad news when went back to calling me Simon. Like the night he said that Satan had got his wish to sift us all like wheat. Some sifting I had gone through! That charcoal fire would always haunt me.

If I hadn't gone over to it to warm my hands ... but then it's impossible to know. 'Simon, son of John, do you love me more than these others do!' Love? Once I had walked on water just to be near him! Now I wasn't too sure of myself. More than the others? I sidestepped: 'Yes, Lord, you know that I love you.' He said: 'Feed my lambs.' Just like another morning after another huge haul of fish when he said I would be fishing for people. Only this time it was all in slow motion. My blinding impulsiveness was gone. I could see the past which had brought me to the present moment: and the future too was coming into view. And it hurt.

Three times he drew it out of me. Painfully. I had never known that hurt could be so deep. That other morning by the lake I was caught up in such a blinding whirl that I felt it was a sort of dying. This morning it hurt so deeply that I knew it was the pain of death. No mistaking it, Simon was dying. I felt everything slipping out of my control. He was taking over.

'Lord, you know everything: you know that I love you.' I had nothing of my own left ... not even my sins. The weight was gone. With wide open eyes I accepted all that his eyes were saying – forgiveness ... new life ... new responsibility. 'Feed my sheep.' My dead bones knitted together under a new flesh. Peter was born.

I remembered how he had once prayed for me: that I would be a rock for all the others. There was no pride for me in this. It was simply that he wanted to live on in me and support the others through me. That is why he changed me and my name. He knew that I had let go. He said that it would always be so and that I would stretch out my hands and let another lead me ... Shepherding is all about leading. And if I am to lead others I must be willing myself to be led. It is very different to fishing. Fishing was brutal in a way. The pulling and the hauling suited my old impulsive strength. I am not afraid. Jesus lives and I know I am not on my own.

Fourth Sunday of Easter

John 10: 27-30

Jesus said: 'The sheep that belong to me listen to my voice; I know them and they follow me. I give them eternal life; they will never be lost and no one will ever steal them from me. The Father who gave them to me is greater than anyone, and no one can steal from the Father. The Father and I are one.'

First Reflection

My sheep listen to my voice

Writers about the Holy Land have been intrigued by the various calls and whistles that shepherds use and the unfailing response of sheep to them. Several flocks may be intermingled overnight in the same shelter. Morning will bring no problem in sorting out the flocks. A shepherd makes his peculiar call and straightaway his flock, and only his flock, will follow him out. In answer to the call a leader sheep begins to move and all the others will follow. Jesus said: 'The sheep that belong to me listen to my voice; I know them and they follow me.'

One must periodically ask oneself: whose voice do I follow? Whose standards do I seek to emulate? Loud voices shout at us today from many sources … peer pressure, pop culture, advertising, political slogans, secularism and so-called liberalism. The way of a disciple is to follow the voice of the Lord. The life of faith is a response to a call. Indeed the whole bible is an ongoing story of call and response. Creation itself can be understood as God calling Adam out of nothingness.

At the beginning of revelation Abraham heard the call of God to venture forth in confidence. He became father of many nations. Moses heard the call, overcame all obstacles and led the people forth into freedom. Often the personal call had to be expressed outwardly in a journey someway symbolic of the inner pilgrimage. Thus Mary, immediately after receiving God's call at the annunciation, set out in faith to visit Elizabeth.

And in the life of Jesus, he received his call when the Spirit descended upon him at the Jordan. His journey began when the Spirit led him first into the wilderness and then into the Galilean ministry. Jesus in turn called disciples, some of whom he called more intimately, to become shepherds of his flock. The risen Lord shared his Spirit with these disciples and called them to carry on his mission: 'As the Father sent me, so I am sending you.' They too would journey forth in answer to the call.

The church is the community of believers who follow the voice of the risen Lord. He lives on in intimate relationship with his followers. He knows them individually and calls each one into an intimate relationship. Many hear a deeper call drawing them into a fuller commitment of life to the mission of Jesus ... some to proclaim his word ...or to carry on his works of compassion... or to take a partner in married love where fidelity reflects the unchanging and unifying love of the Blessed Trinity.

The harvest is great and the labourers are few. More than half the parishes of the world today have no resident priest: the mission of Jesus needs many more voices. While people are hungry, while the sick need tenderness and caring, the compassion of Jesus needs many more hearts and hands. While fidelity in love is often unknown, the world needs the witness of Christian marriage as a light showing the possibility of unconditional trust. The life of a true disciple is directed by listening to the voice of the God who calls. We need the discipline of reflecting on our daily involvement to discern how the Lord is calling us to respond and represent him there. Vocations Sunday is an occasion to reflect on one's own experience of the Lord's call: and to encourage others to understand their lives as being open to the call of the risen Lord. Christ is alive ... in his voice which calls generous disciples to lead others forward in his name.

Second Reflection
The Lord is my shepherd

The thought of God as shepherd developed into a psalm which has ever been a favourite prayer, even of people far removed from pastoral life.

'The Lord is my shepherd; there is nothing I shall want.' Who is your leader? Whose way do you follow? Whose voice do you listen for? The disciple follows the Lord and listens for his voice. He is absolutely confident that with the Lord on his side he will lack for nothing essential.

'Fresh and green are the pastures where he gives me repose.'

As the heat of the day builds up the shepherd leads his flock to the shaded areas. There they will rest during the warmest hours of the day contentedly chewing the cud. The disciple seeks the shade of the Lord's protection from the pressures of life. Daily he must rest with the Lord, chewing his word contentedly, prayerfully reflecting on what the day has brought.

'Near restful waters he leads me,
to revive my drooping spirit.'

Sheep have difficulty in drinking from the swiftly flowing mountain streams so the shepherd has to find a still pool or make one for them. The stream is an image of the activities of life. God is present everywhere and in our activities, but often the pace is so fast that we cannot drink of his presence. Like the sheep we too need the pool of stillness. In restful prayer he revives our drooping spirits.

'He guides me along the right path; he is true to his name.'

The shepherd leads the flock from the front: the sheep follow in his way. How can a sheep get lost? Usually it is by nibbling away in the wrong direction. Christ our shepherd offers us guidance in his words and way of life. His words and actions are the signs or evidence for faith. He is true to his name, Shepherd, in being the way, the truth and the life. And since he is one with the Father, his way leads to the Father.

'If I should walk in the valley of darkness,
no evil would I fear.
You are there with your crook and your staff;
with these you give me comfort. '

Here is a powerful expression of strong faith. Sheep country is in mountainous territory. It a sheep falls into a fissure between rocks or fails to jump across a defile, the shepherd will use his crook with its hooked head to pull up the fallen sheep. Wild dogs and ravenous wolves prowl in the shadows of the valley. The shepherd's staff is the sheep's protection. The good shepherd is prepared not merely to risk danger but even to lay down his life for his sheep. That is an image of the sacrificial love of Jesus for us. No matter how dark the valley, how eerie the situation, or how terrifying the prowling monsters, the true disciple never loses confidence in the love and care guaranteed by the faithful shepherd.

'You have prepared a banquet for me
in the sight of my foes.'

The reward for going through the valley of darkness is the banquet of a fresh pasture. Before letting the sheep graze there the shepherd will first have cleared it of poisonous plants and shrubs. These are thrown upon stone pyres to dry out in the sunshine. In the sight of his enemies, the poisonous plants, the sheep can enjoy the sweet grass in perfect safety. The disciple's banquet is the eucharist, the bread of life, which strengthens the soul against all enemies.

'My head you have anointed with oil,
my cup is overflowing.'

At the end of the day the sheep return to the fold and, one by one, they are examined by the shepherd. Scratches and bruises are treated with olive oil. Heads are plunged into a jug of cool water, right up to the eyes which are soothed from the irritations of dust.

'Surely goodness and kindness shall follow me
all the days of my life.
In the Lord's own house shall I dwell
forever and ever.'

Fifth Sunday of Easter

John 13: 31-35

When Judas had gone Jesus said: 'Now has the Son of Man been glorified, and in him God has been glorified. If God has been glorified in him, God will in turn glorify him in himself, and will glorify him very soon. My little children, I shall not be with you much longer. I give you a new commandment: love one another; just as I have loved you, you also must love one another. By this love you have for one another, everyone will know that you are my disciples.'

First Reflection

A New Commandment

Where is the Risen Lord to be met? The liturgy each Sunday in this Easter season directs our thoughts to the various situations where the Lord is present and active in our midst. Over the past weeks we have reflected on his presence in the church's mission of forgiveness, in the faith of those who do not see yet believe, in the universal mission of the church, in the breaking of bread, in the pastoral responsibility of Peter and in the voice of the Lord as the shepherd whom we follow.

The answer today is that the Lord is to be found in the community where people love one another with his love.

Judas left the table fellowship of those who shared in the breaking of bread with Jesus. John expresses the awfulness of his decision by saying that night had fallen. Judas, leaving the Light of the world, was opting for darkness. That night indicated the beginning of the process which would culminate in the death of Jesus. But Jesus entered the darkness of death only to conquer it. So, the departure of Jesus really marked the beginning of the return of Jesus to glory.

Sadness would overwhelm the hearts of the disciples when they began to realise that Jesus would no longer be present physically with them. He consoles them with the encouraging message of a new and greater mode of presence in the times after his resurrection. At his return to the Father's glory, elsewhere called his lifting up, he will draw all people up. He promises a higher level of life. This new life will be governed by a new commandment: 'Love one another, just as I have loved you, you must love one another.'

In what sense is this a new commandment? After all, wasn't the command to love one's neighbour clearly taught in the Old Testament? What is new in the words of Jesus is the standard of love ... 'as I have loved you' ... a love that gives unto death, a love that excludes nobody. The love of Jesus is not confined to neighbours or close friends. His sort of love includes enemies and those who might have been unjust to us. His love is not turned off by the wrongdoing of others. It is a river that refuses to be polluted by the poison of others. Also new will be the source of this love, the Holy Spirit, soon to take up residence in the hearts of the disciples.

As baptised Christians we are called to be the active members of the body of Christ on earth. The lifestyle of the early Christians gave a powerful witness to the presence of the Lord among them. 'See how these Christians love one another.'

The First Reading in today's liturgy is John the Seer's vision of new Jerusalem, coming down from God, as beautiful as a bride all dressed for her husband. 'You see this city? Here God lives among people. He will make his home among them; they shall be his people, and he will be their God; his name is God-with-them ... Now I am making the whole of creation new.' (Apoc 21:1-5)

While those words of vision refer primarily to heavenly life after death, we see the beginning of this new life in the church where Spirit-filled people make the love of Jesus visible and tangible. Truly God is with them.

In his First Letter John expands on the idea. 'God is love, and whoever remains in love remains in God and God in him.' (1 Jn 4:16)

Where is the Risen Lord to be encountered? The answer coming through today's readings is that the Lord's presence is to be seen and felt where disciples follow the example of his total love. The church is the beautiful bride of Christ, loved by him and giving birth to love throughout the world in her many children.

Risen Lord Jesus, may your Spirit invade our hearts and lift us up beyond our sinful limitations. May your love be the energy of all our activities so that we might reflect the beauty of your face unto the glory of the Father.

Second Reflection
Reflecting his glory

All created things bear the marks of the Creator and can lead us to God's glory. St Paul wrote to the Romans: 'Ever since God created the world his everlasting power and deity – however invisible – have been there for the mind to see in the things he has made.' (Rom 1:20)

This April morning I see the glory of God reflected on the dewy grass and in the colours of the garden, daffodil yellow and tulip red, purples and greens, each flower being an unique expression of the glory of God. Below the garden wall the glassy Barrow saunters at an easy pace through our flat midlands on its journey back to the ocean.

The wise man of old, Qoheleth, commented on the constant journeying of water back to the ocean of its origin. 'Into the sea all the rivers go, and yet the sea is never filled, and still to their goal the rivers go.' (Ecc 1:7) As the water which came from the bosom of the ocean journeys back to the ocean, so does every created thing need to return to its Creator.

The exciting colours, the delicate intricacy of each design and the subtlety of each scent were all born in the mind of the Creator.

They are glorious because they have come from God, who is glory. In the eye of the beholder they are newly glorious when they are allowed to point away from themselves in a return to their divine source.

All created things then bear the marks of the Creator: they are like the footprints of God proclaiming that He has passed this way.

But redeemed humanity is called to be more then the footprint of God. We are adopted into a sharing of the life of the Son. St Paul sings of God's blessed plan for us: 'Blessed be God the Father of Our Lord Jesus Christ ... who chose us in Christ ... determining that we should become his adopted sons ... to make us praise the glory of his grace.' (Eph 1: 3-6) It is our calling to be like Him who is the 'image of the unseen God' and the 'perfect copy of his nature.' Image here means being a mirror of God's beauty and glory. God's plan for the present era is that his glory should be most nobly reflected on earth through the lives of those who follow Christ's commandment of love. While every created thing is a footprint of God's passage through the world, in a special way the 'little children' of divine adoption are called to be living mirrors of God by imitating the love of Jesus Christ.

'No one has ever seen God,' wrote St John, 'but as long as we love one another God will live in us and his glory will be complete in us.' (1 Jn 4:12) The compassion and caring of God come to people through human hearts which are given over to Christ's way.

'God is love and anyone who lives in love lives in God and God lives in him.' (1 Jn 4:16) The new commandment, the vocation of people in the new life of Easter, is to complete the love of God! 'No one has ever seen God; but as long as we love one another God will live in us and his love will be complete in us.' (1 Jn 4:12)

As an electric current is rendered ineffective if there is any break in the circuit, so the energy of God's love is cut off from people when we fail to love them. The circuit is completed and the energy flows when we bring his love to one another.

Jesus Christ may not be walking our roads today in his physical body: but the power of his love and glory can be known 'by this love you have for one another.'

Sixth Sunday of Easter

John 14: 23-29

Jesus said to his disciples, 'If anyone loves me he will keep my word, and my Father will love him, and we shall come to him and make our home with him. Those who do not love me do not keep my words. And my word is not my own: it is the word of the one who sent me. I have said these things to you while still with you; but the Advocate, the Holy Spirit, whom the Father will send in my name, will teach you everything and remind you of all I have said to you. Peace I bequeath to you, my own peace I give you, a peace the world cannot give, this is my gift to you. Do not let your hearts be troubled or afraid. You heard me say: I am going away, and shall return. If you loved me you would have been glad to know that I am going to the Father, for the Father is greater than I. I have told you this now before it happens, so that when it does happen you may believe.'

First Reflection

My peace I give to you

The minds of the disciples were numbed and confused when Jesus spoke to them of his impending departure. Love finds it so hard to let go of the loved one. Jesus explained to them how it was necessary to let go of his physical presence so that he could release even greater gifts to them. They were promised very special gifts from Father, Spirit and Son.

The Father's gift would be an inner sense of his love: an intimate, at-home relationship with the very Creator of all.

The Spirit's gift would be the light of faith to understand the teaching of Jesus.

And the Son's gift would be *shalom*: not a worldly imitation of peace, but his own inner strength which enabled him to face the conflicts of his departure and the pain of the cross.

The popular philosophies of West and East offer imitations of peace, useful in their own way, but not totally authentic.

The hedonistic West offers peace like the soothing of an irritation. Take a painkiller, distract the mind as an escape from boredom, release all pent up energy, calm the nerves with soothing music, ease the pressure with drink or pills which dull the senses. These ways offer an escape but not an authentic inner strength. Escapism my remove the itch for a while but it does nothing to cure the wound.

The East offers a journey into inner tranquillity which is like a submarine seeking the depths of the sea far below the storms on the surface of life. The source of all pain and misery is said to be desire: so the remedy for pain must be through control of our desires. Techniques of muscular relaxation, breathing exercises and the mental repetition of simple, soothing sounds have been perfected as means of control.

The painkilling of the West may be legitimately used: and the inner tranquillity of the East may be gainfully sought. But the Christian disciple is ultimately to seek peace in the gift of God's love to the soul. The shalom of Jesus, which he bestowed on his disciples, grows out of intimacy with God who lives in us.

The word intimacy has its roots in the Latin word for fear. Intimacy means a relationship that can face into the risks and fears, the pains and cost that the relationship will bring. Intimacy grows out of a trust that is so strong between the parties that together they can face into better or worse, richer or poorer, sickness or health

Because of his intimacy with the Father, Jesus could speak of peace on the night when he knew apprehension, disappointment and fear. His unfailing source of trust was his sense of the Father's will: 'Not my will, but thine be done.' The peace which he spoke of had nothing to do with escaping the reality of pain: it was the strength to face the cross.

The totality of his life was a union of intimacy with the Father's will. Even when the parts creaked and groaned in the storms of darkness and suffering, still his house stood firm. In the Father's will was his foundation, his inner strength and source of peace. The poet, Dante, attributed the joy of the blessed in heaven to their doing God's will. 'In his will is our peace,' they told him.

The evangelist who recorded the words of Jesus' promise of peace knew how much the disciples were to live with pain, suffering and persecution unto death for their belief. Like their Master, they would find their peace in intimate union with the Father ... with God who had set up home in their hearts.

'Do not let your hearts be troubled or afraid.' The parts of life my be painful and terrifying at times, but the totality of life is firm, for God is at home in the heart.

'God is within, it cannot be shaken.' (Ps 45)

Second Reflection
Letting Go

In a backstreet room in New York, on a stifling August evening, an old man lay dying, gasping for breath. In vain did an air conditioner hum and crane its neck this way and that.

One of the watchers at the bedside had twined a rosary beads around the fingers of his right hand. The other hand tightly grasped a little silver casket to his heart.

The family knew its unusual treasure: a fistful of earth from his native western isle; an island where good earth was scarce on the skeleton of rocks swept clean by regular Atlantic rainstorms. He had taken up that fistful of earth the night before he left, sixty years ago. It was first deposited in a crumpled brown paper bag, later in a glass jar and eventually in the little silver casket, which was the only item of luxury his life ever afforded. He had survived in the city, held body and soul together, reared a family, but never achieved enough to return home. With every passing year the fistful of earth grew more precious as it brought him back to the Eden of memory … the freedom of the salty wind, the soft vowels of his native tongue, the wild release of the seagull's cry when borne on a giant hand of air. In later years the family offered to pay for his journey, but he was afraid to go, afraid of shattering his dreams.

He was drifting away from the droning of the prayers … as in a boat down an underground channel. It was dark but the boat was drifting along towards a place of light where he saw a great door. But it was just above his reach. A man on duty came out and offered a lifting hand. But he was clasping his fistful of earth too tightly and the boat lurched forward as the current bore it away.

He came towards another door. This time a group of people, so like his own parents and neighbours of childhood, appeared and called.

He reached towards them, checked for a moment to secure his casket and then failed to make contact with them as the current carried on in its relentless way.

A third door … and here was a little child. Startled at the danger for the child above the swirling waters, he seemed to leap towards the child's arms. He had landed. And there inside the door was an island so like his own but many times more beautiful. When the watchers at the bedside saw the silver casket fall from his grasp and the dry earth spilling on the floor, they knew that he had gone home.

Letting go of Jesus was so painful to the apostles that their minds were virtually numbed to what he was saying. They desperately wanted to hold onto their fistful of earthly contact with him. 'If you loved me you would have been glad to know that I am going to the Father.' Love, if it is true and unselfish, knows when to let go. Absolute trust in God demands the risk of letting go of our last fistful of earth. Francis Thompson wrote of his fear of giving in to the Hound of Heaven: 'For though I knew His love Who followed, Yet was I sore adread Lest, having Him, I must have naught else beside.' Our fistful of earth can take many forms:

– pride in our prestige and achievements;

– a stubborn insistence on our rights;

– a self-pity which seeks to justify sinful compensations;

– the repressed anger which holds on carressingly to memories of past hurts.

With keen understanding St Francis described anger as a sin against poverty, since hurt memory is like a purse that selfishness will hold on to. 'I am going away and shall return.' Before he can come back to us we have to let go of our fistful of earth. The heart that is open and waiting for him is shown by empty hands.

The Ascension of the Lord

Luke 24: 46-53

Jesus said to his disciples: 'You see how it is written that the Christ would suffer and on the third day rise from the dead, and that, in his name, repentance for the forgiveness of sins would be preached to all the nations, beginning from Jerusalem. You are witnesses to this. And now I am sending down to you what the Father has promised. Stay in the city then, until you are clothed with the power from on high.' Then he took them out as far as the outskirts of Bethany, and lifting up his hands he blessed them. Now as he blessed them, he withdrew from them and was carried up to heaven. They worshipped him and then went back to Jerusalem full of joy; and they were continually in the Temple praising God.

First Reflection

Worship, Joy and Praise

Each of the synoptic evangelists gave his own nuance to the Ascension story. Matthew emphasised the promise of the Lord to be with the disciples to the end of time. Thus he would be true to the name Emmanuel, God is-with-us, the name by which the conception of the child was announced to Joseph on the opening page of Matthew. Mark highlighted the messianic triumph of Christ when he was taken up to heaven to the right hand of God while the apostles go out to preach in his power. Luke harked back to the manner of the departure of Elijah, who was taken up to heaven in a chariot of fire, but whose spirit came to rest on his disciple, Elisha (cf. 2 Kngs 2). He described how Jesus was carried up to heaven and was worshipped by the disciples: and that he was sending down to them what the Father had promised.

One would labour in vain trying to fit together the jig-saw details of the various accounts. Even the one writer, Luke, differs between his gospel and Acts. A photographer deputed to capture the scene would have had insurmountable problems about the day and location. Luke in Acts says it was forty days after Easter day but in his gospel it seems to happen on Easter day. Luke's gospel situates the departure on the outskirts of Bethany and in Acts he says the Mount of Olives, whereas Matthew has it taking place on a mountain in distant Galilee. The diverse details are no more than wrappings around the mysterious event. The essence of the various stories are certain theological truths on which the evangelists are in full agreement. The first truth being celebrated today is the return of Jesus to the Father in heaven: this is what John calls his glorification.

A second reason for celebration is the promise of power from on high to enable the disciples become witnesses of the Lord to the ends of the earth. A third aspect of the celebration is our final hope ... that we can look forward to the return of the Lord. 'Jesus who has been taken up from you into heaven, this same Jesus will come back in the same way as you have seen him go there.' (Acts 1:11) Luke draws attention to the reaction of the disciples. They worshipped Jesus: they went back to Jerusalem full of joy: and they were continually in the temple praising God. What John would call believing, Luke describes as worship, joy and praise. If throughout the liturgical year one has listened to the teaching of Jesus, wondered at his miracles, journeyed through the testing days of Lent and shared the pains of the passion, then it is fitting now to celebrate the triumph of Jesus in worship, joy and peace. We bow in worship as we recognise his uplifting in divine glory. There is joy in the thought of how he transformed death into the dawn of new life. And God is to be praised every day in the proclamation of his great works.

Second Reflection
Peter Remembers

Ever since that morning of the hundred and fifty-three fish I hardly knew myself. Such peace and quiet strength I had never known. Some were anxious about me. I noticed them at times watching, wondering when I would bark a command or explode in temper. But I was at peace. And waiting.

The great dreams were back. One hundred and fifty-three fish ... I was waiting on his words where to cast the net again. Feed his lambs, feed his sheep! Me, a shepherd! He had a sense of humour. I no longer resented his departure. Gone were the nightmares about tombs and charcoal fires. I had let go of my guilt and shame. The lightness of peace was something new to me. I tried to explain it all to the others. And tried to show that he had to die and go away. John of course understood it all before I did. Thomas too, in his own way. But some of them were very slow to fit the pieces together. It was odd that I was the one offering patient explanations. Witnesses to the ends of the earth!

The impulsive Simon would have immediately jumped into the first ship going anywhere but would have ended up nowhere. In my new life as Peter I waited. And prayed. Long before, we had asked him to teach us to pray. Now it was happening. We were praying. If anyone wanted proof of the rising of Jesus, here it was … Peter was patiently waiting … and praying! New life was a fact.

Two great memories helped to keep us together. Somebody had mentioned Elijah. Together we went back over the story of how he was taken up to heaven in a chariot of fire but his prophetic spirit came to rest on his disciple, Elisha. That story helped us to make sense of things. It gave us hope. And hope gave us patience.

And then too there was the presence of Mary. She came in with John but I think she would have come in any case for now we felt that she was a mother to us all. Nobody had to mention Cana but that wedding feast was always forefront in our minds when Mary was around. She was part of that story where water was changed into wine. Her presence reminded us that it could happen again… to us. And her favourite saying was: 'Nothing is impossible to God.'

And so, we waited … and prayed. And for nine days of deep peace I knew the tranquillity of a child in the womb of a loving mother.

Seventh Sunday of Easter

John 17: 20-26

Jesus raised his eyes to heaven and said: 'Holy Father, I pray not only for these, but for those also who through their words will believe in me. May they all be one. Father, may they be one in us, as you are in me and I am in you, so that the world may believe it was you who sent me. I have given them the glory you gave to me, that they may be one as we are one. With me in them and you in me, may they be so completely one that the world will realise that it was you who sent me and that I have loved them as much as you love me. Father, I want those you have given me to be with me where I am, so that they may always see the glory you have given me because you loved me before the foundation of the world. Father, Righteous One, the world has not known you, but I have known you, and these have known that you have sent me. I have made your name known to them and will continue to make it known, so that the love with which you loved me may be in them, and so that I may be in them.'

First Reflection

Images of the Father

John writes as the skylark sings ... ascending and descending on warm currents of air in a spiral of song, bubbling forth rich notes which are repeated in different combinations but which never quite reach a final statement of simple melody.

High above the earth, John, the skylark, sings of the union of the Father and the Son in heavenly glory. The song descends to earth when the Son is sent and manifests heavenly glory and love to the disciples. As they catch the divine melodies their lives become part of the song and they pass on the notes of harmony and unity to the rest of the world. People observe how these Christians love one another and then they too are drawn up into belief in the Son. And in believing that the Son was sent by the Father, they are drawn upwards to where the song first began ... in the Father.

The model and source of unity is the intimate relationship of the Father and the Son. The Father sent the Son into the world so that all who believe in him might share in the glory of their divine life. Baptism makes us children of the Father, called to grow into the likeness of Christ.

One of the great stories of John's gospel is the wedding feast at Cana where Jesus changed the water into wine. In the abundance of that miracle the great wedding being celebrated was the union of God and humanity, the joining of the families of heaven and earth.

As a marriage reaches consummation in the partners' reciprocal act of total giving and receiving, so was Calvary the hour of consummation when the life of Jesus was totally given up and returned to the Father.

The children of the consummation are those who are born again through belief in Jesus, under water and the power of the Holy Spirit. Children inherit the inner characteristics and show the outward features of both parents ... earthly and heavenly. We are children of the earth who live in the limitations of the flesh, bearing the common ailments of a sinful society, inheriting the wounds of the past and breathing in the polluted air of an imperfect culture. But for all that, the likeness of God is in us too.

St Paul in many places wrote of the image of God that we are called to reflect. 'Those who love God are the ones he has specially chosen long ago and intended to become true images of his Son.' (Rom 8:29) And this is how he described living up to our baptismal life: 'You have stripped off your old behaviour with your old self, and you have put on your new self which will progress towards true knowledge the more it is renewed in the image of its creator.' (Col 3:9-10) A process of growth is set in motion at baptism. Christian life is the proper progression from planting to growth to maturity.

The miracle at Cana showed that the power of Jesus could change water into wine. So would it transform the features of our earthly existence into heavenly likeness. The change at Cana took place in an instant: the transformation of life into heavenly likeness is a lifelong process of growth. And so, Jesus prayed for his disciples: 'Father may they be one in us as you are in me and I am in you ... May the love with which you loved me be in them so that I may be in them.'

Christian life is the process of allowing the beauty of God's love increasingly to shine out through our lives.

Second Reflection

Peter remembers the prayer

We went back to Jerusalem as Jesus had told us. There we waited and prayed. We talked too, remembering Jesus in different places, what he had said to various people, piecing together the incidents that happened. I was constantly amazed at John's memory. He was always a deep one. He kept recalling things Jesus said that last night with us. I must admit that I could recall very little except Judas going out and the black bile of hatred that knotted in my gut. Although I had no clear knowledge of what he was about to do, I had this vague, eerie sense of something terrible.

But now as John talked, brighter memories began to take shape. Jesus had drifted away from us into a strange world. He was in a mysterious communion with the Father but we could hear what he was saying. I remember feeling a bit embarrassed for it was like eavesdropping on a conversation. Pieces we could hear clearly and then we would miss bits. Then he began to pray for us and as his voice strengthened I felt that he wanted us to hear as well as the Father. It seemed to be all about being one. He kept saying it in different ways. And now, in the upper room, I thought about it.

As a fisherman I had spent many a contented hour clearing my slow brain as we rested on the oars until a break on the surface was the signal for action. I drifted back to the night of his trial. I could see now that my betrayal happened because I was not one in the way that Jesus was one with the Father. I was not one ... I was a different person wherever I found myself. With Jesus I was a passionate friend who would die to defend him. But once away from him I put on a different personality and swore that I had never heard of him.

I now understood that the inner strength of Jesus was his unflinching oneness with the Father. This gave him an inner core of peace, a strong centre that could never be split up. Sin must be the result of our lack of inner oneness. Being one person here and another person there. But Jesus had prayed for us! That we would be at-one in ourselves, true to his name, consecrated in the truth. If we could be strong in ourselves as individuals, then we could be strong for each other too. If we were to represent Jesus we would have to be very united and supportive among ourselves.

Another occasion came up out of memory. He had prayed

for me especially … that I might be strengthened and in turn strengthen the others. That memory of his prayer for me warmed my heart and firmed up my backbone. I moved into action and organised the election of a replacement for Judas. Someone who was a witness to the rising of Jesus, that's what we needed. Matthias was elected. The fullness of the tribal number was complete again. It bolstered up our flagging spirits to see us one and entire again. It showed that we were looking ahead, that we were waiting, not in desperation, but ready to move into action.

I felt my own inner self totally healed and at-one. As a group, our old jealousies had disappeared. There was a new spirit of co-operation and we were one as never before. Could we pass on this inner peace and desire for oneness to others? God would show us if we waited and prayed … if we rested on our oars and awaited his inspiration.

Pentecost Sunday

John 14: 15-16. 23-26
Jesus said to his disciples 'If you love me you will keep my commandments. I shall ask the Father and he will give you another Advocate to be with you for ever. If anyone loves me he will keep my word, and my Father will love him, and we shall come to him and make our home with him. Those who do not love me do not keep my words. And my word is not my own; it is the word of the one who sent me. I have said these things to you while still with you; but the Advocate, the Holy Spirit, whom the Father will send in my name, will teach you everything and remind you of all I have said to you.'

First Reflection
Pentecost – The Harvest

The name Pentecost denotes the fiftieth day. Seven weeks, a full season of growth, have been completed: it is time for harvest. Pentecost coincided with a Jewish feast which was at once a nature feast and a religious memory. The nature feast was the celebration of the grain harvest: the religious memory celebrated the covenant established in the law given to Moses on Mount Sinai. The seed which had died in the soil of Calvary had now produced a hundred-fold. And the word of God which was inscribed for Moses on tablets of stone is now at home in the hearts of the disciples who live by the new commandment of Christ's love.

Pentecost is the fulfilment of the old dispensation and the first harvesting from the seeds planted by Christ. The mission of Jesus blossomed into the mission of the church. And the power of the Holy Spirit which filled Jesus is now at work in the disciples. It is the birthday of the church. The immediate impact on the apostles was radical and dramatic. Previously they were locked behind closed doors, fearful and unsure of what to do. Now they emerge in broad daylight, full of courage, charged with conviction, with a very clear sense of their mission. The promised power from on high has descended upon them.

The proper word to describe the effect of Pentecost is enthusiasm ... which literally means God-is-in. God is at home in the souls of the disciples of Jesus and stirs up in them a clear sense of their new identity as children of God. In today's second reading St Paul tells the Romans: 'The spirit of God has made his home in you ... The spirit you received ... is the spirit of sons, and it makes us cry out, "Abba, Father!" The Spirit himself and our spirit bear united witness that we are children of God.' This gift of Christian identity is the light of faith. The Spirit is also the source of the gift of hope. Jesus promised the Spirit as a courtroom advocate, who would give counsel to the disciples in their conflict with the world.

The Advocate is also the consoler who lifts the minds of the disciples from depressing circumstances to the memory of the teaching of Jesus. 'The Advocate, the Holy Spirit, whom the Father will send in my name, will teach you everything and remind you of all I have said to you.' And it is the Spirit who raises the soul's love up to the supernatural plane where it shares in Christ's own love. Again it is Paul who clarifies the teaching. 'The love of God had been poured into our hearts by the Holy Spirit which has been given to us.' (Rom 5:5) And to the Corinthians he confides where the motivating power of his apostolate comes from: 'the love of God overwhelms us.' (2 Cor 5:14) The correct grammatical analysis of that text indicates that Paul is referring to Christ's own love which lives in him and must be expressed.

The light of faith: the strength to hope: and the ability to love as Christ did – these are beyond our natural powers. Faith, hope and love are given when the Holy Spirit is at home in the soul. The church is the community of faith, hope and love. The mission of Jesus has blossomed into the mission of the church. It is the birthday of the church: a day to celebrate in praise, thanksgiving and joy.

Second Reflection
A Powerful Wind and Tongues of Fire

How does one describe something invisible as the wind? The New Testament writers wrote of the Holy Spirit through the use of symbols and by describing the effects of the Spirit's power in the lives and works of Jesus and the disciples. A symbol is something we refer to in order that it might point beyond itself to a greater reality. For instance a piece of coloured cloth is more than a mere cloth when it is the flag of a country. The great symbols in the Pentecost story were wind and tongues of fire. 'They heard what sounded like powerful wind from heaven.'

The movement of the wind recalled the story of creation. In the beginning, God's spirit, or breath, hovered over the primeval waters. When God fashioned man of dust from the soil 'he breathed into his nostrils a breath of life, and thus man became a living being.' (Gen 2:7) And in Ezechiel's vision of the valley of dry bones, it was when the breath entered the bones that they began to live. Breathing was a sure sign of life. People understood that the breath of life was on loan from God until he called it back again.

The wind of Pentecost was powerful. Just as the breath of the risen Lord over the disciples bestowed on them his own living mission of reconciliation. In the new creation of the resurrection age the powerful wind of Pentecost is a symbol of the life of God in the souls of the disciples.

The air that we breathe is allowed to vibrate on vocal chords, expand in sound chambers and the sound is given shape by tongue and lips. The mind invests the sound with a meaning and words are born. Tongues of fire were the second symbol of Pentecost.

The fearful silence of the apostles gave way to an eloquence that astonished and moved the teeming multitudes in Jerusalem. Differences of language proved no obstacle to these inflamed tongues and each nation heard in their own language. In the old story of Babel's challenge to God, the people were scattered in punishment by the confusion of different languages. But in the new story of Pentecost different nations are united as they understood the words of the divinely inflamed tongue. The tongues appeared to be fire. Fire brings light and symbolises the warmth of love. Fire is a powerful element of change. John the Baptist described his conversion of people as the change effected by water. But the one who was to come after him, the one more powerful, would baptise people by the Holy Spirit and fire.

The heart that is afire with divine flames enlightens the mind with the clear conviction of our new relationship with the Father: 'God has sent the Spirit of his Son into our hearts: the Spirit that cries, "Abba, Father."' (Gal 4:6)

The enlightened mind must speak. Tongues must proclaim the deeds of God ... sometimes even beyond the rational choosing of words, according to the mysterious words of Paul: 'The Spirit too comes to help us in our weakness. For when we cannot

choose words in order to pray properly, the Spirit himself expresses our plea in a way that could never be put into words,
and God who knows everything in our hearts knows perfectly
well what he means, and that the pleas of the saints expressed
by the Spirit are according to the mind of God.' (Rom 8:26-27)

The creating and re-creating breath of God blew like a powerful
wind. Dead bones knitted together.

Hearts extinguished by fear were fanned into tongues of
flame. The church had come alive.

Trinity Sunday

John 16: 12-15

Jesus said to his disciples: 'I still have many things to say to you but they would be too much for you now. But when the Spirit of truth comes he will lead you to the complete truth, since he will not be speaking as from himself but will say only what he has learnt; and he will tell you of the things to come. He will glorify me since all he tells you will be taken from what is mine. Everything the Father has is mine; that is why I said: All he tells you will be taken from what is mine.'

First Reflection
Christian Prayer

Today's gospel is taken from the last supper discourse when Jesus spoke of his impending return to the Father. His physical departure would not leave the disciples orphaned or bereft of his presence: rather, it would open up a new mode of divine presence. The Holy Spirit would come into the minds and hearts of the disciples in what can best be called a new creation.

Trinity Sunday is an opportunity to consider the vital movement of all Christian prayer and of the liturgy in particular. We cannot appreciate what liturgy is about without some understanding of the inner movements of divine life. Jesus described his mission as a journey down into our world and then back up in a return to the Father. 'I came from the Father and have come into the world and now I leave the world to go to the Father.' (Jn 16:28) There is no other way to the Father but through the Son's return. We are privileged to share in that return by the power of the Holy Spirit given to us. 'When the Spirit of truth comes he will lead you to the complete truth.' (Jn 16:13) The essence of Christian prayer is our sharing in the return of glory to the Father, through the Son, by the power of the Holy Spirit.

In particular, the eucharistic liturgy is the living remembrance of Jesus Christ, who was the Word of God touching the lowest areas of human life, even death in disgrace, out of which he rose and returned to the Father. At Mass, the mind listens to the word of God in the readings. In the light of the word, the needs of the community are gathered together in the petitions of the faithful. Bread and wine are prepared as gifts to symbolise the return of our lives and of all creation to the Father. Then in the solemn words and actions of the Eucharistic prayer the journey of the Word down into our world and back to the Father is remembered. And in the biblical sense, to remember God's actions is to make them present again. The ceremony reaches a climax of intimacy in holy communion.

Our arms would never be long enough to stretch across the infinite space to heaven. Nor would we ever be worthy to show our faces before the all holy face of God. But the Son has reached down in mercy to us: and the Spirit of uniting love has raised us up. And so, in the light of the Son's teaching and in the power of the Spirit we have the courage to utter the essential word of Christian prayer: 'Father.' 'The Spirit himself and our spirit bear united witness that we are children of God … and it makes us cry out, "Abba. Father!"' (Rom 8:15)

Christian prayer is unto the glory of the Father: it is a movement undertaken in the name of Jesus Christ, the Son: and it is only through the power of the Spirit that is given to us that we are raised up in mind and heart to share in this movement. This movement of prayer is seen in its purity in the liturgical remembrance of Jesus Christ. Glory be to the Father, through the Son, by the power of the Holy Spirit.

Second Reflection
The Ocean of God's Life
My favourite image of the Blessed Trinity is the ocean. Its vastness suggests infinity: its ceaseless movement speaks of eternity. Its depths are an awesome mystery: yet to relax every muscle and float with the waves is intimacy. A stormy sea shows terrifying power: yet to be absorbed in a calm ocean sunset is about the quietest moment you'd ever experience. The twice-a-day miracle of the sea's coming in and going out expresses the inner movements of the triune God.

The deep and mysterious bosom of the ocean is like the Father, the first principle of all being. From this living bosom proceeds the incoming tide – as the Son proceeds from the Father. The incoming tide reaches our shores – as the Son was sent to earth in our flesh. The pockmarks of work and play on the sands of our world are totally erased under every high tide. The work of Jesus was a cleansing wave of mercy and forgiveness on the sands of life. When its mission is done, the tide then dies away and returns to the ocean – as the Son eternally returns to the Father.

Science tells us that the sea is drawn by the magnetism of the moon as it hovers over the waters of the world. But I prefer to think that its flowing to and ebbing from is under the power of the Holy Spirit who has ever hovered over the waters as the breath of God.

The breath of warm air over the ocean causes the water to evaporate. The vapour rises and is borne on the hand of the breeze towards the lands of the world, upon which it will fall in the bounty of rain. But all water is eager to return to its source. Our lakes and rivers, our kettles and cups, our tanks and basins temporarily restrain the homeward flow of the water that we might avail of its million uses. But the journey of return goes on, as two writers of wisdom noted: 'All that comes from the earth returns to the earth, what comes from the water returns to the sea. ' (Sir 40:11) 'Into the sea all rivers go, and yet the sea is never filled, and still to their goal the rivers go.' (Ecc 1:7) As Jesus returned to the Father … as the water returns to the ocean … all of creation must return to its creator. Every created thing is a symbol of the creator, that is, part of a movement beyond itself to a greater reality. If you look at a flower and see only the flower, you are only partly living. But if you look at a flower and in that flower you see the beauty of the creator, then you are somebody caught up in the return to the fullness of living. Since human beings are endowed with free will, our return to the creator is in the free response of love. That is why the new commandment of re-created humanity is about love.

Contemplation begins when we start to realise that we are not simply distant observers of the ocean … but that the waters of life are flowing in and through us. Jesus spoke of the coming of the three Divine Persons to live in us … 'we shall come to him and make our home with him.' (Jn 14:23) The meaning of sanctifying grace is that God dwells in the soul. Since the mission of Jesus Christ and the coming of the Holy Spirit, humanity has been re-created on a new level of life. The mission of Jesus was the tide which cleansed our shores. And the Spirit of Pentecost is the Love of God which draws us back to the Father's bosom.

The movements of God which we observe in creation, as the

sea flows in and ebbs back to its source, are now to be found within the sanctified soul.

The contemplative observes the created word and hears the word of the creator echoing in the soul ... as 'deep is calling on deep in the roar of the waters.' (Ps 41)

The contemplative who prays before the Blessed Sacrament is not under the strain of searching for words, but knows that the bread means that God is our companion (that is, a sharer of bread) at the table of the heart. The contemplative who reads Sacred Scripture hears God speaking from within .

'On that day you will understand that I am in my Father and you in me and I in you.' (Jn 14:20)

The Body and Blood of Christ

Luke 9:11-17

Jesus made the crowds welcome and talked to them about the Kingdom of God; and he cured those who were in need of healing. It was late afternoon when the Twelve came to him and said. 'Send the people away, and they can go the the villages and farms round about to find lodging and food; for we are in a lonely place here.' He replied, 'Give them something to eat yourselves.' But they said, 'We have no more than five loaves and two fish, unless we are to go ourselves and buy food for all these people.' For there were about five thousand men. But he said to his disciples, 'Get them to sit down in parties of about fifty.' They did so and made them all sit down. Then he took the five loaves and the two fish, raised his eyes to heaven, and said the blessing over them; then he broke them and handed them to his disciples to distribute among the crowd. They all ate as much as they wanted, and when the scraps remaining were collected they filled twelve baskets.

First Reflection

Luke and Bread

The story of how Jesus fed the multitude, as told by Luke, prefigures the ministry of the apostles in the Christian community. The actions of Jesus in taking, blessing, breaking and distributing the food would become the eucharistic actions. The work of the apostles was foreshadowed when Jesus told them, 'Give them something to eat yourselves.'

Bread is surely the most relevant symbol of hope for a world in which half the population suffer from shortage of food. Little wonder that Jesus should choose bread as the memorial sign of his presence and care in the world.

Although in our western society doctors more often ask patients to cut back on their intake of food and drink, Luke, the physician, is fascinated by food. Every chapter of his gospel has mention of food or eating. It has been remarked that Luke presents Jesus either going to a table, at a table, or coming from a table. Robert J. Karris, in his book, *Luke: Artist and Theologian*, (Paulist Press), has a fascinating chapter on the theme of food.

The conception of Jesus is celebrated in the canticle of Mary as God filling the starving with good things. Then Jesus was born in Bethlehem, which means the house of bread. His first cot was a feeding trough borrowed from animals.

Before commencing his public ministry he fasted for forty days. In fasting, he manifested his solidarity with the hungry of the world. He relied absolutely on the providence of the Father rather than turn stones into bread. He responded to the tempter's first attack that man does not live on bread alone. Thus he recognised the value of fasting in giving priority to the leading of the Spirit over the demands of the flesh. Later, however, Jesus was very critical of those who abused fasting as a way of winning the esteem of others.

There were meals of celebration, as in the house of Levi, and at the return of the prodigal son. And there were meals to relax with friends, as with Martha and Mary. There are several references to meals on the Sabbath, the day of rest.

Jesus was the guest who brought to the table more than he received. At various tables he brought pardon to the sinful woman, friendship to Zacchaeus and faith to the two disciples on the road to Emmaus. Much of his teaching was imparted at meals. There he drew attention to the foolish pride of those who vied for the places of honour at table. He taught that our tables should be anticipations of the final messianic banquet with special consideration being given to the beloved poor of God. Lazarus, the beggar at the gate, is the personification of God's beloved poor.

Jesus told a story about God as the master who dons the apron to serve the faithful servant. And at the last supper Jesus moved among the apostles as one who serves.

The behaviour of Jesus at table so challenged the accepted pious traditions that he drew condemnation upon his head. He was accused of being a glutton and a drunkard. There was a loud complaint that he 'welcomes sinners and eats with them.' Karris comes to the provocative conclusion that Jesus got himself crucified by the way he ate.

When he taught his followers a prayer which would express their Christian identity, the petition for today's needs is a request for bread. And Jesus arranged that the celebration of his memory would be in a meal: 'Do this in memory of me.' The risen Lord was recognised by two disciples at the breaking of bread. And would you believe what he asked of the dumb-founded apostles when he appeared to them in the Upper Room: 'Have you anything here to eat?'

This theme of food continues into the Acts of the Apostles. The breaking of bread was one of the cornerstones of the early community. And when Peter was establishing his credentials as a witness his claim was: 'We have eaten and drunk with him after his resurrection from the dead. ' (Acts 10:41)

The day when Jesus fed the multitude in the lonely place was like a summary of his mission. He welcomed the crowds ... even though they were wrecking his plans for a day of retreat with the apostles. He talked to them about the kingdom of God. He brought healing to those who needed it. And he fed them in their hunger.

Bread is a symbol of the outreach of God to his children in welcome, enlightenment, healing and sustaining.

'We begin our day by trying to see Christ through the Bread and during the day we continue to see him beneath the torn bodies of the poor.' (Mother Teresa)

Second Reflection
The Real Presence

We speak of the real presence of the Lord in the Blessed Sacrament. I've met many people who are confused by the expression. In popular usage when we say something is real we mean it actually exists as opposed to an imaginary or fictitious existence: or that something is genuine as opposed to counterfeit or sham. Some people wonder then that when we speak of the Lord's presence in the Blessed Sacrament, do we imply that there is something less real or less genuine about his presence in the Christian community, or in the scriptures, in moments of intimate prayer or in other ways.

The word *real*, as used in eucharistic theology, is a transliteration of the Latin term *realis*, which means pertaining to a material thing. The 'real presence' indicates the special presence of God in a particular material thing or place. Perhaps the Latin term might be more effectively translated as the 'thinged' presence or the specially located presence of God.

There is a long tradition of believing in the special presence of God in sacred locations. Although God is everywhere and the span of the heavens above cannot altogether contain him, yet the revealed biblical word tells of a succession of sacred things or places which were a special meeting place with God for the people.

Moses met with God in the burning bush and on the sacred mountain. Later the Ark of the Covenant was a mobile sanctuary which expressed the presence of God who had entered a covenanted relationship with the people. When the nomadic people settled, the sacred thing was the Tent of Meeting. Later there was the Temple with the sacred precinct of the Holy of Holies.

God was present in an utterly unique way in the flesh of Jesus Christ. The body of Jesus Christ replaced the Temple as the special place of God's presence. And at the last supper, Jesus prepared for the coming time when his physical body would no longer be present. Then he gave the consecrated bread and wine to the disciples: 'This is my body which will be given for you; do this as a memorial of me.' (Lk 22:19) The Eucharist is now the special, sacred meeting place of God with his people. God, who is everywhere, accommodates his presence according to our needs. The presence of the Lord in the sacred host answers three basic needs for us: as a centre for our belief, a focus point for our senses, and a source of our religious emotions.

Our theological belief in the presence and activity of God in our lives comes to a centre of focus in the Sacred Bread. When we eat ordinary bread, it is changed into us: but when we eat this Bread, we are changed into Him, whose body the bread has become. In Chapter 6 of John's gospel, the teaching of Jesus about the eucharist is presented as the testcase of faith. 'For my flesh is real food and my blood is real drink. He who eats my flesh and drinks my blood lives in me and I live in him.' (Jn 6:55-56) Those who did not accept this belief no longer walked with Jesus.

The Blessed Sacrament exposed for veneration is a powerful focusing point for the attention of our senses. It satisfies our need to focus sight, the most powerful of the senses. Our minds, teeming with distractions, are helped to hold together in a strong focus.

Discreet use of lighting, colours, flowers and artistic symbols can aid our attention. The discipline of reverential gestures can calm the obsessive haste of one or arrest the slovenly indolence of another. The fragrance of incense in uprising clouds can generate an atmosphere of prayer rising to God. And the good example of others in veneration is a challenge and support to us.

The Eucharist is also a source of our religious emotions. Towards the Blessed Sacrament we are drawn back to God in expressions of adoration, love, thanksgiving, asking and repentance. As an aid to our memories, the first letters of these motions spell ALTAR.

Who is there before our gaze? It is the Lord! It is the Word of the Father, born in the flesh of Blessed Mary, and now become Bread for us. These three moments of divine presence can be expressed in one simple prayer: Word, made flesh, made bread.

Second Sunday of the Year

John 2:1-11

There was a wedding at Cana in Galilee. The mother of Jesus was there, and Jesus and his disciples had also been invited. When they ran out of wine, since the wine provided for the wedding was all finished, the mother of Jesus said to him, 'They have no wine.' Jesus said, 'Woman, why turn to me? My hour has not come yet.' His mother said to the servants, 'Do whatever he tells you.' There were six stone water jars standing there, meant for the ablutions that are customary among the Jews: each could hold twenty or thirty gallons. Jesus said to the servants, 'Fill the jars with water', and they filled them to the brim. 'Draw some out now,' he told them, 'and take it to the steward.' They did this; the steward tasted the water, and it had turned into wine. Having no idea where it came from – only the servants who had drawn the water knew – the steward called the bridegroom and said, 'People generally serve the best wine first, and keep the cheaper sort till the guests have had plenty to drink; but you have kept the best wine till now.'

This was the first of the signs given by Jesus: it was given at Cana in Galilee. He let his glory be seen, and his disciples believed in him.

First Reflection
The Wedding

'Three days later there was a wedding at Cana in Galilee.' We do not know the names of the couple who were married there. But it matters little because the real wedding being celebrated in the story of that third day was the union of God and humanity in Jesus… the marriage of heaven and earth. Before Jesus, God's relationship with the Chosen People was like the courtship before marriage – a time of preparation. The old religious system is represented in the story by the six stone water jars standing there. The water was that used for the ablutions which were a prescribed preparation for the feast. Stone jars were regarded as very clean. But an exaggerated insistence on ritual cleanliness was part of a system that had left the people with hearts like the

108

jars... made of stone. These jars numbered six, still short of seven, the number of fullness or perfection. Now the water was changed into wine as an indication that the preparatory courtship had reached the day of marriage, and that the hearts of stone would be replaced by hearts of flesh. The best wine was kept until these latterdays.

The miracle at Cana was a first sign of the glory of Jesus. This first glimpse of his glory drew his disciples to believe in him. His glory would be fully revealed, his hour would come, when he would be lifted up from the earth on Calvary as he returned to the Father's mansions. Thus lifted up, he was to draw all people to himself, embracing all people as his bride, loving them to the end. In going to his Father's house on the third day, he brought home humanity as his wedded bride.

The courtship and wooing of the people in the Old Testament prepared for the wedding of the new covenant. If the old religious system is symbolised by the water of ablution, the new religion is characterised as the wine of a celebratory banquet. This banquet is ever fresh in the Eucharistic memory of Jesus. To remember is to proclaim that the deeds of God are not confined to one transient day but belong to an eternal now. The Eucharist is the living memory of the wedding of heaven and earth. 'Father, calling to mind the death your Son endured for our salvation, his glorious resurrection and ascension into heaven ...'

The wedding which was first glimpsed at the changing of water into wine at Cana, was consummated on Calvary in the death-glorification journey of Jesus to the Father. And we who gather in faith at the Eucharistic remembrance are the children of the consummation.

'Like a young man marrying a virgin, so will the one who built you wed you, and as the bridegroom rejoices in his bride, so will your God rejoice in you.' (Is 62:5)

Second Reflection
Mary

In the stories of Cana and Calvary Mary is seen in an intermediary role of unique importance. At Cana she is not mentioned by name but she is called 'the mother of Jesus' and she is addressed by Jesus as 'woman'. These two titles embrace the rich extent of her role. The title 'mother of Jesus' certainly refers to her: but it is sufficiently open to allude also to the Jewish people, the racial womb from which Jesus came. The entire Old

Testament period in its incompleteness and longing is caught up in Mary. She becomes the expression of the nation. Everything is summed up in the utter simplicity of her statement: 'They have no wine.' Thus Mary becomes the link in the story between Jewish incompleteness and fulfilment in Christ.

The only other place where John refers to Mary is on Calvary. Cana and Calvary are linked as in both places Jesus addresses Mary as 'Woman.' 'Woman, why turn to me ? My hour has not come yet.' When his hour has come on Calvary, he says to her: 'Woman, this is your son.' If he had called her 'Mother' on these occasions he would have expressed her relationship with him alone. The title 'Woman' helps to broaden the perspective to her universal motherhood. As mother of all she is the new Eve. The first Eve in her disobedience played a part in the fall of humanity. But Mary, as the new Eve, speaks words of obedience: 'Do whatever he tells you'. And in her obedient faith she plays a significant role in the reconciliation of God and humanity, the wedding of heaven and earth. She came to the wedding on Calvary as the mother of the Bridegroom: there she became also the mother of the bride, the mother of all humanity. At Cana Mary showed all a mother's sensitivity and caring instinct when she sensed that something was amiss. She identified the source of the potential embarrassment and delicately brought the need to her Son's attention: 'They have no wine.' In her role as mother of humanity she is sensitive to all the needs and anxieties of her children on earth. One can be sure that she continues to intercede for our needs: 'They have no wine.'

Holy Mary, mother of loving kindness, pray for us.

Third Sunday of the Year

Luke 1: 1-4; 4: 14-21

Seeing that many others have undertaken to draw up accounts of the events that have taken place among us, exactly as these were handed down to us by those who from the outset were eye witnesses and ministers of the word, I in my turn, after carefully going over the whole story from the beginning, have decided to write an ordered account for you, Theophilus, so that your Excellency may learn how well founded the teaching is that you have received.

Jesus, with the power of the Spirit in him, returned to Galilee; and his reputation spread throughout the countryside. He taught in their synagogues and everyone praised him.

He came to Nazara, where he had been brought up, and went into the synagogue on the sabbath day as he usually did. He stood up to read, and they handed him the scroll of the prophet Isaiah. Unrolling the scroll he found the place where it is written:

The spirit of the Lord has been given to me,

for he has anointed me.

He has sent me to bring the good news to the poor

to proclaim liberty to captives

and to the blind new sight,

to set the downtrodden free,

to proclaim the Lord's year of favour.

He then rolled up the scroll, gave it back to the assistant and sat down. And all eyes in the synagogue were fixed on him.

Then he began to speak to them, 'This text is being fulfilled today even as you listen.'

First Reflection
Introducing Luke

Today's gospel could well be called 'Introductions'. In two separate extracts we have Luke's introduction to his writing and then his introduction to the public ministry of Jesus.

Luke's opening verses borrow the formal style of some classical Greek writers. He addresses his work to Theophilus, Lover of God, a name which can include anybody who sets out in loving search to know more about God.

His stated purpose is to show how well founded is the Christian message of salvation. He indicates the three stages in the growth of his message: the events that happened, the handing on of the message and eventually the effort to put it in writing. The gospels are based on fact, not on fiction: on the historical events of the life, teaching and saving mission of Jesus of Nazareth who died and rose again.

Jesus left no written documents but his followers proclaimed his message. The formation of the Christian teaching in the local communities is the second stage of development. Luke, writing some fifty years after these events was not himself a firsthand witness but he used what was handed down by eye witnesses and preachers of the word. There is a pious legend that one of Luke's sources was Mary, the mother of Jesus.

The third stage of development is what the gospel writer does with the material to hand. Luke decided to write an ordered account of what was handed down. The four evangelists may be compared to four cooks who set about baking cakes. They all go to the same shop for the ingredients: the shop is the life and saving work of Jesus, what Luke calls the events that took place. Will we get four identical cakes from the one source? Most unlikely because the cooks will differ in the mixing and in the sort of cake they want. One goes all the way with a rich Christmas cake, another opts for a light fruit-cake, another for a sweeter gateaux. Similarly, the four evangelists tell the story of Jesus in quite different versions. One hugely influential factor was the pastoral situation of the local Christian community in which the evangelist lived. The writer's ability and personal character also come to light in their writing.

Among the characteristics of Luke's writing we note his prayerfulness, emphasis on the mercy of God, and the care of God for the poor and downtrodden. Luke has more instances of prayer and more teaching about prayer than the other writers. His gospel gives us many of our familiar prayers: the canticles of Mary, Zechariah and Simeon used daily in the Prayer of the Church; the Our Father, the first half of the Hail Mary, the five joyful mysteries of the Rosary and many short prayers like that of the publican in the temple and the repentant thief on Calvary.

Luke is the evangelist of the mercy of God, giving us the repentant woman who washes the feet of Jesus with her tears, the story of the Prodigal Son, the repentant thief, the humble publican whose short prayer of repentance pierces the clouds. I am lifted up every morning when we take the Benedictus of Zechariah to celebrate 'the loving-kindness of the heart of our God who visits us like the dawn from on high'.

The care of God for the poor and outcasts is announced by Jesus at the opening of his preaching mission in Nazareth. It is a time of God's grace as he brings good news to the poor, liberty to captives, sight to the blind and freedom to the downtrodden. The heroes of the story are lepers, shepherds, tax collectors, public sinners, Samaritans and pagans, all outsiders to the system. Luke highlights the important roles given to women, notably Mary, Elizabeth, Martha and Mary, the women who were involved with Jesus and the apostles in his public ministry, and the women of compassion on the road to Calvary.

Luke's pages teem with people. He does not give us long sermons like Matthew, nor long discourses as in John. The teaching of Jesus is in shorter contacts with people and much of the teaching is then embodied in people. For instance, the deprived Lazarus is the embodiment of the Beatitudes while all the dangers of wealth are found in the rich man at whose gate poor Lazarus sat. Always pay attention to the verbs in Luke for these tell us the actions of God and the reactions of people to what Jesus did. Usually we see how they were moved to wonder and the praise of God.

One other feature of Luke is the focus on meals. It has been said that in Luke, Jesus is either at a table, going to a table or coming from a table. And in his second book, the Acts, one of the four cornerstones of the early Christian community was the breaking of bread.

With all this emphasis on prayer, on mercy, on care for the poor, on preaching at the popular level and celebration at the table, Luke has been called the first Catholic. Certainly Catholic devotional life can relate very comfortably with Luke's language of the heart.

As we walk the road with him this year may we have the experience of the disciples on the road to Emmaus. May our hearts take flame as we come to know the Lord in his word. May we recognise him in the breaking of the bread. And then, enlightened by his word, and nourished by his sacred bread, may we actively witness before others.

Second Reflection

Introduction to Jesus

The opening words ascribed to Jesus by each evangelist can tell us much about the writer's intention. Matthew and Mark have Jesus announcing the closeness of the Kingdom and the accompanying exhortation to repent and believe the good news.

John has Jesus reaching out to the human quest: 'What do you want? Come and see.' Luke has Jesus in the synagogue at Nazareth reading from Isaiah: 'The Spirit of the Lord has been given to me.' It is good news for the poor and downtrodden. It is the Lord's year of favour, indicating a time of abundant grace. Three strands are woven through the text: the action of the Holy Spirit, the care of God for the poor and downtrodden, and the impact of the God's power today.

Luke is the evangelist of the Holy Spirit. John has the great promises of the Spirit but Luke's story is energised by the action of the Spirit in Jesus and later in the Christian community. Luke tells of the Holy Spirit overshadowing Mary, indicating divine presence and power. The blessed words of Elizabeth and Simeon are uttered when they are filled with the Spirit. From the moment of the adult emergence of Jesus at the Jordan he is filled with, led by, empowered by the Spirit.

In Ezechiel's famous vision of the valley of dry bones, it is when the breath or spirit of God enters them that new life appears. There is nothing secretive about it for there is a loud clattering as bones are joined together. New sinews promise strength, skin bestows adornment and the divine breath grants the miracle of life.

The good news proclaimed under the power of the Spirit at Nazareth addressed the dry bones of inner poverty, captivity, blindness and oppression. Where are these symptoms today? Around us on every side. Counsellors and psychiatrists have long waiting lists. Healing services, whether religious or secular, are guaranteed to fill church or hall. Lives of desperation are no longer kept quiet.

Jesus put aside the written scroll and announced the presence of the Spirit here today. The immediacy of God's presence is conveyed by Luke in his repeated use of the adverb today. 'Today is born to you a Saviour ... we have seen strange things today ... salvation has come to this house today ... today you will be with me in paradise.' The benefit of constantly pondering on the scriptures is that familiarity with what God did in the past enables us to recognise what God is doing today.

Jesus taught people to relax in the smile of God's favour. And they found that they could let go of their chains of bondage. What a day of liberation it is when you discover that the chains restricting you have no locks on them except for the rigidity of your own grip! Once the love of God made known to us in Jesus is discovered, you let go the tight grip and the chains fall off.

Jesus brought God-news to the poor, the news that God is loving, caring, compassionate and forgiving, because his favour smiles upon us. If I am privileged to savour this God-news, then the challenge arises: to what extent do I pass on this portrait of God to others. Not so much by words, which may be pious but hollow, as by what I am. A question to live with – what is the God-news proclaimed by my life to others today

Fourth Sunday of the Year

Luke 4: 21-30

Jesus began to speak in the synagogue, 'This text is being fulfilled today even as you listen.' And he won the approval of all, and they were astonished by the gracious words that came from his lips. They said, 'This is Joseph's son, surely?' But he replied, 'No doubt you will quote me the saying, "Physician, heal yourself" and tell me, "We have heard all that happened in Capernaum, do the same here in your own countryside."' And he went on, 'I tell you solemnly, no prophet is ever accepted in his own country. There were many widows in Israel, I can assure you, in Elijah's day, when heaven remained shut for three years and six months and a great famine raged throughout the land, but Elijah was not sent to any one of these; he was sent to a widow at Zarephath, a Sindonian town. And in the prophet Elisha's time there were many lepers in Israel, but none of these was cured, except the Syrian, Naaman.' When they heard this everyone in the synagogue was enraged. They sprang to their feet and hustled him out of the town; and took him up to the brow of the hill their town was built on, intending to throw him down the cliff, but he slipped through the crowd and walked away.

First Reflection

Actions and Reactions

This passage describes the gracious proclamation of the Good News by Jesus and the swelling current of negative reactions among his own townspeople

After reading from Isaiah about the power of the Spirit in the Lord's year of favour, Jesus handed the scroll back to the attendant and announced, 'This text is being fulfilled today even as you listen.' Sacred Scripture is the word of God on paper but it is not meant to remain in the book. It has to be taken from paper and applied to life. Like seeds in a packet, the sacred words lose their life-force if they are not taken out of the packet and planted in the earth. By studying the scriptures we become familiar with God's actions in the past so as to recognise the divine presence and action in our present situations. The same God who acted in the past is present in our lives today.

The initial reaction to the words of Jesus was very positive. People were astonished. His words were regarded as gracious, filled with God's goodness. But see how quickly the mood is soured. Luke takes us on a whole journey of emotions from universal approval, through growing doubt, into anger and eventually into violence.

It is left to the reader's imagination to put flesh on the story, to notice the nudges and winks, to hear the disapproving grunts and cynical guffaws. After the initial approval, local jealousy began to plant the seeds of doubt. First to speak is somebody who sounds like the voice of caution: 'This is Joseph's son, is it not?' In other words, don't be swept off your feet by all this sweet talk.

The begrudger can usually mask his cynicism under a rough humour which serves to rally allies. And out they come from their corners. The voice of parochial jealousy is heard, masked in a tone of pious admiration. 'We heard all that happened in Capernaum ...' and then his voice hardens a little, 'Do the same here in your own countryside.' It takes very little imagination to hear the guffaws of the boys at the back. They have an outlet now for their local resentment.

Sensing the negative mood, Jesus makes the immortal statement. 'No prophet is ever accepted in his own country.' It is not a new story. It happened years before to the great holy man Elijah and to Elisha. Each of them had a poor reception at home but they brought God's healing to people outside the nation.

They think it audacious of Jesus to couple himself with those hero prophets of history. And sorer still is the implication that Jesus is on a mission beyond the confines of Israel. Anger is now beyond control and violence takes over.

They sprang to their feet and hustled him roughly out of the town. The swaying journey up to the brow of the hill anticipates another day, another angry crowd, another hill. The escape of Jesus is rather vague. 'He slipped through the crowd and walked away.' An angry mob will not easily let the object of its wrath slip away. Luke is really hinting at the later day when Jesus would pass through this world and its anger on his journey back to the Father.

The episode is consolation to those whose commitment to a good cause is meeting with resentment, jealousy and opposition. They are in the good company of Jesus who testified that prophets do not normally get a good reception from their own neighbours. From my desk I can look out at the channel which feeds the water to the upper reaches of Sheephaven Bay. When the current is very strong there are swirling eddies at either side causing slight currents in the opposite direction, a force to be availed of when rowing a boat against the main current. Similarly, currents of goodness invariably cause negative movements in counter direction.

The experience at Nazareth, the hometown of Jesus, is a challenge to us to examine how we respond to the talents of those around us.

Are we jealous, threatened, insecure in comparing ourselves?

Do we rejoice to see others get on well? Do we support them? Do we help them to find their talents and to develop them? Is it our joy to accept the prophets among us?

Second Reflection
Rejection of Jesus … Rejection of the Church

Faraway hills are green. We can spend our lives pining for the ideal situation to come about. Like the woman who waited and searched for the ideal man: eventually she found him, only to discover that he was searching for the ideal woman! The people of Nazareth began to doubt Jesus because he was too human for them, too much one of themselves. 'The son of Joseph! Listen to him? Now, I'd go to him for a table or a set of chairs. He has a great name with the farmers. What's that slogan over the door … 'Our yokes are easy and our burdens light.' A good carpenter maybe, but a preacher! Where did he get these notions? Will you listen to his fancy claims !'

In much the same way there are people today who find the church too human. They can allow no room for failing or foible in Pope, bishop, priest, teacher, sister, brother, neighbour, or anybody else who goes to church. How often must one listen to the critic who is put off by the bad example of the crawthumpers. Would that the same critic were even half as observant of the good example of others. It is fashionable to knock the past as if nothing good existed in the church before Vatican II. Old formation systems can be criticised but many good men and women cut their teeth there.

And while one might criticise the spirituality of recent centuries as being too concerned with a privatised holiness, yet these same times produced the worldwide missionary expansion of the church and a great flowering of the apostolates of caring, nursing and education. The people of Nazareth found Jesus too human for them. If critics today wish to find fault with the church they won't have far to look. Personally, I am glad it is such a frail, human community ... because there is room for me in it.

By the way, if you discover the perfect church in the morning, you are bound in conscience to join it immediately. Only remember – once you have joined it, it will no longer be perfect.

Fifth Sunday of the Year

Luke 5:1-11

Jesus was standing one day by the Lake of Gennesaret, with the crowd pressing round him listening to the word of God, when he caught sight of two boats close to the bank. The fisherman had gone out of them and were washing their nets. He got into one of the boats – it was Simon's – and asked him to put out a little from the shore. Then he sat down and taught the crowds from the boat.

When he had finished speaking he said to Simon, 'Put out into deep water and pay out your nets for a catch.' 'Master,' Simon replied, 'we worked hard all night long and caught nothing, but if you say so, I will pay out the nets.' And when they had done this they netted such a huge number of fish that their nets began to tear, so they signalled to their companions in the other boat to come and help them; when these came, they filled the two boats to sinking point.

When Simon Peter saw this he fell at the knees of Jesus saying, 'Leave me Lord; I am a sinful man.' For he and all his companions were completely overcome by the catch they had made; so also were James and John, sons of Zebedee, who were Simon's partners. But Jesus said to Simon. 'Do not be afraid; from now on it is men you will catch.' Then, bringing their boats back to land, they left everything and followed him.

First Reflection
The Sense of Sin

After the hostile reception accorded to him at Nazareth, Jesus embarked on a mission of preaching and healing in the lakeside towns and villages. He was well received and crowds were flocking to him. The time was ripe to call some of them to a deeper discipleship so that they might in time carry on his work. It is typical of Luke's personal style to capture the moment by focusing on the deep experience of one person, namely Simon Peter.

After fishing all night without success, at the request of Jesus they put out the nets again and pulled in a miraculous catch. For

Simon Peter this glimpse of the greatness of the Lord was an overwhelming experience. It recalls the experience of Isaiah, used for the First Reading on this Sunday, in which he experienced the total otherness or holiness of God, in the light of which he felt wretched and unclean. Simon Peter's reaction was to fall at the knees of Jesus protesting his unworthiness: "Leave me, Lord; I am a sinful man."

Sin is a problem today. Rather, the problem is that sin is not a problem for the majority of people. Hearing confessions, one wonders if people are committing sins any more, so little have they to confess. It is more than fifty years since Pope Pius XII said that the greatest sin of our age is the lack of the sense of sin.

On the surface level of conscience sin is understood as the transgression of some obligation by thought, word, deed or omission. The obligation is recognised as a commandment, a precept of the church, a directive of legitimate authority, or in the duty of one's state in life. These transgressions can be given specific names such as lies, theft, disobedience or anger: and these can be counted, at least to an approximate number.

These counted acts are like the bad apples on the tree. A second level of conscience seeks the poisoned roots which are causing the rot. There is a traditional list of seven poisonous roots usually called the capital sins: pride, covetousness, lust, envy, anger, gluttony and sloth or laziness. Every act of sin can be traced back to one or other of these poisoned roots. On this level of conscience sin is seen in areas of character which need healing and strengthening.

But there is a deeper level of conscience which grows out of awareness of one's relationship with God. When Isaiah and Peter received a personal experience of God they were overwhelmed by the sense of their sinfulness. A mature conscience makes one sensitive to who one is in response to God's love. We read of saints who would weep for their sinfulness even though they were not committing what the rest of us might call sins. Saint Francis wept because 'love is not loved'. In the light of a more intimate experience of God, to say 'I am a sinner' is deeper than to say 'I have sinned'. The focus of attention is more on who I am in response to God than on what I have done.

In former times there were long queues for confession every week and people had lists of specific sins. This was when the experience of authority dominated people's lives. Authority figures in politics, teaching, medicine, family and church were above questioning. People could then draw the sense of sin out of disobedience to the supreme authority of God.

But times have changed and, in today's culture of self, authority is resented as an invasion on one's personal space and choice. Personal experience and freedom of choice are the chief guidelines. The authority of experience has replaced the experience of authority.

In this mental condition how can conscience be challenged? The old sense of sin as disobedience is not working. For many people who return to the Sacrament of Reconciliation, what makes sense to them is to examine their lives in terms of areas of character where they acknowledge their need of God's forgiveness and healing grace. They are drawn to examine conscience in the light of desirable virtues, perhaps as outlined in passages of scripture.

The greatest factor obscuring the sense of sin is the diminishment of faith. A rockface may be hard and water may be soft, but the constant dripping of water will wear away that rockface. Constant exposure to secularistic thinking, as in television's portrayal of life as an area where God is utterly irrelevant, is bound to erode faith, unless one takes counter measures like a disciplined prayerlife.

When Simon Peter glimpsed the power of God in Jesus, he experienced a deep sense of his own distance from God through sinfulness. 'Leave me, Lord; I am a sinful man.' Yet this moment of distance from God is the result of the most intense experience of the nearness of God. Smart critics like to make cynical remarks about Catholic guilt. But the fact is that guilt is the appropriate response to having done wrong and the denial of appropriate guilt is not correct. For Isaiah and Simon Peter, a sense of guilt was part of their experience of the grandeur, love and beauty of God. A true sense of sin is the shadow side of the light of God experienced in faith.

Second Reflection
Peter remembers that morning
The day I made my first move to follow Jesus began with anything but religion in my mind. I was tired after a night's work and frustrated with our failure. The nets had to be freed of weeds and then folded away. I was in no mood to meet anybody before I'd put a bite of breakfast in. Then a good sleep and I might feel human again. James and John knew me well enough

to keep a safe distance. Andrew? Where had he got to? Voices …
people coming out of the morning haze. So early in the day?

It was Jesus, the teacher from Nazareth. That explained
Andrew's disappearance. You'd think he might have told me.
Jesus … a man of God surely. He healed my own mother-in-law
of a raging fever. Now the very sight of him soothed the cross-
ness in my craw. The crowd kept pushing forward and then he
sat on the prow of my boat. I felt honoured that my boat should
be his rostrum. There was a depth, peace and inner strength in
him which reached into people. And I can see him there so relaxed, dangling his feet playfully in the water, talking away. My
humour warmed by the minute. The crowd showed no sign of
moving off so it seemed a good idea to push offshore some distance.

Then he said to put out the nets! My weary back objected. I
knew there wasn't a fish for miles in that light. And the thought
of folding up those nets again… Funny how landlubbers think
that you just throw out a net and it fills up with fish every time.
'Master, we laboured all night long …' Yet he had done us a
great favour and he was a guest in my boat so I owed him on the
double, gratitude and courtesy … 'but if you say so, I will pay
out the nets.' So, I did my best to look enthusiastic. Suddenly the
floats dipped heavily. The surface was an eruption of silvery
splashes. The weight on the rope was nearly capsizing us.
'James … John … here … hurry, the nets are tearing.'

Years of fishing behind me and now I was as excited as a
child. One boat full to the gunwales. Two. Unbelievable ! Nearly
sinking, so greedy to land the lot. Balance was vital but we just
managed, not a fish was lost. It was only when my feet touched
solid ground once more that I came back to reality. Was I dream-
ing ? No, the fish were there leaping about. What happened?

Who is *he*? And what am I? Blindly clinging to his tunic,
afraid to let him go. Yet a million miles distant. Hardly knowing
what words were coming out. Overcome. Dying, ceasing to be
… so small, so poor, so useless. So much wasted time, so many
faults, such weakness. Sin, sin, sin. Deep, deep abasement.
Nothing left. Distant from all.

Then I grew conscious of a gentle warmth in his hands
stroking my hair. A surging sense of healing in courage and
light. 'Do not be afraid!' So gentle, so uplifting. Death undone, a
new creation. 'From now on it is people you will catch.'

What else could one do that day but make the magnificent,
blind gesture of leaving everything to follow him!

Sixth Sunday of the Year

Luke 6: 17, 20-26

Jesus came down with the twelve and stopped at a piece of level ground where there was a large gathering of his disciples, with a great crowd of people from all parts of Judaea and Jerusalem and the coastal region of Tyre and Sidon who had come to hear him and to be cured of their diseases.

Then fixing his eyes on his disciples he said:

How blessed are you who are poor: the kingdom of heaven is yours.

Blessed are you who are hungry now: you shall have your fill.

Blessed are you who are weeping now: you shall laugh.

Blessed are you when people hate you, drive you out, abuse you, denounce your name as criminal, on account of the Son of man. Rejoice when that day comes and dance for joy, look! – your reward will be great in heaven. This was the way their ancestors treated the prophets.

But alas for you who are rich: you are having your consolation now.

Alas for you who have plenty to eat now: you shall go hungry.

Alas for you who are laughing now: you shall mourn and weep.

Alas for you when everyone speaks well of you! This was the way their ancestors treated the false prophets.

(The New Jerusalem Bible)

First Reflection

Blessed by God

Jesus set out to preach the ideals of the reign of God's ways in peoples' hearts. For starters he had to challenge many of the assumptions which supported the religious values and moral principles of the existing religion.

Matthew's version of this great sermon portrays Jesus as the great teacher of the new covenant and so he situates Jesus on a mountain, standing with authority over the people. Luke prefers a more humble stance, and so, he pictures Jesus as coming down to a piece of level ground. As I heard a man once describe it in sporting terms, Jesus was establishing a level playing pitch for all.

People came to be cured of their diseases. Dis-ease means the loss of peace of mind. The most fundamental experience of peace is in the tranquillity of harmony with God in all things. Where this harmony is disrupted, then peace is shattered, and dis-ease sets in.

As he opens up the vision of life in harmony with God's reign, Jesus first has to challenge the accepted concepts of what it means to be blessed by God. The words of Jesus are revolutionary in the sense that he turns upside down the notion of blessedness that people accepted. Thankfully, *The New Jerusalem Bible* has restored the word blessed instead of happy. To be blessed indicates the state of receiving the loving kindness of God, whereas happiness expresses an emotional state which may have nothing to do with one's relationship with God.

The Jewish mind that he addressed thought that the signs of God's blessing were in prosperity, power, prestige and popularity. These marked the lifestyle of those who were in the front of synagogue or assembly. As one cartoon put it, if you were blessed in the Old Testament, you knew it, your neighbour knew it and your bank manager knew it! What a shock to the system it must have been when Jesus spoke of the blessedness in God's eyes of those who were poor, powerless, broken or victims of injustice!

The prevailing Jewish concept of blessing went back to the early days before they had a belief in life after death. Lacking the knowledge of eternal reward or punishment, their sense of divine justice demanded that God's blessings had to be manifested in this life.

In the beatitudes, the state of belonging to the kingdom or reign of God is referred to in the present tense ... the kingdom of God is yours. But the beatitudes of consolation all use the future tense. Jesus does not promise prosperity and success in this life, something contrary to the claims of many of the so called evangelical preachers.

Lest the blessed state of the poor be lost in spurious explanations, Jesus warns those who are enjoying worldly prosperity that they are in danger of being so self-occupied that they have no room for God. Alas for you who are so rich now that you have no idea of your need for God. Alas for you for whom life is all about the craic, alas for you whose theme is how-great -I-am. Alas for you who are taken in by shallow popularity. Your minds are far from the true values of life. The prophets you follow are false.

Later this year, on the Twenty-Sixth Sunday of the Year, we will come across the parable of the rich man and Lazarus. The lifestyle of the rich man makes him the personification of the four warnings of Jesus. Whereas the lot of poor Lazarus makes him the personification of the beatitudes. Destitute and broken in this life, yet he is the one who receives all the consolations of the next life. What is very significant about this parable is the name of Lazarus, which means God has had compassion.

The blessings of God reach out in a special way to those who are poor, hungry, broken-hearted and deprived of justice. On the other hand, those who settle for the riches and pleasures of this life are not properly disposed to receive God's best gifts. Jesus set out a level playing pitch for all.

Second Reflection
Space for God

Disciple: Master, I've been thinking about your preaching, especially about the beatitudes. Now, I admire your idealism no end, but don't you go a bit beyond common sense here?

Master: What do you mean?

Disciple: You know what you say about the poor and hungry, the depressed and the victims of injustice. You can't be serious when you call them blessed... Don't tell me that they wake up every morning happy with their lot. Sorry if I sound offensive, Master, but I just cannot see your point.

Master: No offence taken. Just try to look at it the other way around. The wealthy nations – do you think that they have found contentment and happiness? Have they found a meaning that gives purpose to existence. Aren't they burying their minds in distraction, afraid to face the deep questions. Or is the world gone out of control? To say that does not think much of our Father.

Disciple: Right, I agree that money and booze and the bright lights bring more problems than happiness to life. But you did say that the poor and the depressed are the blessed people. I cannot see what you are getting at.

Master: Put it like this. Imagine a really sumptuous banquet. Those who come hungry to the table are lucky, aren't they? But tough luck on those whose appetite has been sated because they have been nibbling away at junk food.

Disciple: Well put, Master. You were always good with parables. So the junk food is all that materialism and sensuality and sensationalism. The rich he sent empty away – I can see that part, but I still do not see how he has filled the hungry with good things. Is it only when we die? It really turns me off when religion is preached as pie in the sky when you die. It is not being honest about the problems of life.

Master: Reward in heaven is only part of it. I also mean happiness here and now.

Disciple: Now that is precisely my search. How are they happy now? How can poverty, hunger or injustice be regarded as a blessing?

Master: When they make space for God in a person's heart, that's how. My Father wants to share his life and love with you all but you are too preoccupied and filled up already. When your hands are too full with trifles, he has to give you a little rap on the knuckles to make you open up.

Disciple: I think I can see what you are getting at.

Master: The poor are those who know how empty they really are. They have learned to hunger and yearn and hope. That opens up the way for God to come in. Those who experience sadness and disappointment are learning that the soul is satisfied only with eternal values. Those who know what 'goodbye' means, what it is to let go, what it means to die – they learn that every exit is also an entrance, that every death is a door to new life. Those who experience darkness learn that there is more to life than superficial, passing experiences. You know how it takes darkness to let you stretch your eyes to the distant stars.

Disciple: Isn't it like a sponge? If it is full already, it cannot absorb any more. So God has to put the squeeze on our sponge before we can absorb his greatness.

Master: Good stuff. Now you are the one coming up with the appropriate parable. But I think you would never have come to this wisdom unless you first experienced the poverty of your questions. Which only proves my point that the poor, the hungry and the emptied people are really blessed.

Disciple: Thanks, Master. I see now that being emptied for God is the first step to true happiness.

Seventh Sunday of the Year

Luke 6:27-38

Jesus said to his disciples: 'I say this to you who are listening: Love your enemies, do good to those who hate you, bless those who curse you, pray for those who treat you badly. To the man who slaps you on one cheek, present the other cheek too: to the man who takes your cloak from you, do not refuse your tunic. Give to everyone who asks you, and do not ask for your property back from the man who robs you. Treat others as you would like them to treat you.

If you love those who love you, what thanks can you expect? Even sinners love those who love them. And if you do good to those who do good to you, what thanks can you expect? For even sinners do that much. And if you lend to those from whom you hope to receive, what thanks can you expect? Even sinners lend to sinners to get back the same amount. Instead, love your enemies and do good, and lend without hope of return. You will have a great reward, and you will be sons of the Most High, for he himself is kind to the ungrateful and the wicked.

Be compassionate as your Father is compassionate. Do not judge, and you will not be judged yourselves; do not condemn, and you will not be condemned yourselves; grant pardon, and you will be pardoned. Give, and there will be gifts for you; a full measure, pressed down, shaken together, and running over, will be poured into your lap; because the amount you measure out is the amount you will be given back.'

First Reflection
A Kingdom of Love

Jesus had an dream. He called it the Kingdom of God. In his dream he saw the world as a great mirror which reflected the beauty and love of God. He came to tell of his dream to people whose small minds had never glimpsed the great power of love. They could not see beyond hurts and injustices. They kept shouting for their rights. Their love was limited because every hurt or wrong was an obstacle which blocked the flow.

The greatest of their wise men had formulated a noble ideal in the Golden Rule: never do to another what you would not wish done to yourself. But this rule did not go far enough for Jesus. A negative statement which set out what one should not do was too limiting for his vision. He knew the Father's love in all its breadth and depth and tenderness. He knew that love is a power, not a limitation. So he spoke of love as a positive energy not to be halted by enmity and hatred, nor by the discomfort of abuse in word and deed. It is a generosity that gives more rather than less. It makes you stand in the shoes of your brother or sister to look out at the world through their eyes. Then you will understand their pain and you will be slow to condemn or pass sentence.

Love is as much greater than injury as goodness is greater than evil. Therefore love will always find the power to forgive. It does not wait for conditions to be perfect. It does not say: 'I will begin to love when ... or if ...' Love is too important an attitude to be made wait on another person's answer. As the Father's love is creative, so must Christian love take the initiative in reaching out to the others. The dream of Jesus saw a world where the Father's unconditional love would be reflected in the lives of his children on earth. He saw the barriers of distrust removed and the legacies of hatred dissolved. He saw the hurts of life healed by compassion and the wounds of misunderstanding healed by forgiveness. The power to transform the world into his dream would be love. He lived according to that vision and power. And his rule of life was a new commandment, love one another as I have loved you.

It was a message taken to heart by twenty-seven year old Etty Hillesum at a time when she was awaiting inevitable arrest and transportation to a concentration camp with her fellow Jews. In her diary for 20 July 1942 she wrote: 'They are merciless, totally without pity. And we must be all the more merciful ourselves. That's why I prayed early this morning.'

(*An Interrupted Life: The Diaries and Letters of Etty Hillesum* 1941-1943, Persephone Books, London)

Second Reflection
Peter Remembers

It's no great secret the trouble I've always had with my temper. So you can imagine how I felt when Jesus started talking about loving your enemies and turning the other cheek. I had al-

ways accepted an eye for an eye, a tooth for a tooth. Equal retaliation was a fair policy. My only problem was a tendency to get
the retaliation in first! Jesus was so calm and sure of what he was
saying that I was swept along by his words even if my whole
way of life was under question. He spoke out of a different vision to anything I had ever suspected. Was his view of life true
and beautiful ... or totally naïve?

I must jump ahead in my memories ... up to a formula we developed later in the community: he took, he blessed, be broke
and he gave. Four actions. It all started with the bread and fishes.
He did the same actions at the last supper.

At some stage we began to realise that God repeated these
four actions in his dealings with people. At that time we had
been chosen and taken. I thought I was ready to move out into
giving, stage four, no time for stages two and three. But what
could I have given them? Only Simon – and who would have
wanted to hear Simon! What power had Simon? Only after the
stages of blessing and breaking would I have something to give
... power in the name of Jesus. We came into the stage of
blessedness when we were gradually drawn into his own vision
of life and his own set of values.

It took me many disappointments, failures and breakings before I would let go of everything and hand over to him totally.
Then I had something to give. Rather, Jesus in me had something to give. There came a day when out of my emptiness and
fullness I could say to a crippled man: 'I have neither silver nor
gold, but I will give you what I have: in the name of Jesus Christ
the Nazarene, walk.'

So, if I may repeat some advice I have written elsewhere (cf 1
Pet): if he is asking you to be broken, do not be afraid. If you can
have some share in the sufferings of Christ, be glad, because you
will enter a much greater gladness with him when his glory is
revealed. Remember that no one can hurt you if you are deter-
mined to do what is right. Love one another, have compassion
and keep yourself in the background. Never pay back one
wrong with another, or an angry word with another one; instead, pay back with a blessing. This is what you are called to do.
And you'll find that the blessing will come back on yourself,
generously multiplied. God is never outdone in generosity.

Eighth Sunday of the Year

Luke 6:39-45

Jesus told a parable to his disciples. 'Can one blind man guide another? Surely both will fall into a pit? The disciple is not superior to his teacher; the fully trained disciple will always be like his teacher. Why do you observe the splinter in your brother's eye and never notice the plank in your own? How can you say to your brother, "Brother, let me take out the splinter that is in your eye," when you cannot see the plank in your own? Hypocrite! Take the plank out of your own eye first, and then you will see clearly enough to take out the splinter that is in your brother's eye.

There is no sound tree that produces rotten fruit, nor again a rotten tree that produces sound fruit. For every tree can be told by its own fruit: people do not pick figs from thorns, nor gather grapes from brambles. A good man draws what is good from the store of goodness in his heart; a bad man draws what is bad from the store of badness. For a man's words flow out of what fills his heart.'

First Reflection
Occupancy of the heart

Today we hear our third lesson from the Sermon on the Plain. First, Jesus set a level playing pitch for all by radically questioning the sense of who enjoyed God's blessing, the rich or the poor. Then, as we saw last Sunday, he set the example of the Father's unconditional love as the model we should aspire to. His message today challenges the internal authenticity of our hearts. 'For a person's words flow out of what fills his heart.'

Some years ago articles were being written on whether Jesus ever showed a sense of humour and if humour has any place in religious services. Surely the hugely exaggerated examples brought to mind by Jesus in this passage had the audience in laughter. Who could remain deadly serious at the picture of a plank sticking out of somebody's eye? Or the prospect of figs growing on thorns or grapes on brambles? One can hear a tone of gentle teasing as he says the word 'Hypocrite'.

131

Gentle humour can prove far more effective than cold confrontation in teaching a lesson. And the lesson here is a very important one. It is a challenge to make us ask what occupies our innermost heart. The context in the gospel is where Jesus has spoken about having a positive flow of love which refuses to be poisoned by enmity or hostility. Now he goes on to say that the way that we judge others and speak about them reveals more about ourselves than the person we are talking about.

The First Reading chosen to accompany today's gospel is full of wisdom.

In a shaken sieve the rubbish is left behind,
so too the defects of a man appear in his talk.
The kiln tests the work of the potter,
the test of a man is in his conversation.

If the heart is occupied by something other than love, it is bitterness that comes out in conversation. Jealousy is a common, negative reaction to the good fortune of another. Jealousy is like a poisonous plant that grows off a good source. Other negative forces that can occupy the heart are resentment, prejudice, memory of past hurts, hatred or lack of mercy.

One item sure to be found in the sieve's accumulation of rubbish is the projection of our own inner darkness or areas of repression. Projection is the way that a small frame of film is thrown up by the projector in a greatly enlarged picture on the screen. The large plank that I criticise in another person may well be the projection of some splinter in my own darkness. Always remember that while we point the finger of condemnation at another person, there are three fingers pointing back at ourselves. So often at meetings or in conversation, one has to sift through what is said to see whom the speaker is getting at.

Bitterness of heart is a blindness that leads only to stumbling on the way. Etty Hillesum, whom we quoted last week, notes wisely that every atom of hate we add to this world makes it more inhospitable. The sermon of the Lord is an alternative vision of life. The original plan of God was about people living in the likeness of God. The ideals of Jesus challenge us to come back to the Father's unconditional love.

Who occupies the innermost heart? If Christ and his love are the well that we draw from, then our judging and conversation will be full of his light. 'A good person draws what is good from the store of goodness in his heart; a bad person draws what is bad from the store of badness. For a person's words flow out of what fills his heart.'

Second Reflection

Peter Remembers

May I say something in my own favour. Everybody knows about my temper – I freely admit to that. But to my credit I will say that I always change back very quickly and I never carry resentment for long periods.

Jesus knew exactly how to humour me. He must have seen the frustration and anger building up in me. Frustration … because I was bursting to go out and do something for him … anything, just to prove myself worthy of my new appointment as apostle. But anger was beginning to boil up as I listened to his words about no retaliation, no violence, loving your enemies. Oh, he could be so impractical, so removed from reality! He was reading me like an open book. I heard him say : 'Can one blind man guide another?'

I saw myself in his words. I began to relax, even to smile to myself. He kept the humour going. Everybody laughed at his crazy picture of the fellow with the plank in his eye. We were all a bit tensed up at his idealistic teaching. Laughter certainly eased the air. 'Hypocrite!' he said, teasingly. Later on we were to hear him use that word in a very hard tone. But here he was gentle, understanding, almost playful as he said it. Isn't it amazing how you can see yourself in a little story? If someone tries to confront you with the truth you defend yourself in an argument. But a story … you can't answer back a story. I would have to be patient.

I was far from being a fully trained disciple. There would be no fruit on my branches until I had put down good roots. That day I always remember as the first time I made a conscious resolution to be more patient, to think before I spoke, to wait awhile before jumping into action. I know I've broken that resolution a million times but I have renewed it a million and one times. And as long as resolution is one ahead of fall, you are winning.

Over the years my thought goes back to Jesus … my roots are there. I am no poet but I have a few lines which express my memory of the patience of Jesus. Christ suffered for you, and left an example for you to follow the way he took. He was insulted but he did not retaliate with insults; when he was tortured he made no threats but he put his trust in the righteous judge. He was bearing our faults in his own body on the cross so that we might die to our faults and live for holiness; through his wounds you have been healed. (1 Pet 2:21-24)

Ninth Sunday of the Year

Luke 7: 1-10

When Jesus had come to the end of all he wanted the people to hear, he went into Capernaum. A centurion there had a servant, a favourite of his, who was sick and near death. Having heard about Jesus he sent some Jewish elders to him to ask him to come and heal his servant. When they came to Jesus they pleaded earnestly with him. 'He deserves this of you,' they said, 'because he is friendly towards our people; in fact, he is the one who built the synagogue.' So Jesus went with them, and was not very far from the house when the centurion sent word to him by some friends: 'Sir,' he said 'do not put yourself to trouble; because I am not worthy to have you under my roof; and for this same reason I did not presume to come to you myself; but give the word and let my servant be cured. For I am under authority myself, and have soldiers under me; and I say to one man: Go, and he goes; to another: Come here, and he comes; to my servant: Do this, and he does it.' When Jesus heard these words he was astonished at him and, turning round, said to the crowd following him, 'I tell you, not even in Israel have I found faith like this.' And when the messengers got back to the house they found the servant in perfect health.

First Reflection
Astonishing Faith

Luke's gospel is something more than an historical account of the career of Jesus. Its style is kerygmatic: that is, it is a proclamation of the great deeds of God. Hence he frequently mentions the amazement or astonishment of the audience or spectators who have witnessed the power of God in what Jesus said or did. The story of the Roman centurion is the only instance where Luke attributes astonishment to Jesus.

What evoked this astonishment? Jesus called it faith: 'Not even in Israel have I found faith like this.' The single word, faith, covers the centurion's attitude to God and to his fellow man and reveals also how he regarded himself.

Before God he showed absolute confidence. The world of

military authority, with which he was familiar, became a parable of the absolute power of God whose word can do all things.

Towards his fellow man he was caring, sympathetic and sensitive.

He cared deeply for his sick servant. Even though he was an
officer of the occupying forces, he obviously respected Jewish
ways for he had built the local synagogue. And he showed a delicate sensitivity by sparing Jesus a Jew's scruple about entering
the unclean home of a gentile. Such noble attitudes towards God
and others could only be found in one who was humble in this
attitude toward self. His confession of unworthiness has been so
highly regarded in the church that it is used in the liturgy as the
soul's preparation for the gift of the Eucharist. One could not
find a more appropriate prayer than this: 'Lord, I am not worthy
…' We do not receive the Lord on merit, as a prize for being
good. Who could ever merit the immense privilege of Holy
Communion?

We approach the sacred table as people who are weak, people who tire and stumble on the pilgrimage of life. The Lord, in
the outreach of his love wishes to be our companion on the road.
And companion literally means one who shares his bread with
us.

In our neediness we come to be fed and strengthened. Our
sense of unworthiness does not keep us away because we have a
balancing confidence in the word of Jesus, 'You say the word
and my soul shall be healed.' The Eucharist celebrates the Word
of God reaching down to our life so as to lift it up … in the remembrance of the dying and rising of Jesus Christ. Who can receive this uplifting, healing Word? Only those who are like that
Roman centurion … a person of absolute confidence, combined
with delicate neighbourliness and a deep sense of personal unworthiness. These qualities all together … that's what Jesus
called faith … and it astonished him.

Second Reflection
Intermediaries
The centurion used the local Jewish elders as intermediaries
with Jesus because he felt deeply unworthy of approaching him,
and because he was sensitive to the protocol of Jewish relationships with gentiles. Some time later, when the risen Lord sent
out the disciples to carry on his mission of reconciliation, he was
in effect appointing them intermediaries between God and

mankind. The Acts of the Apostles testifies to the power of God working through the apostles. People came to them for healing just as they had earlier come to Jesus.

From the early days of the Christian church, the veneration of the great witnesses of faith, the saints, included a belief in the power of their prayers on our behalf. The idea of the intercession of the saints must be properly understood. Intercession means standing between God and the one who is in need. It does not mean that one employs a substitute to pray in one's place. No substitute can replace one's own prayer relationship with God. Nor does it diminish the position of Jesus Christ as the unique mediator with the Father. 'There is only one mediator between God and mankind, himself a man, Christ Jesus, who sacrificed himself as a ransom for them all.' (1 Tim 2:6)

The fact that the centurion used the local Jewish elders to present his petition to the Lord in no way expresses a lack of confidence in Jesus. On the contrary, the centurion was a man with the utmost confidence. But he used the mediation of others because of his sensitivity to his own deficiencies, personal and racial.

When we enlist the intercession of Mary or the saints on our behalf, we are certainly not expressing any lack of confidence in God, nor are we saying that God cannot be approached directly. As with the centurion, the use of intermediaries reflects our own deficiencies.

We are deeply aware of the power and love of God but we recognise our unworthiness before him. It is not a matter of thinking that we might one day be deserving of God's loving action in our regard. The use of intermediaries is simply a further expression of our personal unworthiness.

The work of the intermediaries is to bring God to us and to help us come to God. The saints bring God to us through their teaching and the inspiration of their lives. They help us come to God since they are our brothers and sisters in the communion of saints, and they care about us and continue to pray for us. They inspire us by their holy lives, instruct us by their teaching and give us God's protection in answer to their prayers. (cf *Preface of Pastors*)

Tenth Sunday of the Year

Luke 7:11-17

Jesus went to a town called Nain, accompanied by his disciples and a great number of people. When he was near the gate of the town it happened that a dead man was being carried out for burial, the only son of his mother, and she was a widow. And a considerable number of the townspeople were with her. When the Lord saw her he felt sorry for her. 'Do not cry,' he said. Then he went up and put his hand on the bier and the bearers stood still, and he said, 'Young man, I tell you to get up.' And the dead man sat up and began to walk, and Jesus gave him to his mother. Everyone was filled with awe and praised God saying, 'A great prophet has appeared among us; God has visited his people.' And this opinion of him spread throughout Judaea and all over the countryside.

First Reflection
Arise

This is a story of grief and hope: of human grief which is lifted and transformed by the compassion of Jesus. Luke never tires of telling us of the immense compassion of God for the poor and broken-hearted.

The raising of the widow's son shows Jesus to be the Lord of life and death and it prepares the mind for the story of his resurrection.

He is not some distant, aloof Lord, but his nearness is shown by his pity for the grieving mother. Not only was this widow bereft of family companionship but, as this was her only son, she was now utterly destitute, since she had lost all property rights which could be held only in a male name. But Jesus felt sorry for her.

And when he put his hand on the funeral bier he was breaking the laws of contamination through contact with a corpse. Compassion, however, is a virtue beyond the restriction of laws. So he said: 'Young man, I tell you to get up.'

The early Christians remembered the important sayings of Jesus. They stored them in their hearts, pondered on them and lovingly lingered with them. The words of Jesus are a constant source of life and inspiration.

Grief is an experience that we all have to go through. But it need not mean that we cease to live inside. The wisdom of the East has a saying that we cannot prevent the birds of grief from flying overhead but we can prevent them from nesting in our hair.

We are drawn down into grief at any bereavement, for when a loved one departs, part of our heart goes too. We grieve also at the temporary absence of a loved one. Or, sometimes we are so shattered by failure that we fear we cannot start ever again. Or if we are deeply betrayed, how can we ever trust again? In some instances it is a deep-seated shame or guilt which drags one down into perpetual night. When our inner self feels consigned to the grave, then we need to hear again the voice of the Lord commanding our youthful spirit to arise: 'O soul of youth, I tell you to get up.'

As the psalmist expressed it so beautifully: 'Even darkness is not dark for you and the night is as clear as the day.' If the great dark realm of death is not removed from God's uplifting power, then neither are the little, dark areas of life. The mission of Jesus was to raise up the fallen, restore courage to flagging hearts and offer renewal of life.

In this life there is no fall so final that it is beyond the power of Jesus to enable one to start again. There is no sinful state beyond the reach of his pure,merciful hand. And there is no such word as 'hopeless' for one who believes in Jesus Christ.

'I tell you to get up … I say to you arise.' The words of Jesus are to be stored up and lovingly echoed in the mind.

Second Reflection
God has visited his people

The garden in June is teeming with life. Lush grass grows again immediately after mowing. Precious little seedlings are hidden in a tangle of weeds and must struggle for survival until I have the chance to rescue them. Areas which were bare a few weeks ago are now covered in a luxuriant carpet of life. Hidden bulbs and corms have flourished and the sleeping plants have revived. The Creator has come to visit us again and has left his footprints in green and red and yellow and blue and in every shade in between. Nature's annual revival reminds me of the gospel message of victory over death.

At Nain, Christ's lordship over life and death was shown in an awe-inspiring incident. Power over death was such a sign of God's presence that here, for the first time, Luke refers to Jesus as the Lord, a title hitherto given only to God.

One can easily imagine how the people felt. To see someone raised from the dead! The dead man got up and walked. Jesus gave him to his mother. Yet one fancies that there was some greedy next-of-kin there that day whose crocodile tears abruptly ceased as the return of the son snatched back the property rights from his grasping hand.

But the general reaction of the people was one of awe. And they clearly saw the presence of God in the event: they were moved to praise God. 'A great prophet has appeared among us; God has visited his people.'

Writers at the time spoke of the world being under the reign of the devil, 'the prince of this world.' But when God visited the world in Jesus Christ, the power of the Kingdom of God began a victory march through the world, pushing back the enemy lines.

Life was considered the creation on God: death was thought of as the home territory of the devil. But Jesus was destined to enter the abode of death and there conquer evil on its own pitch.

The three instances when he raised people from death were declarations of his power and intention. He is the Lord of life and death … 'I am the resurrection and the life.'

The garden in June with its flourish of renewed life is a mirror of Jesus at Nain, the Lord of life and death. It too can be a source of awe and praise of God.

Every morning, in the Benedictus canticle, the Prayer of the Church celebrates God's visit to the world in Jesus Christ: 'He has visited his people and redeemed them.'

Eleventh Sunday of the Year

Luke 7:36- 8:3

One of the Pharisees invited Jesus to a meal. When he arrived at the Pharisee's house and took his place at table, a woman come in, who had a bad name in the town. She had heard he was dining with the Pharisee and had brought with her an alabaster jar of ointment.

She waited behind him at his feet, weeping, and her tears fell on his feet, and she wiped them away with her hair, then she covered his feet with kisses and anointed them with the ointment.

When the Pharisee who had invited him saw this, he said himself, 'If this man were a prophet, he would know who this woman is that is touching him and what a bad name she has.' Then Jesus took him up and said, 'Simon, I have something to say to you.' 'Speak Master,' was the reply. 'There was once a creditor who had two men in his debt; one owed him five hundred denarii, the other fifty. They were unable to pay, so he pardoned them both. Which of them will love him more?' 'The one who was pardoned more, I suppose,' answered Simon. Jesus said, 'You are right.'

Then he turned to the woman. 'Simon,' he said, 'you see this woman? I came into your house, and you poured no water over my feet, but she has poured out her tears over my feet and wiped them away with her hair. You gave me no kiss, but she has been covering my feet with kisses ever since I came in. You did not anoint my head with oil, but she has anointed my feet with ointment. For this reason I tell you that her sins, her many sins, must have been forgiven her or she would not have shown such great love. It is the man who is forgiven little who shows little love.'

Then he said to her, 'Your sins are forgiven.' Those who were with him at table began to say to themselves, 'Who is this man, that he even forgives sins?' But he said to the woman, 'Your faith has saved you; go in peace.'

Now after this he made his way through towns and villages preaching and proclaiming the Good News of the Kingdom of God. With him went the Twelve, as well as certain women who had been cured of evil spirits and ailments; Mary surnamed Magdalene, from whom seven demons had gone out, Joanna the wife of Herod's steward Chuza, Suzanna and several others who provided for them out of their own resources.

First Reflection

The Repentant Woman

If I have any regret about the New Testament it's that none of the writers was a woman. We miss the feminine understanding of the story of Jesus Christ. Luke is the writer who comes closest to feminine sensitivity. Immediately after this story of the repentant woman he draws our attention to the role of several women in the ministry of Jesus.

Luke sometimes pairs off the story of a man with a corresponding episode about a woman. Invariably the woman will be shown as more open to faith than the man. For instance, Zechariah and Mary both received angelic annunciations but his doubting is in sharp contrast to her faith and obedience.

Much of the important action in Luke's gospel takes place at tables. In this story we meet the man who is master of the table. He is a Pharisee, somebody very concerned about the rightness of life and very much given to warning people about the danger of contamination ... or the occasions of sin.

In one way he represents the power of the male world. He had the initiative, organisational ability and necessary wherewithal to invite guests to a banquet. It was customary to invite some special guest whose wisdom would enrich the table. Simon – it's significant that we are told his name but not the woman's – had sufficient influence to get Jesus as his star turn. Simon was a religious man with power and influence. But later in the story his weakness will be revealed.

A woman came in. Unnamed, she is one of Luke's anonymous little people, so dearly loved by God. But even worse than having no name, she actually had a bad name in the town. A bad name doesn't just happen: it has to be spread. Whose tongues did the spreading? I bet it was all the 'good' people.

This 'bad' woman needed to put her life together ... to reach reconciliation within herself. By God's grace she found the source of reconciliation ... in Jesus, come to save sinners.

See how this woman goes to confession. Her language is made up of tears and touch. Her actions are with kisses and an extravagant anointing. Did Jesus ask her 'How many times?' or that most naive of questions, 'Did you take pleasure in it?'

Lucky for her that she did not come along centuries later in search of reconciliation. A wooden grill would not have understood her tears nor responded to her deep need for touch. In addition to his purple stole, every minister of reconciliation should come equipped with a spare packet of Kleenex!

The story comes back to the man. 'He said to himself' … it's always a bad sign when you start talking to yourself: it shows there's a big argument going on inside: an argument with that part of life you're repressing. And when we are attempting to deny part of our reality, one of the defence mechanisms we employ is to shelter behind a law. It protects our feeling of righteousness.

The law said that a rabbi should stay at a safe distance from any woman in public. Now here was a woman with a bad name, and this man, Jesus, is letting himself be touched by the evil creature. Thus Simon is staying in his head, judging and assessing guilt. His mental powerhouse is now shown to be the trap that imprisons him for he is incapable of responding with feminine heart to the situation.

How can one break through the defensive screen? Jesus uses the story of the two debtors to unhinge the prison door. He invites Simon to come out from behind his defensive screen by responding to a question. Not about debts or correctness of behaviour, but about love. 'Which of the two will love him more?' Jesus sees the entire encounter, not as an issue about sins and contamination by bad people, but as a day when love is released from beneath the crushing burden of guilt and debt. She must have been released of a terrible burden, such is the extravagance of her love. 'Her many sins must have been forgiven her, or she would not have shown such love'.

Simon, the conscientious Pharisee, worked hard on the duties of his love for God. But the anonymous feminine heart discovered that religion begins in letting God love us.

As a man ordained to priestly ministry in the Church I feel uncomfortably close to Simon the Pharisee. What challenges me is that many of us who frequently, even daily, occupy seats at the table of the Lord , may be very distant from his heart because of our cold judgments and unfeeling principles. Jesus may be far closer to the hearts of some who are barred from receiving him at the altar. Like the unnamed woman, they may not sit with him at table, but they know of his mercy and they come from behind him to touch him in prayer.

Perhaps it's better to have loved extravagantly, though not always properly, than to have lived ever so rightly, though not lovingly. Best of all, of course, is to live rightly and to love extravagantly.

Second Reflection
The Sunshower

On the Mount of Olives, at a spot which looks across the Kedron Valley towards the temple area of Jerusalem, there is a little chapel called 'Dominus Flevit,' recalling the tears Jesus shed over Jerusalem. The chapel is designed in the shape of a teardrop. On each of the four corners of the roof there is a stone jar, recalling the custom that a woman would save up her tears to be the most precious sign of her devotion to her loved one.

The sinful woman who came into the meal at Simon's house brought an alabaster jar of ointment. But her gift of her tears to Jesus was far more precious and personal. She poured her tears over his feet. Jesus recognised that her tears were her greatest expression of devotion and love. She is a great example of the sorrow for sin that leads to healing.

The guilt one feels on account of sinfulness leads to sorrow. But sorrow can be either a healing process or a destructive emotion.

St Paul distinguished these two ways of reacting to the pain of correction: 'To suffer in God's way means changing for the better and leaves no regrets, but to suffer as the world knows suffering brings death.' (2 Cor 7:10)

Destructive sorrow is well called remorse, which comes from the Latin word for taking a bite out of something. Remorse eats away the life of the soul, reduces hope, deflates confidence and deadens prayer because it makes one feel only a hypocrite before God. As one progressively eats in on self the load of guilt increases and the fear of falling again paralyses any hope of improving. It is like a team going onto the pitch defeated before they start. In Judas one can see a savage remorse which ate into his selfhood unto the final act of self-destruction.

Sorrow unto healing, repentance, does not delve into self in the pursuit of justification but reaches out to the mercy of God.

It has caught the loving glance of Christ just as Peter did after his fall. It has learnt to rejoice in the boundless extent of God's mercy as Paul did ... 'However great the number of sins committed, grace was greater.' (Rom 5:20)

Repentance is a sorrow unto God because it has learnt to use even one's sins in a constructive way. One of the great skills of judo is to twist the force of your opponent's attack into working against himself. Applied to the spiritual life this means making one's sinfulness work unto growth. Think how frustrating it must be to the tempter to see his moment of victory snatched away from his grasp!

Our experience of sin and weakness can undo much of our pride and give us a solid foundation of humility. Most of us would be unbearably proud were it not for our humiliations. The pain of our failures can make us less inclined to cast stones at others. The flower of compassion can grow best on the dungheap of wasted opportunities. According to Hebrews, every priest who intercedes between mankind and God must be compassionate ... 'he can sympathise with those who are ignorant or uncertain because he too lives in the limitations of weakness.' (5:1) Our frailty can cause us to pray more. Whereas remorse deadens prayer and makes one hide from God, repentance increases one's dependence upon God and draws one to pray all the more.

Above all, admission of our sinfulness makes us greatly appreciate the merciful love of God. The sinful woman loved much because she was forgiven much . The prodigal son came to know the extent of his father' s love when he was humiliated by his experiences. The mature believer uses the sacrament of reconciliation as an occasion of sorrow which yields to the praise of God's mercy. Like the sunshower ... when the sky's tears show us the rainbow of God's forgiveness and give way to the dancing brightness which dazzles the eye. Jesus recognised that the woman who came into the feast loved much because she had been forgiven much ... forgiven so much that she poured out her precious jar of tears on those feet, which were beautiful in the good news of peace which they brought.

Twelfth Sunday of the Year

Luke 9: 18-24

One day when Jesus was praying alone in the presence of his disciples he put this question to them, 'Who do the crowds say I am?' And they answered, 'John the Baptist; others Elijah; and others say one of the ancient prophets come back to life'. 'But you,' he said, 'who do you say I am?' It was Peter who spoke up.

'The Christ of God,' he said. But he gave them strict orders not to tell anyone anything about this.

'The Son of Man,' he said, 'is destined to suffer grievously, to be rejected by the elders and chief priests and scribes and to be put to death, and to be raised up on the third day.'

Then to all he said, 'If anyone wants to be a follower of mine, let him renounce himself and take up his cross every day and follow me. For anyone who wants to save his life will lose it; but anyone who loses his life for my sake, that man will save it.'

First Reflection

Alone … with others … and God

'Jesus was praying alone in the presence of the disciples.' In this neat sentence Luke has expressed how Jesus was present in three worlds at once. Alone, he was present to his own inner thoughts, feelings and stirrings. He was also present to his disciples and through them he was in contact with the mind of the wider society which they had met. And being in prayer, he was present to the Father. It is worth reflecting on how this time of prayer for Jesus meant being in touch with his own inner thoughts and stirrings and with those of the people around him.

Many of us have been educated to regard such inner thoughts and feelings as obstacles to prayer. Little wonder that the most commonly admitted problem in prayer is distraction. There seems to be a tendency to regard prayer as some sort of a pure, unearthly experience removed from our imaginations, feelings and vague stirrings. That it is part of the pursuit of a

God in the unearthly-up-there. But the incarnation tells us that since God has put on human flesh he can be found in the imperfect-in-here situation. Distractions need not be an obstacle to prayer: they can be used as pointers to where God wants to lead us. The psalmists found the basis for prayer in every sort of human experience. If our prayer takes no account of our inner stirrings and feelings, then it runs the risk of not being the true prayer of our lives. The first place where we encounter God and listen to him is in our daily experience of life.

Imagination will quickly carry us off from where we wanted to pray. But treat imagination with respect: it may be the only form of expression available to the blind stirrings deep in the mind. Remember the biblical stories where God used dreams to convey his message. Imagination may be the fool of the house, according to St Teresa, but the clown was the one person allowed to break through the pomposity and pride of the court.

It is a grand form of prayer at the end of the day to sit alone with your thoughts ... in the presence of God. Invoke God's light as you reflect on the day. Then, as your thoughts and feelings come up, listen to God who has been with with you throughout the day ... even if you have scarcely paid attention to him. Let the shape of the day's events emerge. What sort of feeling is surfacing? Stay with your feelings long enough to allow the deep-seated, blind gut stirrings to come up. Is it pain ... vague dissatisfaction... anger ... an unforgiven hurt? Is it fear of the impending future ... or a blind anxiety whose cause is not clearly recognised? Or is the feeling about the day very positive ... happy ... a joy waiting to be expressed? Is it tiredness ... perhaps the sort of fatigue which no amount of sleep will remove? In the prayer of Jesus the pain of the distant cross was beginning to emerge in his feelings: but also the hope of rising again. We also see that his prayer took in the reactions of other people to his identity and mission.

As you ponder on your day, whatever impressions, feelings, emotions or thoughts emerge, bring them all before the Blessed Trinity. Glorify the Father through all these experiences: they are today's part of your journey back to your Father. The Incarnate Son has touched the world of all our experiences. He has been through human pain and joy, anxiety and confidence, enmity and love, anger and peace. He is the Bread of sustaining help on our pilgrimage. By the gift of the Holy Spirit, God is in us ... and must be involved in all the inner life which our reflection has brought into the light of awareness. 'Thou in toil art comfort sweet, Pleasant coolness in the heat, Solace in the midst of woe.' (Sequence of Pentecost)

In this prayer of pondering on my day, I am alone, with the aftertaste of my encounters with others today, in the company of the Father, Son and Holy Spirit.

Second Reflection
Peter Remembers

Galilee was our own area. But our days with Jesus there were numbered, though we did not realise that yet. Excitement was at fever pitch, which suited me fine. Opinions about Jesus varied. But on one point they were unanimous: the power of God was visiting the world through him as much as, nay more than, in the days of Elijah or any of the great prophets of the past.

He wanted our little group to have a few days of quietness. But there was no getting away from the crowd. They had come down from the towns in the hills, curious and excited, careless of plans for food or lodgings. We thought we had seen everything until Jesus fed them all, at least 5,000, with just 5 loaves and 2 fishes. Was there any limit to the man? I always remember the challenge in his voice when he said to us: 'Give them something to eat yourselves.' Emptyhanded, I stood there, for once stuck for a word to say. And after he had multiplied those loaves and fishes, the broken pieces left over filled up exactly 12 baskets, one for each of us, and one for each tribe. I was quite excited when John hinted to me the significance of it all. We were each being given a basket of the miraculous bread to give to the hungry tribes: a hint of our mission.

Eventually the crowd dispersed and we were at last alone with him. It was one of those strange times when a quietness which was beyond us took possession of him. It had to do with prayer. He was with us in a way but we knew that there was something in him that we could not reach. He listened intently to what we had to say about people's reactions to him. Then he shot a quick question at us. 'But you, who do you say that I am?' I had the answer out before I knew I was speaking. 'The Anointed One of God.' I know that I could never have said it better. He was all that we had longed and waited for. He accepted what I said with the satisfied look of a teacher whose pupils have got it right at last.

But – and there was always a 'but' when he had that strange

look of prayer about him. But – he started saying all sorts of strange things about being rejected and put to death and rising on the third day. In my ignorance at the time I wouldn't hear of anything so terrible happening. Now, years later, with the benefit of hindsight, I can see what he was telling us. In our excitement we were thinking of him in the hope of the restoration of the glory days of David. But there was so much more that we had overlooked. It did not suit us to think in terms of Isaiah's Servant of God, innocent yet rejected, but by his wounds healing many. Or Zechariah's words about people looking in tears upon one whom they had pierced. And he went on to say that it would not be all days of glory for us either. He said a lot of tough things about the necessity of giving up selfish interests, even losing one's life for his sake. I couldn't fathom it at the time. But later events opened up his meaning to us. We who gathered up the 12 baskets of the miraculous bread of Jesus would have to be ready to let our lives, like bread, be broken and given too.

Thirteenth Sunday of the Year

Luke 9:51-62
As the time drew near for him to be taken up to heaven, he resolutely took the road for Jerusalem and sent messengers ahead of him. These set out, and they went into a Samaritan village to make preparations for him, but the people would not receive him because he was making for Jerusalem. Seeing this, the disciples James and John said, 'Lord, do you want us to call down fires from heaven to burn them up?' But he turned and rebuked them, and they went off to another village. As they travelled along they met a man on the road who said to him, 'I will follow you wherever you go.' Jesus answered, 'Foxes have holes and the birds of the air have nests, but the Son of man has nowhere to lay his head.'

Another to whom he said, 'Follow me,' replied, 'Let me go and bury my father first.' But he answered, 'Leave the dead to bury their dead; your duty is to go and spread the news of the kingdom of God.' Another said, 'I will follow you, sir, but first let me go and say goodbye to my people at home.' Jesus said to him, 'Once the hand is laid on the plough, no one who looks back is fit for the kingdom of God.'

First Reflection
Jesus of the resolute face
The ministry in Galilee reached its climax in Peter's profession of faith in Jesus as the Christ. In today's gospel we commence Luke's long section on the journey of Jesus to Jerusalem.

Luke is interested in Jerusalem not only as a geographical location of events but as the place of destiny for Jesus in the divine plan. The time was drawing near 'for him to be taken up to heaven.' In the Jewish heart Jerusalem was the desired place of pilgrimage. The narrative of Jesus' journey to Jerusalem will be used by Luke as a framework for teaching the way of Christian pilgrimage.

Luke notes the resolution on the face of Jesus as he took the road to the city of his destiny. He sent messengers ahead of him, thereby anticipating the days to come when the Spirit would set

149

missionary hearts on fire to be his witnesses to the ends of the earth. The rest of today's gospel teaches how his messengers must have the same resoluteness of purpose as Jesus.

In Samaria they met with hostility, just as the future missionaries would encounter opposition and persecution. James and John, harking back to the deeds of Elijah perhaps, wanted to call down fires from heaven. Jesus turned and rebuked them for this thinking was devilish. Fires from heaven there would be: not fires of vengeance and destruction though, but fire like tongues of divine love to inaugurate the Christian mission.

As they travel the road, various individuals step momentarily into the story like characters in a play flitting briefly across the stage. As in all good stories the characters are three, and each encounter is a lesson on the conditions of the pilgrimage.

'Foxes have holes and the birds of the air have nests, but the Son of Man has nowhere to lay his head.' Christian pilgrims are a future-people who keep moving forward. What we have here is not lasting. The soul thirsts for the eternal streams and must ever move on.

'Leave the dead to bury their dead; your duty is to go and spread the news of the kingdom of God.' A difficult text for balanced interpretation. While it is very noble to carry out family duties, the call to spread the news of the kingdom of God may be a more urgent duty on the person who is so called. The load of family duties can be discharged by the others who have not received the powerful energy of a missionary vocation. Missionaries of all times, from Abraham down to our own day, have bravely ventured forth from family and homeland for the sake of the Good News.

In the third encounter on the road Jesus stresses the need for singleminded concentration on the mission. 'Once the hand is laid on the plough no one who looks back is fit for the kingdom of heaven.' In the primitive agriculture of the time, one hand was used for steering the unruly oxen, while the other had to hold steady the structure of the plough. It demanded concentration and the coordination of muscle and eye to achieve a straight furrow. A distracted life and sloppy performance would not be worthy of God.

In my mind's eye I picture Jesus of the resolute face. His eyes are set on the first hill to the south, beyond which is another hill, and another, until eventually there is Jerusalem, city on a hill. 'On the holy mountain is his city, cherished by the Lord.' (Ps 86)

The strong look on the face of Jesus challenges the dedication of his followers. We must count the cost and give priority to God in the event of a clash of loyalties.

The story of Elisha in today's first reading is an example. When he left his life as a ploughman he slew his ploughing oxen for a feast, using the wood of the plough for the fire. There would be no going back. That is how the pilgrim goes forward towards the city of destiny.

In the Middle Ages the idea of a pilgrimage to the heavenly Jerusalem was a very popular way of understanding the Christian life. Blessed Henry Suso in his writing represents that spirituality of pilgrimage. The pilgrim travels a while, halts and works for his keep, then packs his bags and journeys on again. His eyes are set resolutely towards Jerusalem. In his heart he keeps on repeating the pilgrim's prayer:

'O Jesus, I am nothing, I have nothing, I desire nothing, but to be with thee in Jerusalem.'

Second Reflection
Peter Remembers

We had been all around the towns and villages of Galilee. Then Jesus got Jerusalem on his brain. Pilgrimage to Jerusalem was always a big thing with our people. We had all done it in our time. But Jesus really seemed to get all worked up over it. We readily caught the mood because we felt sure that it had something to do with taking over the kingdom.

I know he had made all sorts of predictions about being rejected, but we paid no heed as we felt it was only a tactic to cool down our ardour or something like that. We set face for the south, but once started he seemed to be in no great hurry. He could have done the whole journey comfortably in less then a week, but he zig-zagged, halted when occasion demanded, preached, healed and sent us off to preach at times.

He knew as well as we did that Samaria would be hostile. He could easily have avoided it like many others who travelled on the far side of the Jordan. One village ran us out with sticks and stones. You can imagine my temper, but for once I was not the one who put his foot in it. James and John beat me to it. One thing about those boys, they always did things in style. No half-measures there. It was the mother's influence. She was an ambitious lady. They saw themselves every bit as powerful as Elijah in the old days. 'Lord, do you want us to call down fire from heaven to burn them up?' I could hardly believe my ears. My rage would have been to strike out with stone for stone and stick for stick. But these boys thought they had the power and the right to call down fire from heaven. They were not asking Jesus to do it ... they were offering to do it for him! The composure of Jesus in the moment of crisis was always amazing. He said a curt 'no' to James and John and calmly told us to shake off the dust of that town from our feet and off we went to the next place.

Later, a day would come when we were to see fire come from heaven: not fires of retribution, but tongues of fire from the Spirit: a fire of love and warmth and light. But that was still a long way off.

Fourteenth Sunday of the Year

Luke 10: 1-12, 12-20

The Lord appointed seventy-two others and sent them out ahead of him, in pairs, to all the towns and places he himself was to visit. He said to them, 'The harvest is rich but the labourers are few, so ask the Lord of the harvest to send labourers to his harvest. Start off now, but remember, I am sending you out like lambs among wolves. Carry no purse, no haversack, no sandals. Salute no one on the road. Whatever house you go into, let your first words be, "Peace to this house!" And if a man of peace lives there, your peace will go and rest on him; if not it will come back to you.

Stay in the same house, taking what food and drink they have to offer, for the labourer deserves his wages; do not move from house to house. Whenever you go into a town where they make you welcome eat what is set before you. Cure those in it who are sick, and say, "The Kingdom of God is very near to you." But whenever you enter a town and they do not make you welcome, go out into its streets and say, "We wipe off the very dust of your town that clings to our feet, and leave it with you. Yet be sure of this; the kingdom of God is very near." I tell you, on that day it will not go as hard with Sodom as with that town.'

The seventy-two came back rejoicing, 'Lord,' they said, 'even the devils submit to us when we use your name.' He said to them, 'I watched Satan fall like lightning from heaven. Yes, I have given you power to tread underfoot serpents and scorpions and the whole strength of the enemy; nothing shall ever hurt you. Yet do not rejoice that the spirits submit to you; rejoice rather that your names are written in heaven.'

First Reflection
Missionary Lifestyle

The instruction of Jesus to the seventy-two missionaries was more about their lifestyle than the content of their words. The Christian message must be lived before it is preached. The message would be seen in the lifestyle.

They were sent in pairs so that their own mutual sharing and caring would witness to charity ever before they spoke of it. They were to go with the gentleness and innocence of the lamb rather than the stealth and violence of the wolf. And their first greeting to all would be of peace. The extent of the harvest would invest their mission with an urgency permitting of no dalliance or socialising along the way. Nor should they delay wherever the message was unacceptable but they should hasten to the next place.

Their words about God would first be authenticated by their own trust in him. They were to travel without purse or haversack or sandals, totally trusting that God and good people would look after their needs. Their life on every level should proclaim a God who is sufficient to our desires, who can be trusted in our needs and whose love is real and urgent.

They would be agents of God's power to heal and reconcile. Through their ministry the power of God's kingdom would be very near people. And such indeed was the experience of those disciples who came back rejoicing at the vanquishing of evil before their very eyes. But they were reminded by Jesus that this was done, not in their own power, but in the power of him who chose them and sent them out.

Christian mission must be in the living before it is in the speaking: in action before it is in doctrine. Pope Paul VI wrote: 'For the Church, the first means of evangelisation is the witness of an authentically Christian life, given over to God in a communion that nothing should destroy and at the same time given over to one's neighbour with limitless zeal.' He also touched on the particular suspicion of empty words that people have today: 'People today listen more willingly to witnesses than to teachers, and if they do listen to teachers, it is because they are witnesses.'

The message must be lived before it is spoken. 'What you are thunders so loudly that I cannot hear what you are saying.'

Second Reflection
Like Lambs among Wolves

The courage to go out like lambs among wolves can only be drawn from the belief that God's power is very near. When the seventy-two disciples were sent out to proclaim peace they were given this assurance by the Lord: 'The kingdom of God is very near to you.'

Heroic peacemakers, like Francis of Assisi, Ghandi and

Martin Luther King were inspired and sustained by their belief in the power of goodness to triumph over all the machinations of evil. Francis utterly disregarded all dangers as he crossed the lines between the Crusaders and the army of the Sultan. He believed that the way to justice was not through the use of superior power but by the proclamation of goodness and brotherhood. Later in his life, when Assisi was rent asunder by the dispute between the mayor and the bishop, Francis did not dally with the rights and wrongs of the case but from his sick-bed he sent his brothers to sing of the blessedness of those who overcome wrongdoing by granting pardon.

Ghandi drew strength and vision from the Sermon on the Mount and especially from the beatitudes. He maintained this gospel faith unshaken even when evil continued to rear its violent head. Anybody who attempts to take seriously the path of gospel goodness can expect to be tested by the backlash of evil.

Martin Luther King, likewise was constantly faced with all the ugliness that discrimination, exploitation, and bitter memory could come up with. His suffering was a process of purification through which he grew ever closer to God as the source of his vision and strength.Towards the end of his life he seemed to be walking more in his visionary land of peace than in the ugly society around him.

Peace can be built only on the foundation of justice. The injustices which stem from discrimination, exploitation and deprivation of rights must be eliminated before peace can grow.

Then the growth of peace requires the climate of forgiveness and reconciliation – as Francis correctly intuited at Assisi. The real blessedness of those who proclaim peace in Christ's name is seen in their power of healing.

There can be no reconciliation with others until the scars of memory are healed. That is why Jesus gave the seventy-two the power to cure the sick. Angry words and destructive deeds will have left deep wounds within the heart. A great percentage of life's ailments flow from the stresses and anxieties that are caused by these inner wounds. What is required is a healing that reaches deep into the human spirit. This inner healing is the work of the Holy Spirit, who is the power of the kingdom. The seventy-two were told by Jesus that the victory over evil that they had witnessed was due entirely to heavenly power: 'Yet do not rejoice that the spirits submit to you; rejoice rather that your names are written in heaven.' The extent of evil and the constant highlighting of depressing news leaves many people despairing of ever seeing peace. But the good news is that the power of God's kingdom is at hand. 'The kingdom of God is very near to you.'

Fifteenth Sunday of the Year

Luke 10: 25-37

There was a lawyer who, to disconcert him, stood up and said to him, 'Master, what must I do to inherit eternal life?' He said to him, 'What is written in the law? What do you read there?' He replied, 'You must love the Lord your God with all your heart, with all your soul, with all your strength, and with all your mind, and your neighbour as yourself.' 'You have answered right,' said Jesus, 'do this and life is yours.' But the man was anxious to justify himself and said to Jesus, 'And who is my neighbour?' Jesus replied, 'A man was once on his way down from Jerusalem to Jericho and fell into the hands of brigands; they took all he had, beat him and then made off, leaving him half dead. Now a priest happened to be travelling down the same road, but when he saw the man, he passed by on the other side. In the same way a Levite who came to the place saw him, and passed by on the other side. But a Samaritan traveller who came upon him was moved with compassion when he saw him. He went up and bandaged his wounds, pouring oil and wine on them. He then lifted him on his own mount, carried him to the inn and looked after him. Next day, he took out two denarii and handed them to the innkeeper. 'Look after him,' he said, 'and on my way back I will make good any extra expense you have.' Which of these three, do you think, proved himself a neighbour to the man who fell into the brigands' hands?' 'The one who took pity on him,' he replied. Jesus said to him, 'Go and do the same yourself.'

First Reflection

Loving Action

On the road to Jerusalem Jesus taught the way of discipleship. The spiritual life is like a tripod supported on the legs of prayer, study of our religion and love expressed in action. Today's gospel shows love in action. The next two Sundays will address the other legs of the tripod.

Love is a word that is used very often but also very loosely. The whole purpose of religion is to guide us towards total love of God and love of other people. The parable of the Good

Samaritan brings out the practical nature of authentic love. The priest and the Levite, both of them professionally dedicated to God's service, passed by the victim in need. Presumably, their excuse was that contact with blood or with a corpse would have rendered them ritually impure and unworthy of service in the temple. Bogus piety is a regular cop-out from action.

The response of the Samaritan shows love in action. He saw; he felt pity; and he did something to remedy the situation.

The first step in love is in seeing people, in paying attention to them. We open up the shutters of our aloofness when we see and hear people. By attentiveness we hear them knocking on our doors, seeking entry into our lives. We are expert at keeping people out. Certain people are barred because of prejudice or discrimination. Or we shrink from the demands on our time, so we are too busy to attend to their knock. We might even shelter behind a rule, 'This is no time to come ...' or, like Robert Frost's neighbour in his poem, we claim that good fences make good neighbours.

The second step is to answer the knock and to let the person in. The Samaritan was 'moved with compassion' for the injured traveller. The two pious men saw the victim but moved to the other side. Compassion means accepting the pain of the other and responding to it. When others knock on our door, compassion lets them it, and is willing to reach out to them, whether they are asking us to share tears in their sorrow, or celebrate with their thankfulness, to give to their emptiness or to receive from their fullness.

Deep attentiveness to others will enable us to be sensitive not only to what they say but, more importantly, to what they need to say but cannot. Just as Jesus not only heard the question, 'Who is my neighbour?', but he was also sensitive to the restricted person behind the question. He answered the questioner rather than the question. He gently opened up his mind to the answer through the inviting possibilities of the story.

The third step of the good neighbour was to take practical action. Feeling is empty if it does not bear fruit in action. When the compassion of the Samaritan met with the needs of the ransacked victim, the result was the practical generosity that reaches into the pocket, forgets about personal convenience and gives.

One of life's great excuses is waiting around for the ideal opportunity. The cartoonist Robert Short, father of the Charlie Brown family, drew a pictured story with this punchline: 'I love humanity ... it's people I can't stick!' Love begins at home, with the people we meet every day.

The First Reading today reminds us: 'The law that I enjoin on you today is not beyond your strength or beyond your reach. The Word is very near to you, it is in your mouth and in your heart for your observance. Now is the favourable time. Today is the day to pay attention, to feel and to give.

Second Reflection
The Use of Story

This parable is a very good example of the power of story-telling. 'You must love your neighbour as yourself ... but who is my neighbour?' Jesus might have answered the question directly in a short statement. But he was more concerned about responding to the person behind the question. The question revealed the restricted mind of the questioner. A definition of neighbour might have answered the question but it would have done nothing for the questioner. By telling a story Jesus was able to shock him out of his smug self-righteousness before inviting him to explore fresh possibilities about religious observance.

In stories like this the hero invariably is the third character. 'Once upon a time there was this priest ... and a Levite ... and ...' All expect the third character to be a Jewish layman, but no, they are jolted by the unexpected. More than a jolt, it is a severe shock when they realise that the hero of the story is a Samaritan – a despised, half-pagan renegade. A fully fledged pagan would have been held in higher regard.

Jesus anticipates that the lawyer's casuistic mind will set about defending the priest and the Levite on the grounds that they were prudently avoiding the possibility of contact with a dead body, which would have rendered them ritually impure and thereby barred from exercising their religious functions. He disarms the lawyer's defence by throwing back to him the central question, which is about neighbourliness. And having broken through his smugness by the shock in the story, Jesus can now invite him to think afresh about the question.

'Which of these three, do you think, proved himself a neighbour?' The new formulation of the question reflects the fresh approach. The emphasis is shifted from defining the restrictions of neighbourly love to exploring the demands of love. 'The one who took pity on him,' he answered.

He is still afraid to mouth that despicable name, Samaritan.

Yet the story has begun to make its point in the admission that this semi-pagan in his own way of practical love was closer to the central law of religious observance than those who scrupulously observed religious ritual.

The use of a story enabled Jesus to open up an entirely new way of thinking for the lawyer. To use the terminology of modern research, he invited the lawyer to move from a mode of thinking restricted to the left brain into the right brain mode.

Left brain thinking seeks control of things by analysis and definition, by dividing and conquering. The lawyer, trained in casuistry, was an expert in this field. Hence his initial reaction was to seek a definition of neighbour. But a definition is always restrictive as it sets out the limits beyond which the term does not apply. The left brain is happy with this restricted area which can be controlled. Right brain thinking seeks the possibilities of the subject and its connections with the larger reality. When we move into the right brain mode we are exposed to losing control and we are open to risk.

The lawyer was invited by Jesus to leave the safe, controlled world of casuistry and discover the realm of love where exciting possibilities live side by side with demands, risks and vulnerability. At the end of the exchange the lawyer has reached the position where he can be invited by Jesus: 'Go and do the same yourself.'

The stories of Jesus are never only stories. Each story is an invitation to us to enter into it, find our place there and discover our life afresh. Sometimes the discovery is shocking: but always the word offers hope of growth.

Sixteenth Sunday of the Year

Luke 10: 38-42

Jesus came to a village, and a woman named Martha welcomed him into her house. She had a sister called Mary, who sat down at the Lord's feet and listened to him speaking. Now Martha who was distracted with all the serving said, 'Lord, do you not care that my sister is leaving me to do all the serving by myself? Please tell her to help me.' But the Lord answered: 'Martha, Martha,' he said, 'you worry and fret about so many things, and yet few are needed, indeed only one. It is Mary who has chosen the better part; it is not to be taken from her.'

First Reflection
Listening

The resolute journey of Jesus towards Jerusalem comes to a moment of restfulness in the house of Martha and Mary. Last Sunday, the neighbourly Samaritan exemplified the practical action of love. Today, the listening Mary is an example of paying attention to the Lord, or deepening our faith through the study of our religion.

The digital-watch is typical of the mind of today. It is never still but ever frantically chasing the present moment to the hundredth part of a second. So frenzied is its chase for the elusive now, that it is out of touch with past and future. It typifies the mind of today, frantic in its search for the instant experience but lacking the patience and sense of context which are necessary for wisdom. Some ninety years before the days of our dancing digits, the novelist Thomas Hardy wistfully recalled the age when one-handed clocks sufficiently subdivided the day. He loved to recapture those country lanes not made for hasty progress and regretted what had been lost to life in the doubtful progress of society. In the same vein T.S. Eliot reflected upon the price paid to progress.

The endless cycle of of idea and action,
Endless invention, endless experiment,

Brings knowledge of motion, but not of stillness;
Knowledge of speech, but not of silence;
Brings knowledge of words, and ignorance of the Word.
(*Choruses from The Rock*)

Listening has always been difficult. The Creator in his vision anticipated our problem and designed us with two ears and one mouth. And that same mouth must perform many other functions, lest it find too much time for idle chatter. The ears are given no other employment except to support spectacles or an occasional pencil. The busy world of today pounds us with noises outside and inside. The outer world passes by at a whirling, accelerated pace. Noise is hugely amplified beyond what our ancestors had to endure. The noises within us come from the clamour of pressures and compulsions. The consumeristic ethic trains us to turn every desire into a compulsion, every want into a need. But the voice of the Master says: 'Few things are needed, indeed only one.'

For many people the work of prayer has to begin with quietening the mind, making space for God, in our time and in our attention. The modern mind is like a postal sorting-office in the aftermath of a strike. When we sort out today's intake there is yet a massive backlog of memories, unidentified pressures, or confused plans, all clamouring for our attention.

So we may need training in the art of quietness. A good way to start is by deliberately paying attention to the gentler sounds. Listen to the sounds that come from the furthest distance. Catch the sounds of things you cannot see. Listen to the wind … sighing or soughing … whining or blowing. Learn to enjoy the gentle pitter-patter of raindrops. Listen every day for birdsong and birdcall. Notice the ticking of things and the expansion or contraction of pipes.

From the gentle sounds it is helpful to attend next to the rhythms of life within us. Get in touch with the quiet rhythm of your breathing … intake … holding … letting go. Pick up the rhythm of your heartbeat … working away unnoticed within you … through last night's sleep … this morning's rising … all day through. Your breathing and heartbeat are far more important than the countless frettings and anxieties which clamour for your attention every day.

Learning how to be quiet and still will dispose us for prayer.Then we can listen to God in one of his many ways of speaking to us. First, 'Be still' … and then, 'Know that I am God.'

Second Reflection

Able to Receive

Meals, in the bible, were sometimes occasions when the hosts discovered that they were more the recipients than the givers. Abraham and Sara were lavish in their hospitality to the travellers at the Oak of Mamre. But that day was remembered more because of what the guests brought – the promise by God of a son in their old age. The widow, at Zarephath, who shared her last handful of meal with Elijah, also received a promise:

Jar of meal shall not be spent

Jug of oil shall not be emptied … (1 Kgs 17:14)

Martha and Mary were hosts to Jesus in their home. Again, the better part was what the guest brought. Mary listened to the precious words spoken by the Word made flesh. The role of Martha, helpful and serving, is absolutely necessary in its own place. So long as it does not become a complex!

People with the Martha-complex are virtually incapable of receiving. And how much poorer life is for that. If you give them a gift they are agitated until they can even the score. Invariably they must make a greater return of favour. They will discover your needs where you never suspected you had any! They will be generous in words of affirmation or praise but most uncomfortable in receiving such from others: yet they are deeply hurt if affirmation is not given. They will be the first to move into action but ill-at-ease if they must wait patiently to receive. They feel strongly that they have little to learn beyond what can be quickly grasped. We, the compulsive doers, profit greatly from the balance that comes with the attitude of 'Let it be done to me.'

Days of rest and times of retreat are most necessary, though not always easy. Playfulness can truly be a re-creation, offering a fresh vision of life and a recharging of energy. It is good to offer others the chance to serve us and give to us. It is good for us to be:

'… out on the road, and going one knows not where

Going through meadow and village,

… one knows not whither nor why. (John Masefield)

It is good to lose control and get lost occasionally. It is good to discover empty time and to know how to be poor. When the Lord visits our lives, the one thing necessary in that precious moment is to know how to listen and receive his gift.

Seventeenth Sunday of the Year

Luke 11:1-13
Jesus was in a certain place praying, and when he had finished one of his disciples said, 'Lord teach us how to pray, just as John taught his disciples.' He said to them, 'Say this when you pray:
Father, may your name be held holy,
your kingdom come;
give us each day our daily bread, and forgive us our sins,
for we ourselves forgive each one who is in debt to us,
And do not put us to the test.'

He also said to them, 'Suppose one of you has a friend and goes to him in the middle of the night to say, "My friend, lend me three loaves, because a friend of mine on his travels has just arrived at my house and I have nothing to offer him"; and the man answers from inside the house, "Do not bother me. The door is bolted now, and my children and I are in bed; I cannot get up to give it to you." I tell you, if the man does not get up and give it to him for friendship's sake, persistence will be enough to make him get up and give his friend all he wants.

So I say to you: Ask and it will be given to you; search and you will find; knock and the door will be opened to you. For the one who asks always receives; the one who searches always finds; the one who knocks will always have the door opened to him. What father among you would hand his son a stone when he asked for bread? Or hand him a snake instead of a fish? Or hand him a scorpion if he asked for an egg? If you then, who are evil, know how to give your children what is good, how much more will the heavenly Father give the Holy Spirit to those who ask him?'

First Reflection
Pray like this
The Christian disciple must be active like the Good Samaritan and listening deeply to the Lord like Mary of Bethany. The third leg of the tripod is prayer, calling on the Lord and knocking on his door for the needs of the world.

The disciples were deeply impressed by the prayerfulness of

Jesus. It was customary for disciples to ask a religious master for a way of prayer to express their newly acquired understanding of God. The lesson of Jesus is a golden moment when we are offered a peep into the dynamics of his relationship with the Father. What marks the advance of divine revelation in the new testament is the revelation of God as our Father. Indeed, Saint Paul wrote that the movement of the Holy Spirit in the baptised person is towards the recognition of God as 'Abba', Father.

The Our Father is not so much a prayer formula to be repeated by rote as an expression of the different moments of our relationship with the Father. It is the prayer of our identity as followers of Christ.

Our Father: By the gift of the Holy Spirit we are adopted children of God, sharing in the return of Jesus Christ to the Father. We are taken up into the inner movements of the Blessed Trinity. In Jesus Christ our prayer shares in the return of the Word to the First Begetter, that is the Father. There are some twenty original prayers of Jesus in the gospel and every one of them begins by addressing God as Father. It is a title of relationship, of nearness, intimacy and trust. Yet this nearness is balanced by the acknowledgement of the holiness of God. God is as near as Father yet as distant as heaven. Prayer takes us towards intimacy and transcendence at the same time.

May your name be held holy.

We cannot add anything to the infinite glory of God but our desire to praise God is itself a gift. This petition is for an increase of faith: that we might be granted an experience of God's holiness and majesty. Then we will be lifted up in praise and adoration. We visualise it as going upwards, the elevation of the heart and mind to God. The holy name of God expresses all that is above and beyond. Repeated humbly, the name of God is a prayer of praise and adoration. Repeated lovingly, it conveys the warmth and tenderness of knowing the Father's love for us, his children.

Your kingdom come.

In contrast to the upwards movement of the first petition, now we ask for a coming down of God's reign to our world. The kingdom or reign of God on earth was the central issue of the ministry of Jesus. He came to cast out the reign of Satan, sin and selfishness. The synoptic gospels present Jesus preaching the good news of the kingdom and revealing the power of God in the world by his works of healing. He established the reign of

God. However, in many of his parables he spoke of the obstacles to growth in souls like hard earth, draught, choking weeds, in the mixture of good fish and bad. The growth of the kingdom is still sort of perfection. We fall very short of having a world run according to the ideals of the Sermon on the Mount. So, our prayer is an earnest desire for the coming down of his Spirit, to take away our hearts of stone, to fill our world with divine love. This petition is for the strengthening of our hope.

Matthew's version of the prayer adds: Your will be done on earth as in heaven. After rising up in praise and desiring the coming down of God to our world, now the movement is inwards, towards the centre of our hearts. On the circumference of life we are engaged in many activities, in work, family, social contacts and so on. We now pray that the will of God will be the steadfast centre of all these activities. It is a petition for an increase of love: that love for God's will might be the guiding power of all we undertake.

These have been the great movements of desire - rising up in adoration, longing for the coming down of God's reign and yearning for God's will at the inner centre of all desire. The petitions that follow express our needs in relation to the different dimensions of time, past, present and future.

The petition for today is 'give'. Utterly dependent on the sustaining hand of God we are needy before him. We come with empty hands and express all our needs in the one word, 'bread'. Our heavenly Father already knows what we need. Prayer is not a matter of filling up gaps in God's knowledge about who needs what. It is we who change through finding the humility to ask and the depth of faith to persevere.

Our prayer for the past is dominated by forgiveness. For all our sins of the past, forgive us, Father. And may we so experience your pardon that we will want to pass on your forgiveness to those who have offended us. Like that woman who loved much because she had been forgiven much.

The only remaining way to look is towards our tomorrows. The future is a source of crippling anxiety to many. But the confident prayer of the disciple is: 'Father, lead us safely through all testing and every crisis. Take us by the hand, lead us through all danger and above all, deliver us from the evil one.

Saint Teresa of Avila was asked by somebody what should she do about contemplative prayer. Her reply: 'Say the Our Father ... and spend an hour at it.' It is the complete expression of the various movements of the Christian disciple towards God and the world: the prayer which expresses our identity as united with Jesus, children of the Father.

Second Reflection
Ask ... Search ... Knock

The master of any art can make it appear very simple. So it was with Jesus as a master of prayer. He spoke in very simple human terms. He gave God a human face. And he described the depths of a disciple's relationship with the Father in familiar stories of hospitality and parental care. We can understand the power of loyalty in human friendships, or the effectiveness of persistence, or the care and protection that are part of a parent's love. That's how God is towards us, multiplied to the power of 'how much more.' Obviously we do not always get exactly what we ask for. Ten people praying for the one job cannot all get the post! Nobody would ever die if it were only a matter of saying a prayer for a cure!

Yet God, as a loving parent, hears every prayer.

The point of petition is not as if God were unwilling to give to us unless we cajoled him or twisted his hand by prayer. Oftentimes the mountains that have to be moved by the prayer of faith are the obstacles in ourselves. The humiliation of having to ask for something breaks in on our unhealthy self-sufficiency .

Repeated asking may force us into facing whether our motivation is unduly selfish. Somewhere along the line God will test the selfishness of our faith: are we using religion to serve ourselves ... or God? When I say 'Thy will be done', may it not sometimes be a camouflaged form of 'My will be done'?

It can be good for us when we have to persist in our asking. What comes to us too easily is often not appreciated. What we have to work hard for is treasured more. The answer to sustained prayer is more likely to be appreciated. It's we who change ... and grow into God's will ... by perseverance in asking, searching and knocking.

The Russian novelist, Dostoevsky, was deeply impressed by the simple belief of many people that the world keeps revolving, day follows night, seasons follow in course, tides ebb and return ... because at any given moment of time there is somebody, somewhere, standing before God in prayer. To intercede literally means to stand between the needs of the world and God, just as Abraham stood before God, bargaining for the people of Sodom.

No prayer goes unheard or unanswered. I may not always get the answer that I want. But I can be sure that God knows who most needs an answer. And my prayer is helping somebody, somewhere. So the world keeps on going around, season follows season, life goes on, because somewhere, all the time, there is somebody at prayer. And sometimes ... that somebody is me.

Eighteenth Sunday of the Year

Luke 12: 13-21

A man in the crowd said to him, 'Master, tell my brother to give me a share of our inheritance.' 'My friend,' he replied 'who appointed me your judge, or the arbitrator of your claims?' Then he said to them, 'Watch, and be on your guard against avarice of any kind, for a man's life is not made secure by what he owns, even when he has more than he needs.'

Then he told them a parable: 'There was once a rich man who, having had a good harvest from his land, thought to himself, 'What am I to do? I have not enough room to store my crops.' Then he said, 'This is what I will do: I will pull down my barns and build bigger ones, and store all my grain and my goods in them, and I will say to my soul: My soul, you have plenty of good things laid by for many years to come; take things easy, eat, drink, have a good time.' But God said to him, 'Fool! This very night the demand will be made for your soul; and this hoard of yours, whose will it be then?' So it is when a man stores up treasure for himself in place of making himself rich in the sight of God. '

First Reflection
Standing with the poor

A plea from a man in the crowd, for Jesus to arbitrate in a property dispute, become the occasion for further instruction on the way of following Christ. Jesus not only heard the man's plea but also the inner voice of a soul too concerned about material possessions. Greed can obscure the soul's need for God. Paul says that greed is the worship of a false god. The story of the rich farmer is the only parable in any gospel in which God speaks. And the first word attributed to God is not too complimentary: he calls the rich man, 'Fool!', a name which implies the denial of God.

Jesus was rich, divinely rich, infinitely rich. Yet he chose to be poor. Why? 'To make you rich out of his poverty.' (2 Cor 8:9)

Jesus was rich ... if we regard power and possessions as part of being rich. For he was Lord of the universe. Yet he chose to be born in the poverty of homelessness, amid the crude comforts of an animal shelter. And on his travels he had nowhere of his own to lay his head.

Jesus was rich ... if we regard an integrated personality as part of being rich. Yet he chose to be among the marginals and outcasts of the system, and he brought peace to the disturbed and possessed.

Jesus was rich ... if we regard health as part of being rich. Yet he came as a physician to the infirm and unhealthy.

Jesus was rich in wisdom and understanding. Yet he submitted to the poverty of being misunderstood and deliberately misrepresented

Jesus was rich in his celebration of life. He restored life to some who had died. Yet he submitted to the ultimate poverty that is death.

Jesus, the Word of the Father, whom the heavens cannot altogether contain, chose the poverty of human flesh, and later the poverty of bread and wine to contain his presence.

The church, as the community of his disciples, has no alternative but to imitate the choice of the Master to be with the poor. In the early centuries, the disciples were largely drawn from the poor, so it was a church of the poor. To be a disciple then, one belonged to a powerless, illegal and oppressed organisation.

When peace was made with the Empire in the fourth century, the church gradually gained political power and accumulated wealth. Over the centuries, it is undeniable that abuses of power were many. Yet the church always had a conscience about the poor and in every age it mothered charitable action for redeeming captives, freeing slaves, helping lepers, founding schools and hospitals, feeding the hungry and protecting people against usury. It was then a church for the poor.

A new era dawned for the church when it lost its last political dominions in the nineteenth century, although it took quite a while to come to terms with the new situation. Today, as the gap between rich and poor appears unbridgeable, and as long as social injustice is accepted as normal, it is no longer sufficient for the church to stand in silence. Giving hand-outs is not enough. The church is taking up a more radical stance and is becoming a church with the poor. The voice of the church is now heard in critical judgement on financial policies of governments and world monetary agencies.

Jesus was rich in many ways but chose to be with us in our needs, so that his poverty might enrich us. The church too is rich in many ways – in possessions, in having a respected voice, in educational experience, in a long tradition of caring ministries and in many more ways. These rich resources are put at the disposal of the poor so that the curse of poverty might be removed and the sickness of injustice be healed.

When the church stands with the poor, only then is it being true to the way of Jesus Christ.

Second Reflection
The Riches of the Poor

Only the poor can rightly read the bible, sincerely pray the psalms, and authentically celebrate the eucharist. In the healing presence of Jesus Christ, the curse of poverty is lifted and its blessedness is revealed. As the prosperous nations lose religion, the poorer countries are increasingly revealing true spiritual wealth. Many who set out to give to the poor were drawn to the humble realisation that they received more than they could give … 'it is in giving that we receive.' The poor countries have preserved many of our lost values such as contentment, inner peace, a sense of the nearness of God, hospitality, neighbourliness, courtesy in greetings and having time to listen to one another. Jesus declared a special blessedness in those who are poor in spirit. Here and now, he said, 'Theirs is the kingdom of heaven.' Among their possessions in the kingdom, the bible is theirs to savour, the psalms are theirs to pray, and the eucharist is theirs to celebrate.

The bible reveals God as being on the side of the poor and oppressed. The heroes of the story are first of all a paltry, insignificant nation, beaten to the ropes by one great power after another. And the later hero of the book is a rejected prophet who was condemned to death as a criminal. Yet God entered into a covenant with that buffeted nation: 'I will be your God and you shall be my people.' And God was in that wounded prophet. Those who are poor and powerless, victims of injustice and misunderstanding, are the very people who are closest in experience to the heroes of the bible. Only the poor in spirit can rightly get inside the mind of the bible.

And only the poor can make their own the wealth of the psalms. 'In God alone be at rest, my soul he alone is my rock, my stronghold.' Anybody whose security is in the size of a bank

account cannot honestly pray these words. 'The Lord is my
Shepherd, there is nothing I shall want.' This is a prayer of unconditional trust in God. Only the empty-handed can pray these
words with sincerity:

I say to God: You are my God,
My happiness lies in you alone ...
O Lord, it is you who are my portion and cup;
it is you yourself who are my prize.

The eucharist too belongs to the poor in a special way. As
long as there is such a serious disproportion in the distribution
of wealth, as long as people are dying from hunger on this plentiful earth of ours, the authenticity of eucharistic celebration for
the rich must be questioned. If Jesus had chosen any other symbol of his memory than bread, the challenge might be less obvious. Ghandi remarked that to a starving people the only authentic way that God dared to come was as bread. If we break bread
in the sanctuary but do not break bread with the hungry and
needy, then our liturgy runs the risk of being a hollow pretence.
Only the poor in spirit can celebrate the eucharist with a totally
free conscience.

Nineteenth Sunday of the Year

Luke 12:32-48

Jesus said to his disciples: 'There is no need to be afraid, little flock, for it has pleased your Father to give you the Kingdom.

Sell your possessions and give alms. Get yourselves purses that do not wear out, treasure that will not fail you, in heaven where no thief can reach it and no moth destroy it. For where your treasure is, there will your heart be also.

See that you are dressed for action and have your lamps lit. Be like men waiting for their master to return from the wedding feast, ready to open the door as soon as he comes and knocks. Happy those servants whom the master finds awake when he comes. I tell you solemnly, he will put on an apron, sit them down at table and wait on them. It may be in the second watch he comes, or in the third, but happy those servants if he finds them ready. You may be quite sure of this, that if the householder had known at what hour the burglar would come, he would not have let anyone break through the wall of his house. You too must stand ready, because the Son of Man is coming at an hour you do not expect.'

Peter said, 'Lord, do you mean this parable for us, or for everyone?' The Lord replied, 'What sort of steward, then, is faithful and wise enough for the master to place him over his household to give them allowance of food at the proper time? Happy that servant if his master's arrival finds him at this employment. I tell you truly, he will place him over everything he owns. But as for the servant who says to himself, "My master is taking his time coming," and sets about beating the menservants and the maids, and eating and drinking and getting drunk, his master will come on a day he does not expect and at an hour he does not know. The master will cut him off and send him to the same fate as the unfaithful.

The servant who knows what his master wants, but has not even started to carry out those wishes, will receive very many strokes of the lash. The one who did not know but deserves to be beaten for what he has done will receive fewer strokes. When a man has had a great deal given him, a great deal will be demanded of him; when a man has had a great deal given him on trust, even more will be expected of him.'

First Reflection
Watching through the night

The journey of faith in the following of Christ would not always be in clear light. So, Jesus encouraged his disciples not to be afraid, reminding them that the Father has promised them the kingdom. If they have freed their lives from material greed, then their desire will be for heaven and their hearts will be in the right place.

The great models of faith in the bible are Abraham and Sara whose story is mentioned in today's Second Reading (Heb 11:8ff.). Trusting solely on God's promise, they left the security of home to venture into the dark unknown. They were promised land and many descendants, but for years they had to endure the darkness of not having even one child. Against all signs to the contrary, they continued to draw their hope from belief in God's promise. Faith enabled them to keep going through the darkness towards the promised future.

Today's parable is about the faithful servants who are rewarded because they persevered in vigilance through the darkness of night.

During the Exodus, the people were led by a pillar of cloud by day and by flame at night. The journey of faith receives sufficient light on God's presence to lead us through the night , whereas the cloud by day represents the mysterious designs of God that we must accept without comprehending. If we look directly into the light of the sun our eyes are darkened. Similarly, the light of the unseen God would be too much for our limited comprehension, so it is a darkness to us.

In the experience of the darkness of faith, one finds it almost impossible to focus attention in prayer, or to enliven the mind with any thought or image. Consolations are absent and inner feelings are dried up. At times one may be a tangle of contradictory impulses: or whipped into a maelstrom of temptation, especially towards despair, anger or impurity. But God is present in the night of faith as much as in the clear daylight. The spiritual life runs parallel to what we see in material nature. The world's time has as much night as day. Our eyes need rest from light. Plants respond to the appropriate balance of light and darkness. The snowdrop needs less daylight than the daffodil, which in turn precedes the tulip. Some plants require more darkness than light, needing more time of rest than activity in their cells.

Thomas Merton noted that in daylight we can see all the objects around us in daily life, but it is only in the dark of night that we can see the distant stars. Darkness stretches our vision. We would too easily settle for mediocre satisfactions unless God shook us up and stretched our desires to infinite possibilities. A God whom our minds could fully understand would not be large enough for the eternal aspirations of the heart.

In daylight faith we advance in knowing what God is like. In nightlight faith we advance in unknowing, that is, in learning the limitations of our knowledge. Then we learn more about what God is not than about what God is. There is a vast body of literature by mystical writers on the darkness which is an essential part of faith. One of the best exponents, Saint John of the Cross, gives this advice: 'Do not be satisfied with what you understand about God. Nourish yourself instead on what you do not understand about Him. Do not base your happiness or delight on what you may hear or feel of him, but rather on what you can neither feel nor hear ... The less one understands, the closer one gets to Him.'

Abraham and Sara set out through the dark unknown on the strength of God's promise. Jesus told the disciples not to be afraid for it has pleased the Father to give them the kingdom. In times of darkness, he tells us to keep our lamps lit and be dressed for action. We keep our lamps lit by at least trying to pray. We are dressed for action when we act in practical love towards those around us. Where your treasure is, there will your heart be also.

Second Reflection
God of the Apron

My God wears an apron! My God was portrayed for me by Jesus in that stunning reversal of roles where the master served the servants. And the actions of Jesus speak more loudly than his words. For when he had gathered the apostles together for their last supper in his company, he was the one who washed their feet and served them. The eucharistic bread is there for me today as a continuing expression of his desire to serve me and strengthen my faltering pilgrim steps. My God is not one to inspire morbid fears or clinging scruples. He is no tyrannical judge whose frightful memory keeps a list of all the black moments of my life. Nor is he a demanding taskmaster who barks at every speck of imperfection in my efforts. My God is extraordinarily well-disposed towards me. It pleases him to give me the kingdom, no less. His delight is in finding me ready to receive ... to take what he will give me.

My God-of-the-apron totally reverses the order dictated by worldly wisdom. Greatness is not to be gauged by wealth, or title, of fame, or the honours one has received. Greatness is in knowing how to receive from God. And what we freely receive we will joyfully pass on to others.

Happy the disciple who has learnt to be a servant ... whose heart is humble enough to let the Lord be generous. 'For it has pleased your Father to give you the Kingdom.'

Twentieth Sunday of the Year

Luke 12: 49-53
Jesus said to his disciples: 'I have come to bring fire to the earth, and how I wish it were blazing already! There is a baptism I must still receive, and how great is my distress till it is over!

Do you suppose that I am here to bring peace on earth? No, I tell you, but rather division. For from now on a household of five will be divided: three against two and two against three; the father divided against the son, son against father, mother against daughter, daughter against mother, mother-in-law against daughter-in-law, daughter-in-law against mother-in-law. '

First Reflection
Testing Times
Jesus did not promise his followers that his way would always be along pleasant roads of sunshine and flowers. On the contrary, he warned them that opposition would be his own lot, and in time, it would come their way too. On an earlier occasion he sent out the seventy-two disciples with the greeting of peace to every house. Peace was his desire for all but he knew that every movement meets with resistance. Every current causes counter currents. Those who would not accept his way would violently oppose it. So there is an irony in the way that he sees opposition and division as the negative reactions to his movement of peace and harmony. Poor Jeremiah, in today's First Reading, was dumped into a well for his preaching.

Jesus spoke of fire and water, images of testing and purification. Fire sorts out the pure ore in the smelter: and it raises the scum to the surface from the purity of jam. Water is an obvious means of cleansing and purification.

The Christians for whom Luke was writing knew how demanding and costly it was to follow Jesus. They were subject to persecution. Many of them had suffered the pain of family rejection and dispossession. There was no cheap or soft way of being a Christian.

Opposition can bring out the best in people. See how a minority group will stick together. If they are asked to sing in church, I guarantee that you will hear them. During the days of communist persecution of the church, a priest from Poland visiting Ireland remarked: 'We have the advantage of a visible enemy and you have the disadvantage of an invisible one.' In our society, while there is no official opposition to religion, yet one may have to show courage to profess and practice it ... to be seen going to church ... to speak up for chastity in relationships ... to wear a religious emblem ... to pray in public... to join some religious organisation. The pressure might come from colleagues, friends, peers, even family members.

In the name of science, the believer may be ridiculed as being naive, gullible or brainwashed. In the name of liberalism, the believer may be scorned as being fundamentalist ... whatever that means. In the name of fudged ecumenism, one might be called archaic for holding beliefs that do not change with the swings in popular opinion.

Jesus visualised families divided over following him. The division of a house calls to mind the system of voting in a democratic parliament. There comes a point where one has to stand up and be counted. A strong opposition party will bring out the best in the government. There is nothing as effective as opposition for bringing out the best in religious commitment.

Jesus sounded passionate about his mission when he spoke of facing fire and water. In the complacency of a large majority, Irish Catholicism has become dull, dreary and without passion. Back-of-the-church stuff and clock-watching liturgy. Where have we hidden the Spirit? Where is the passion and singing of the football terraces? Opposition is causing a slimming of the ranks, but hopefully, a much healthier and more committed body in the long term.

Second Reflection
Conflicting Experiences
Jesus experienced the inner clashing of contrary emotions. He felt the urgency of going forward to send down the fires of Pentecost from heaven to earth. But at the same moment he knew the hesitancy caused by the distressing prospect of Calvary which appeared like a whirlpool of death into which he must plunge. The images of fire and water express his inner feelings. The Old Testament sage, Ben-Sirach, reflected on how opposites can complement each other: 'All things go in pairs by op-

posites and he has made nothing defective; the one consolidates the other ....' (Sir 42:24-25)

Observing the world we live in, we see that night contains the seed of day and day itself grows into night. Mid-winter contains the promise of summer and is chosen for the liturgical celebration of the coming of the Light of the World.

And midsummer's day, which marks the waning of the sun, is the feast of John the Baptist, the light whose brightness would decrease. Oftentimes we need to move in one direction before we begin to appreciate the pull of the opposite pole. It is only in the experience of fear that we learn what courage is.

And it is only in the darkness of night that the light of distant stars can come into our ken.

We learn that every step away is also a step towards something else. And every experience of dying is the beginning of some new form of life.

Opposite experiences not only exist side-by-side but 'the one consolidates the other.' And so, true joy is not eliminated by sorrow. Sorrow can deepen the sensitivity of the soul and increase its capacity for joy. Just as rest increases our capacity for activity: and times of solitude help us contribute more to the community.

It can come as quite a shock to us if we recognise that though we love God dearly, yet there may be resentment and anger towards God seething in our system. Or while we think we trust God absolutely, yet we may be deeply disappointed with the way he has treated us. It will take patience (and good directing) to discern what the conflict has to reveal to us.

We are so geared-up today to expect instant answers that we do not find it easy to have the patience to await the balancing of opposite emotions. But if we run from moments of loneliness we will never discover the beauty of solitude.

If we cannot stay awhile with times of depression we miss the chance for a deepening reflection on life. If we always insist on getting our own way then we miss the possibility of enrichment from others' ideas.

Jesus experienced the opposites of enthusiasm and fear, urgency and hesitation, the one as warm as fire and the other as drowning as water. The disciple of Jesus must learn to live with similarly conflicting experiences. Indeed, the basic pattern of Christian life is a sharing of opposites in the death and resurrection of Jesus Christ.

Nobody has expressed it better than St Paul: 'Always, wherever we may be, we carry with us in our body the death of Jesus, so that the life of Jesus, too, may always be seen in our body. Indeed, while we are still alive, we are consigned to our death every day, for the sake of Jesus, so that in our mortal flesh the life of Jesus, too, may be openly shown.' (2 Cor 4:10–11)

Christian dedication draws energy from the tension created between opposing poles.

Twenty-First Sunday of the Year

Luke 13:22-30

Through towns and villages, Jesus went teaching, making his way to Jerusalem. Someone said to him, 'Sir will there be only a few saved? He said to them, 'Try your best to enter by the narrow door, because, I tell you, many will try to enter and will not succeed.

Once the master of the house has got up and locked the door, you may find yourself knocking on the door, saying "Lord, open to us,' but he will answer, 'I do not know where you come from.' Then you will find yourself saying, 'We once ate and drank in your company: you taught in our streets,' but he will reply, 'I do not know where you come from. Away from me, all you wicked men!'

Then there will be weeping and gnashing of teeth, when you see Abraham and Jacob and all the prophets in the kingdom of God, and yourselves turned outside. And men from east and west, from north and south, will come to take their places at the feast in the kingdom of God. 'Yes there are those now last who will be first, and those now first who will be last.'

First Reflection

The Narrow Door

Jesus knew where he was going in life. Jerusalem was his destiny. Yet he was not so obsessed with the idea as to be blinded to other places. On his way he found time for many towns and villages. He had a clear sense of purpose: but his response to it had the gentleness of free choice and none of the anxiety of compulsion.

He spoke of salvation as trying to enter by a narrow door. The image of a narrow door indicates the need for a clear sense of purpose and the disciplined commitment of moving towards it. It suggests taking responsibility for the direction of one's life rather than drifting along with the prevailing current or wind. It is hardly a compliment to be called narrow-minded, for it suggests the tunnel vision of the bigot who cannot see anything good beyond the scope of his own prejudices. Yet there is a sense in which it is a great strength to operate out of a narrowed vision. Like the marksman who achieves maximum concentration on the target by closing one eye totally and narrowing the vision of the other. There was considerable wisdom behind the old understanding of sin as missing the target of life. In a way, sin is the result of not being sufficiently narrow-minded with our aim.

We live in an age which greatly favours broad-mindedness. But it is also the time when people are finding it very difficult to make a total commitment of life to any cause or to say 'forever'. We are open to such a wide variety of experiences and choices that the prevailing temptation is to want to keep all our options open. The trouble with total commitment is the pain of closing the door on the other options.

So, the weakness of broad-mindedness comes from the wastage of energy which is scattered in too many directions. Dissipation is the inevitable result of the lack of clear purpose and definite commitment.

It is more than mere coincidence that this broad-minded age is when we are constantly hearing of boredom, inertia and depression. It has much to do with the absence of commitment to a clear purpose in life. Energy is plentiful where there is a purpose. You see light in the eye and a bounce in the step of those who know where they are going.

And yet, daily purposefulness may not be enough. Ultimately, we need a comprehensive meaning of life which crosses the bridge of death. It is increasingly being recognised that the deep questions which arise in the second-half of life nearly always have to do with the meaning of life's journey, that is, finding a religious outlook on life.

The pursuit of the chosen direction will involve a disciplined life:
– priorities are clarified;
– sources of help along the way are identified;
– danger points are noted and avoided;
– unnecessary weight is off-loaded;
– purposeless waste of energy and resources is eliminated.

Yet the disciplined approach must not be so rigid that it cannot allow relaxation and a gentle pace. With too rigid a system the journey to God's door would not be enjoyable: and that could hardly be right. A joyless religion is a sure sign of bigotry, which knows far more about hatred than love.

The way of Jesus is the model. He resolutely directed his face and firmly set his feet towards Jerusalem. Yet he was sufficiently relaxed on the way to have time for all the other towns and villages. It may be towards a narrow door that the disciple directs his vision, but once the direction is right, there can be a relaxed and gentle movement forward which allows one to enjoy the journey to God's door.

Second Reflection
Pictures of Heaven

If we reach that narrow door, what awaits us inside? What is heaven like? Is there a hell? If there is, what is it like?

The majority of those who listened to Jesus shared in the belief in life after death which would bring either reward to the just or punishment for the wicked . Jesus spoke to them of the after-life in homely pictures.

In this particular passage three pictures are offered – feasting, meeting with one's ancestors, and faces showing surprise.

(i) Feasting … not surprising, since Luke's gospel is never far from eating and drinking. Association with Jesus is described as eating and drinking in his company. Heaven is imagined as a great banquet. For those who cannot get in the door there is a terrible pain of loss. There is woeful weeping in distress. And there is grinding of teeth expressing all the anger with oneself when the blame for sin is finally admitted as one's own responsibility. Those who are admitted through the door enjoy all that a feast conjures up – good company, relaxation, satisfaction and the mood of celebration.

(ii) The Jews had a very strong sense of their ancestry. Jesus offered the very appealing picture of meeting up with their great ancestors in the faith, Abraham, Isaac, Jacob and all the prophets. It offers us the hope of meeting again our own departed family and friends as well as our forebears through whom the gifts of life and faith came to us down through the centuries.

(iii) When God selects his team we are warned to be ready for some surprise omissions. God alone can read the heart and the deepest motive of the mind. He alone can perfectly judge the response one has made to the graces offered and the difficult circumstances that had to be surmounted. Many who seem to be first in their manifestation of piety and church-belonging may be far back in the line when genuine charity is uncovered … and charity is the only question in this final test. And many who appear to be against the outward standards may finally be seen to have hearts of gold.

As St Augustine noted, there are many in the church who are

not in the kingdom, and many in the kingdom who do not belong to the church. Watch out for the Paddylasts of this life, re-
splendent under their shining haloes: while Holy Joe is squirm-
ing with embarrassment after being shown up as bogus.

Twenty-Second Sunday of the Year

Luke 14: 1, 7-14

On a sabbath day Jesus had gone for a meal to the house of one of the leading Pharisees; and they watched him closely. He then told the guests a parable, because he had noticed how they picked the places of honour. He said this, 'When someone invites you to a wedding feast, do not take your seat in the place of honour. A more distinguished person than you may have been invited, and the person who invited you both may come and say, "Give up your place to this man." And then, to your embarrassment, you would have to go and take the lowest place. No; when you are a guest, make your way to the lowest place and sit there, so that when your host comes, he may say, "My friend, move up higher." In that way, everyone with you will see you honoured. For everyone who exalts himself will be humbled, and the man who humbles himself will be exalted.'

Then he said to his host, 'When you give a lunch or dinner, do not ask your friends, brothers, relations or rich neighbours, for fear they repay your courtesy by inviting you in return. No; when you have a party, invite the poor, the crippled, the lame, the blind; that they cannot pay you back means that you are fortunate, because repayment will be made to you when the virtuous rise again.'

First Reflection

Table-talk

No table was considered blessed unless there was a scholar to sit at it. The body will relish the delights of victual and vine all the more deeply when the meal is salted with lively table-talk. The wisdom of the church has preserved the two tables in the liturgy, source of the word and of the bread. Indeed, it is said that the priest who breaks the bread at the altar without breaking the bread at the ambo, is only half a priest.

In Luke's gospel, Jesus is never far away from a table. And much of his teaching is given at the table. A light and lively exchange can reach beyond the limitations of formal teaching. Table-talk comes in a very different wrapping to sermon-talk.

One can expect sharp observations, humorous caricatures of various poses and all the cut and thrust of lively repartee. And yet, there is a serious level underneath as Jesus invites the listeners to see themselves somewhere in that flow of words.

He had a message for the guests. He sketched the caricature of blatant vying for positions of honour. In that picture all of us are invited to see ourselves as guests insofar as we have been recipients of God's favour. But how quickly we forget that all we have is but what we have received. And, imagining that the credit is our own, we become self-opinionated, pushy, aggressive and vying for prestige and popularity. There will be no room for such behaviour at the messianic banquet.

Then Jesus had a message for the host, the one who would foot the bill that day. It sounds a bit ungracious in cold print: 'When you give a lunch or a dinner, do not ask your friends, brothers, relations or rich neighbours, for fear they repay your courtesy by inviting you in return...' One has to hear the tones of table-talk, for Jesus is speaking tongue-in-cheek somewhat. If taken with deadening literality these words will be misunderstood. After all, we know that Jesus had no objection when it came to dining with his own friends and associates. And see how he exaggerated the fear of ever getting a return of invitation. Pity the perplexed host who is compiling a list of guests, double-checking that nobody gets through who might possibly return the compliment!

The serious message underneath the smile is the challenge to consider those who were excluded from the table. The poor, the crippled, the lame and the blind were even forbidden by law to take part in religious functions. Many of the religious teachers held that there would be no place for the handicapped at the messianic banquet. But at the outset of his preaching Jesus had made the shocking announcement that his mission was primarily to these pariahs of the system.

The humorous touch of Jesus in his table-talk should prepare us for the humour of God at the last banquet. His many mansions will be filled with the jokes of life, for the last shall be first, the humble exalted, the poor fed and the crippled will be dancing for joy. A God who dons the apron to serve at table must be full of surprises. And a God who insists on a day of rest after a week's work cannot be taken too seriously all the time.

Second Reflection
Of Pride and Humility

The seven deadly sins are poisonous roots which are at the source of all wrong behaviour, and first on the list is pride. There is, of course, a legitimate pride in the recognition of true gifts. But disordered pride puts self at the centre of everything. Pride sets self in opposition to others by engaging in comparison, by despising and judging others. Pride sets up self as a little god in place of the true God. 'There is no cure for the proud man's malady since an evil growth has taken root in him' (Ecc 3:28).

The evil growth of pride is always deceptive. In contrast, humility literally means down to earth truthfulness, having its origin in the Latin word humus, meaning the earth.

As novices imbued with youthful zeal for instant sanctity, we had many discussions on humility and this business of taking the lowest seat. We foresaw a big problem. How could one remain humble if one recognised growth in virtue? Could you be proud of your humility? We read of the heroes of the desert and of obscure saints whose lives seemed to be a constant crucifixion of talent and who virtually lusted for occasions of self-abasement. And we were guided by a manual of conduct on how to be self-effacing in conversation or how to yield right of way at table or in the corridor. Fortunately for our survival, sanity prevailed over sanctity once a week on the sportsfield, where honest assertiveness and the will to win surfaced once more.

Some of the proudest people I know have reserved seats at the lowest table. But dare you try to budge them from it. Humility does not mean thinking yourself less than other people. Not does it mean having an underevaluation of your talents. There is nothing so off-putting as that bogus humility. But watch out how subtle and stubborn the preoccupation with self can be underneath that ploy of yielding to others. Quite often, those who constantly profess their unworthiness will be very annoyed if someone else says it for them.

Humility is down to earth truthfulness. The truly humble person recognises one's own talents and good points but is never arrogant because humility recognises these as gifts from God. 'What do you have that you have not received? And if you have not received why do you glory as if you had not received it?' (1 Cor 4-7). Rather than hiding talents, humility is happy to nurture them and use them to celebrate the glory of God.

Humility is not paralysed with the crippling fear of failure because the humble person is not overly concerned with personal success. God is not demanding that we succeed, only that we try our best. Humility refrains from passing derogatory judgement on others from a position of moral superiority: 'there go I but for the grace of God.'

The inspiring ideal of the prophet Micah is to act justly, to love tenderly and to walk humbly with your God. 'Everyone who raises himself up will be humbled, and the one who humbles himself will be raised up.'

Twenty-Third Sunday of the Year

Luke 14: 25-33

Great crowds accompanied Jesus on his way and he turned and spoke to them. 'If any man comes to me without hating his father, mother, wife, children, brothers, sisters, yes and his own life too, he cannot be my disciple. Anyone who does not carry his cross and come after me cannot be my disciple.

And indeed, which of you here, intending to build a tower, would not first sit down and work out the cost to see if he had enough to complete it? Otherwise, if he laid the foundation and then found himself unable to finish the work, the onlookers would all start making fun of him and saying, "Here is a man who started to build and was unable to finish." Or again, what king marching to war against another king would not first sit down and consider whether with ten thousand men he could stand up to the other who advanced against him with twenty thousand? If not, then while the other king was still a long way off, he would send envoys to sue for peace. So in the same way, none of you can be my disciple unless he gives up all his possessions.'

First Reflection
No Half-hearted Response

Luke portrays Jesus as very merciful, sensitive and gentle. Yet when it comes to the question of possessions, whether emotional or material, he is very demanding. He insists on giving unconditional preference to Christ over any other attachment.

Some parts of today's gospel can present us with a problem of interpretation. What is meant by hating your own family? Does every follower of Jesus have to give up every last cent? Are we to take these injunctions literally? Or can they be understood as a device of the preacher's art who presents the audience with a simple either/or option and who does not hesitate to exaggerate for effect?

The first rule in biblical interpretation is to compare the text in question with the rest of the bible. There are so many passages about loving others, even loving one's enemies, that we cannot take the words here to indicate hatred of one's family. What is meant is giving priority or preference to the call of Christ even over family love if this becomes an obstacle to following Christian principles.

On the matter of giving up everything in voluntary poverty, Jesus did demand this of one individual, the rich young man. But we also see Jesus availing of the hospitality of friends and of some rich hosts and he did not demand that they should sell out lock, stock and barrel. Jesus even defended the extravagant expenditure of Mary of Bethany when she anointed his feet.

The point being made by the preacher is that following Christ can be costly and demanding. A disciple must give an uncompromising preference to the will of God over all other considerations. One must be ready to let go of any possession, a family tie, a personal relationship, an ambition, occupation or pursuit if these run counter to the way of Christ.

'I have no love for half-hearted people, my love is for your law', wrote the psalmist.

Great crowds were flocking to Jesus. They came out of curiosity, to seek help, to use him for political ends and for many other reasons. The time had come for him to put it straight to them that following him would be costly and demanding. There would be no half measures like a half-built tower or a war entered with half an army. Like the old joke about the fellow opening one gate at the level-crossing because he was half expecting a train.

This tough, demanding side of Christianity runs directly counter to the permissive culture of today, which cries out for the gratification of every desire or feeling. Pop psychology has sold the religion of self-fulfilment. There is a suspicion that voluntary self-denial is a sign of a pathological condition. There is little understanding of making an option for the life of the spirit over the life of the flesh. Authority is rejected as some outside power attempting to invade my personal space. Hence rules and principles of behaviour are easily disregarded. Only this very day that I write, the radio news featured an item about a recently married priest who wants to celebrate Eucharist for the people. The vox pop taken by the reporter came up with such gems of wisdom as, 'He is a grand man, he should be allowed to do whatever he wants to.'

The contemporary mind is very impressed by great crowds.

The impression is given that numbers constitute the surest criterion of greatness. The popularity chart is the judge of music, the best-seller list the arbiter of literature. It is worth recalling that there is one instance in the gospel of a decision being taken on a show of hands. It was the day that Barabbas was released and Jesus was crucified. The ballot box today carries more weight than objective principles of morality. But matters of truth or morality are far too serious to be left to the opinion poll.

Jesus warned his would-be followers that, before they called themselves disciples, they should first sit down and carefully consider the cost of upholding Christian principles. Obedience and fidelity will, at times, place heavy demands on personal feelings, relationships or occupations. The option of a true disciple will always be for the will of God or Christian principle.

The Book of Revelation contains a hard hitting denunciation of all who make the half hearted effort: 'I know all about you: how you are neither hot nor cold. I wish you were one or the other, but since you are neither, but only lukewarm, I will spit you out of my mouth' (Rev 3:15-16).

Second Refection
The Cost
'I would like to follow Jesus. Will it demand much of me?'

Great crowds accompanied Jesus on his way. They came from field and village, drawn to him by a variety of motives. They were curious to see for themselves the one that others spoke of, they were caught up in the excitement about miracles, they were attracted by the controversies raging. Some came seeking wisdom and answers to problems, others were hoping for healing and others again came with political dreams rekindling. But Jesus, who could read their hearts, was not taken in by the size of the crowd. He spoke to them in uncompromising terms about the cost of following his way.

'But ... the bottom line to the bill? How much will it cost?'

Great crowds today express their admiration for Jesus in his compassion and helpfulness, his fairness and honesty. But many seem not to have noticed his tough, uncompromising determination, and the cost he demanded of anyone who would take him seriously.

'Yes, the cost ... that's what I want to know. '

Even the good things of life often have to be sacrificed if they stand in the way of the better. Getting an exam, winning at sport, every achievement is at the cost of some sacrifice. One must be willing to break off even the precious ties of family relationships if these are restricting the pilgrimage. The life of St Francis of Assisi is a classical instance of where a parent stood in the way of following the call of Christ. His father forced him into a position which left Francis no option but to declare his independence of any claims the parent might have on him. 'Up to now I have called Peter Bernardone my father, but now I can say without reservation, "Our Father in heaven".'

'So, what does it all add up to? What is the total cost?'

The demands of discipleship are so radical that the early church soon began to speak of it in terms of taking up the cross to follow Jesus. And they knew what the cross meant! There must be courage and determination born out of blind confidence in God.

'Blind! Why can't I trust my own understanding and feelings?' Because in your weakness you may be misled. The Book of Wisdom reads (in today's first reading): 'The reasonings of mortals are unsure and our intentions unstable; for a perishable body presses down the soul, and this tent of clay weighs down the teeming mind.' The mind teems with so many preoccupations that we need great detachment to allow us to be occupied by God.

'Detachment? From what?'

From the possession of anything – material, emotional or even spiritual – which would lessen your ability to say 'God is my all, in him alone is my heart at rest.'

'It's beginning to sound very costly. What can I expect as the final cost?'

Some of those who went the full journey with Jesus wrote in depth of their experience. They concluded that it is a way which costs… 'not less than everything.' (T.S. Eliot: *Little Gidding*)

Twenty-Fourth Sunday of the Year

Luke 15: 1-32

The tax collectors and the sinners were all seeking the company of Jesus to hear what he had to say, and the Pharisees and the scribes complained. 'This man,' they said, 'welcomes sinners and eats with them' So he spoke this parable to them:

'What man among you with you with a hundred sheep, losing one, would not leave the ninety-nine in the wilderness and go after the missing one till he found it? And when he found it, would he not joyfully take it on his shoulders and then, when he got home, call together his friends and neighbours? "Rejoice with me," he would say, "I have found my sheep that was lost." In the same way, I tell you, there will be more rejoicing in heaven over one repentant sinner that over ninety-nine virtuous men who have no need of repentance.

Or again, what woman with ten drachmas would not if she lost one, light a lamp and sweep out the house and search thoroughly till she found it? And then, when she had found it, call together her friends and neighbours? "Rejoice with me," she would say, "I have found the drachma I lost." In the same way I tell you, there is rejoicing among the angels of God over one repentant sinner.'

He also said, 'A man had two sons. The younger said to his father, "Father, let me have the share of the estate that would come to me." So the father divided the property between them. A few days later, the younger son got together everything he had and left for a distant country where he squandered his money on a life of debauchery.

When he had spent it all, that country experienced a severe famine, and now he began to feel the pinch, so he hired himself out to one of the local inhabitants who put him on his farm to feed the pigs. And he would willingly have filled his belly with the husks the pigs were eating but no one offered him anything. Then he came to his senses and said, '"How many of my father's paid servants have more food than they want, and here am I dying of hunger! I will leave this place and go to my father and say: Father, I have sinned against heaven and against you; I no longer deserve to be called your son; treat me as one of your paid servants." So he left the place and went back to his father.

While he was still a long way off, his father saw him and was moved with pity. He ran to the boy, clasped him in his arms and kissed him tenderly. Then his son said, "Father, I have sinned against heaven and against you. I no longer deserve to be called your son." But the father said to his servants, "Quick! Bring out the best robe and put it on him; put a ring on his finger and sandals on his feet. Bring the calf we have been fattening, and kill it; we are going to have a feast, a celebration, because this son of mine was dead and has come back to life; he was lost and is found." And they began to celebrate.

Now the elder son was out in the fields, and on his way back, as he drew near the house, he could hear music and dancing. Calling one of the servants he asked what it was all about. "Your brother has come," replied the servant, "and your father has killed the calf we had fattened because he has got him back safe and sound." He was angry then and refused to go in, and his father came out to plead with him; but he answered his father, "Look, all these years I have slaved for you and never once disobeyed your orders, yet you never offered me so much as a kid for me to celebrate with my friends. But for this son or yours, when he comes back after swallowing up your property-he and his woman – you kill the calf we have been fattening."

The father said, "My son, you are with me always and all I have is yours. But it was only right we should celebrate and rejoice, because your brother here was dead and has come to life; he was lost and is found."'

First Reflection
He welcomes sinners

Last week we invoked the first rule of biblical study: that any one text must be taken in relation to the rest of the bible. This week we take on board the second rule: that to understand any text properly, one must take account of the situation and pastoral concerns of the writer. Just as the Jewish people were God's chosen race long years before a word of the Old Testament was written, so too the church was in existence before a word of the new scriptures were written. The bible is part of the church. The New Testament scriptures were written by church members who were influenced by and responding to contemporary pastoral situations.

Luke was faced with a particular pastoral problem about accepting the repentance of lapsed Christians who wanted to return to the community. Clearly there were people who did not welcome them back to the table where the breaking of bread expressed the unity of the members. The writer of the Letter to the Hebrews would certainly not have them back. 'As for those people who were once brought into the light, and tasted the gift from heaven, and received a share of the Holy Spirit, and appreciated the good message of God and the powers of the world to come and yet in spite of this have fallen away – it is impossible for them to be renewed a second time. They cannot be repentant if they have wilfully crucified the Son of God and openly mocked him' (Heb 6:4-6).

To answer those who refused to accept the repentant sinner, Luke sets the scene where sinners seek out Jesus: he welcomes them to table: but the righteous people complained. In this scene Luke gathers three parables of Jesus, each of them about something lost, then found and the finding is an occasion to celebrate.

We note Luke's sensitivity in complementing a story from the man's world of shepherding with a parable about a woman. The third story is usually called The Prodigal Son or occasionally The Generous Father. Really though, it should be called The Unforgiving Brother since the context of the story is the response of Jesus to those who were complaining about his welcome to sinners.

Notice all the negativity in this character. The word he repeats is 'never'. He is angry. He speaks brusquely to his father without any personal title. He cannot use the word 'brother' but refers disparagingly to 'this son of yours'. I'm sure Luke is echoing the uncompromising, angry attitudes he had seen at the local parish meeting.

All this negative energy is in such a contrast to the way that the shepherd went after the lost sheep, the woman searched thoroughly for the lost coin and the father ran towards the returning son, clasped him in his arms and hugged him. All three can be called crazy lovers who do extravagant things. In the world of practical common sense, a shepherd does not leave ninety-nine sheep unguarded in dangerous territory to seek for one. And by the time the woman of the coin had celebrated with the neighbours she called in, she had probably spent more than the actual monetary value of the coin. The father of the wayward son would have done well to take him in quietly by the back door. But his big heart needed to tell everybody and to celebrate. It is with this picture in mind that we say that, while private confession to God is very good, yet the church reflects the mind of Christ in calling us to celebrate in the sacrament.

Answering the pastoral question about taking repentant sinners back to the table, Luke tells us clearly what Jesus would do. 'He welcomes sinners and eats with them.' As Paul writes to Timothy in today's second reading: 'He is a saying you can rely on and nobody should doubt: that Christ Jesus came into the world to save sinners.'

The challenge to us is about taking people who have hurt or wronged us back to the table of our affection. Am I willing to make a move, to seek out the stray, to search thoroughly for reconciliation? Do I allow resentment to harden my heart? Am I stuck in the mud of negative words ... never again ... never in my house ... over my dead body? Do I accept an apology? Do I make it easy for others to apologise? What would Jesus do in the situation? His example is what we are to follow. Sadly, our churches have too many of the 'never people'.

Second Reflection
One is important
One is important to God. The love of God is intensely personal and individual. A man with a hundred sheep is concerned when one is lost. A woman with ten coins searches diligently when one is lost. A man with two sons loses one to his youthful wildness. Daily he shields his ageing eyes which scan the horizon for that one face. Many travellers pass his way and they exchange pleasantries. But there is one for whom his heart is waiting.

One is important to God: 'I have carved you on the palm of my hand.' One name is precious to God: 'I have called you by your name, you are mine.'

So different is the jungle law built into society today. Governments plan for the millions but will trample on the one. Multinational corporations manipulate thousands with little sympathy for the individual. In the cruel world of competition, compassion is regarded as a weakness: its only function is to cover up a mistake. The law of Jesus draws attention to the one, to the littlest one. 'In so far as you did this to one of the least of these brothers of mine, you did it to me.' Judgement itself is based on our attitude to the one, the least one. The kingdom won by Jesus on Calvary is promised that day to one – and he a thief. In the one-to-one dialogue which took place there, that repentant thief is the first person in the gospel to address the Lord by his name, Jesus.

The first lesson to draw is that I am important in God's eyes. Jesus is concerned about one sinner: so much so that the return of one is an occasion for rejoicing in heaven! If I were the only sinner in the world ... Jesus would have done all he did for the one ... for me. I am that important to God. Many people fight shy of intimacy with God ... keep him at a respectful distance!

No – he loves me – he wants to hear the sound of my prayer, the beat of my heart. Imagine, God wanting me!

The second lesson follows naturally: what I receive from God I must pass on to others. Charity begins at home. It can be very safe and undemanding when one pontificates about the problems of lands and peoples miles away. But what of the one to whom I owe an apology … the one about whom my words are always critical … the one I have frozen out of my affections? That one person is precious in God's eyes. If I claim to be serious about God then I must strive to partake in God's special love for each individual.

Brother, Sister, one is important to God: every single one.

Twenty-Fifth Sunday of the Year

Luke 16:1-13

Jesus said to his disciples, 'There was a rich man and he had a steward who was denounced to him for being wasteful with his property. He called for the man and said, "What is this I hear about you? Draw me up an account of your stewardship because you are not to be my steward any longer." Then the steward said to himself, "Now that my master is taking the stewardship from me, what am I to do? Dig? I am not strong enough. Go begging? I should be too ashamed. Ah, I know what I will do to make sure that when I am dismissed from office there will be some to welcome me into their homes."

Then he called his master's debtors one by one. To the first he said, "How much do you owe my master?" "One hundred measures of oil," was the reply. The steward said, "Here, take your bond; sit down straight away and write fifty." To another he said, 'And you, sir, how much do you owe?' 'One hundred measures of wheat,' was the reply. The steward said, 'Here, take your bond and write eighty.'

The master praised the dishonest steward for his astuteness. For the children of this world are more astute in dealing with their own kind than are the children of light.

And so I tell you this: use money, tainted as it is, to win you friends, and thus make sure that when it fails you, they will welcome you into the tents of eternity. The man who can be trusted in little things can be trusted in great; the man who is dishonest in little things will be dishonest in great. If then you cannot be trusted with money, that tainted thing, who will trust you with genuine riches? And if you cannot be trusted with what is not yours, who will give you what is your very own?

No servant can be the slave of two masters: he will either hate the first and love the second, or treat the first with respect and the second with scorn. You cannot be the slave both of God and money.'

First Reflection
Slavery or Stewardship

Money is a great servant, with enormous potential for good: but it makes a tyrannical master if allowed to take over a life.

Jesus never showed any desire to be a possessor. Having left behind the home security of Nazareth, he had nowhere of his own to lay his head. He depended on the generosity of others who would minister the Father's providence to him. He did not condemn rich people as such. There were people of property such as Nicodemus and Joseph of Arimathea among his disciples. And he accepted the invitations of people who were wealthy enough to host a banquet. But he spoke of the serious obligation on the rich to use their wealth to help the poor. And he warned that riches very easily become an obstacle to spiritual wealth. He observed how people quickly lost their freedom and idealism once they started to accumulate wealth. So, he described money as tainted because it can corrupt life.

Traditional wisdom has listed seven capital sins, that is, recognised areas of frailty which are likely sources of evil within us. Second only to pride in that list is covetousness. Covetousness is a compulsive desire to possess more. The more the compulsion grows unchecked, the more one is enslaved. Compulsion does not know the meaning of enough. It is a sort of monster whose hunger grows ever more insatiable the more it is fed. Increasingly the possessor is possessed by the possessions. That is why Jesus said that money can make a slave of the possessor.

And yet, money has enormous potential for good. 'Use money, tainted as it is, to win you friends ... who will welcome you into the tents of eternity. '

Jesus viewed us all as brothers and sisters sharing the world of one Father. In such a view, ownership is really a fraternal stewardship of God's creation. And stewards who are trustworthy in small things will rise to greater responsibilities.

Stewards of God's wealth will be accountable to God for their use of things. 'As often as you did it to one of the least of my brothers...', the poor become the porters of heaven's gates for those who shared with them, welcoming them into the tents of eternity. But 'as often as you neglected to do it to one of the least of my brothers...', the poor will stand in condemnation over the self-indulgent rich.

The prophet Amos (First Reading) warns the rich that God is taking note: 'Never will I forget a single thing you have done.'

Since God is ultimately the owner of everything, is there anything that can unequivocally be called private property? Every talent or material property one possesses is laden with responsibilities. The rights of ownership are carefully protected by law but the responsibility to share God's gifts with others is blandly ignored. The occasional highlighting of a famine or local tragedy will sting the conscience. But we have become so smug that gestures of generosity can sufficiently quieten the disturbing voice. We show very little social or political conscience in addressing the growing gap between rich and poor. The extent and effects of economic poverty today are an indictment of our deafness to the Lord's teaching.

The early Christian community understood that those who shared in the breaking of the bread were obliged to share with the needy members through distribution of their wealth. What does one possess that did not come originally from the Creator, who is Father of all? Every gift of the Creator comes with the responsibility of using it and sharing it.

Second Reflection
Gifts at the Roadside

God has adorned the road of our pilgrimage through the world with many sources of pleasure and comfort, with a wondrous variety of beautiful creations, with many gifts to be tasted and enjoyed. But it would be a mistake to settle for the gift and fail to journey on to the Giver. One of the effects of sin is shortsightedness. We easily forget the distant goal of life's destiny and settle for the comforts at the roadside. But their beauty is fickle, their flame in time turns to ashes, and their taste when over-indulged becomes sour. The pain of Autumn's sadness can be a salutary lesson from Nature. The exciting promise of Spring's young colours is now a faded memory. Daylight wanes and darkness advances a step each evening. We are left with the dying blaze of tree and hedgerow. In our autumnal experiences of life we taste the frustrations of unfulfilled expectations and come face-to-face with the emptiness of having little to look forward to. But Nature's lesson on the impermanence of everything here teaches us to set our vision and hope on more distant and lasting values.

If we settle for material and sensual satisfactions then we are like children on the road who eat too many berries and get sick: or who follow too far on the pleasant path of flowers and get lost: or who play games until night has crept upon them and they cannot find the way home.

The mistake of sin is to settle for the gift and neglect the

Giver. The secret of the saint is in knowing how to use the gifts as a way back to the Giver. Nobody has described it better than St Augustine. 'Late have I loved you, O Beauty ever ancient, ever new ... I sought you outside and in my ugliness fell upon those lovely things that you had made. You were with me and I was not with you, and I was kept from you by those things; yet had they not been with you, they would not have been at all.' (*Confessions*, Book 10)

It took another saint, Francis of Assisi, to show perfectly how it is precisely by owning nothing that one can enjoy everything. Few have ever striven as much as Francis not to be possessed by possessions. Yet no one has ever entered into such a deep relationship with creation as he in his mystical communion of brothers and sisters. His early biographer described how Francis returned everything to God. 'In every work of the artist he praised the Artist; whatever he found in things he referred to the Maker ... In beautiful things, he saw Beauty itself; all things were to him good. He made for himself from all things a ladder by which to come even to his throne.' (2 Celano, 165)

The gifts of God which adorn the road of our pilgrimage are most deeply appreciated by one who does not greedily possess them, but returns them to the Creator in gratitude and praise. Why settle for the little gifts which are but the foretaste of the Giver?

Twenty-Sixth Sunday of the Year

Luke 16:19-31

Jesus said to the Pharisees: 'There was a rich man who used to dress in purple and fine linen and feast magnificently every day. And at his gate lay a poor man called Lazarus, covered with sores who longed to fill himself with the scraps that fell from the rich man's table. Dogs even came and licked his sores. Now the poor man died and was carried away by the angels to the bosom of Abraham. The rich man also died and was buried.

In his torment in Hades he looked up and saw Abraham a long way off with Lazarus in his bosom. So he cried out, "Father Abraham, pity me and send Lazarus to dip the tip of his finger in water and cool my tongue, for I am in agony in these flames." "My son," Abraham replied, "remember that during your life good things came your way, just as bad things came the way of Lazarus. Now he is being comforted here while you are in agony. But that is not all: between us and you a great gulf has been fixed, to stop anyone, if he wanted to, crossing from our side to yours, and to stop any crossing from your side to ours."

The rich man replied, "Father, I beg you then to send Lazarus to my father's house, since I have five brothers, to give them warning so that they do not come to this place of torment too."

"They have Moses and the prophets," said Abraham, "Let them listen to them." "Ah no, father Abraham," said the rich man, "but if someone comes to them from the dead they will repent." Then Abraham said to him, "If they will not listen either to Moses or to the prophets, they will not be convinced even if someone should rise from the dead."'

First Reflection
A disturbing message

Amos, in the First Reading, joins forces with Luke in a scathing attack on smug complacency and soft living. 'Woe to those ensconced so snugly in Zion and to those who feel so safe on the mountain of Samaria.'

One estimate says that some forty thousand children die of malnutrition every day, that is one every two seconds. This is happening in the world of internet and global communication. Getting the Olympics or World Cup to all nations is more important than the technology of food production or primary medical care. If we celebrate the breaking of bread in church but do nothing about feeding Christ in the hungry, then our liturgy is the height of hypocrisy. We have mastered the art of availing of the comforts of religion while being immunised from its challenges.

There is a sanitised version of Christianity in which being saved by Jesus Christ is understood in a totally individualistic sense, with no reference to social obligations. Wealthy business people park their limousines outside some plush hotel and go into their Gospel Breakfast to witness to the prosperity they have enjoyed since handing their lives over to Jesus. Several prominent sports millionaires claim to have found Jesus and success in the same package. They garner even more success when they cope with pressure by handing it all over to Jesus. I would like to think that this handing over includes donating their extravagant salaries and prize-money to Christ in the poor. But the cynic in me harbours doubts.

At the conversion of Zacchaeus, it was when he made his promise to share with the poor, that Jesus said that salvation had come to his house. An incomplete concept of salvation is being used to launder the conscience of the rich.

Luke is the evangelist of mercy, but he is also the evangelist who warns us of the responsibilities that come with money, 'that tainted thing' (16:11). The social principles of the kingdom are set out in the great sermon which begins with the Beatitudes. Jesus radically reversed the Jewish mind that the blessings of life were to be seen in prosperity, power, prestige and popularity. He turned these values upside down by declaring the blessedness in God's eyes of the poor, the hungry, the distressed and victims of injustice.

In today's parable, the rich man enjoyed all the trappings of the false blessings, wealth, feasting, success and being the centre of attention. There is no suggestion that he amassed his wealth through wrong means or shady dealing. His sin was in what he failed to do. Sins of omission are easily overlooked. Charity has to be proactive, looking beyond self, taking the initiative, making the gesture, doing what is possible.

In contrast to the rich man, Lazarus is the personification of the true beatitudes. He is poor, hungering for hand-outs, lacking proper medical care, a victim of neglect and social injustice. But God hears the cry of the poor and it is he, not the rich man, who is blessed in the eyes of God. It is worth noting that Lazarus is the only character in any gospel parable who is given a name: and his name means God has had compassion.

There is a huge gulf between the rich man and Lazarus. Guess which side God is on. It is lamentable to see the righteousness of the self-indulgent rich being laundered by social respectability. Worse again, when religion is used as the laundry. Church membership may let people think that they are on the side of God. But every Lazarus at the gate is a challenge to remember where God is ... at the side of the poor.

Today's Responsorial Psalm is a hymn of praise to God who blesses those who are oppressed, hungry, imprisoned or handicapped in any way. 'Praise the Lord, who raises the poor.'

Second Reflection
Mister Millions and Godhelpus

Mister Millions: They call me Mister Millions ... and I rather like it. My father gave us a good start in life, but it took a lot of hard work to attain our present position. My five brothers and I worked hard before we were strong enough to diversify and build our own personal empires. Money makes money, but only if you have a shrewd brain to know how to use it. At times you have to be ruthless. But that is in self-defence really, because survival works on the principle of weakest to the wall. My conscience is perfectly clear for I have never employed strongarm tactics or gone beyond the accepted rules of business ethics. That stuff always catches up on you and I have no time for it. My friends say I am as tough as they come, but I regard that as a terrific compliment. I know that I have been luckier than most in life. And I am not ashamed of being a religious man who acknowledges that he has been blessed by God in my good fortune and natural acumen. I am openly grateful to God and I pay my priests well. I am known as a soft touch to any good cause.

Actually that soft streak in my make-up is something my friends do not always see.

Take that beggar who lies all day at my gate, what's his name ... *Godhelpus*. It's not a pretty sight I can tell you. Yet for more years than I care to count I have let him take up his station there. He smells to high heaven and seems to draw dogs around the place. Scavengers like himself. You know what they say ... it takes one dog to know another.

I don't know how he offended his creator to deserve that fate, nor is it any of my business to enquire. I'm a fair-minded man and that's his own story. He can feed off the tasty leftovers which the servants give him every day, on my instructions.

I will always let him at my gate because he is crippled and he cannot do much for himself. Most of the other beggars have only themselves to blame. They are lazy by nature and utterly improvident.

Something I have often discussed with my friends at table... you could sell your whole estate and give every penny to the poor and, do you know what, they'd be back next week for more with not a penny left. Improvident, that's what they are.

I don't work as hard now as before. Time to enjoy the good things of life. A man deserves a break. I give employment to many cooks, servants, tailors and entertainers. Any one of them would tell you how I pay them well. The one person on my paylist that I find disagreeable is that buffoon of a doctor who wants me to give up this and cut back on that. I've been around long enough to know how to enjoy life without his solemn voice. I refuse to listen to fools.

Godhelpus: Nobody seems to remember my real name now. It's my own secret. And since it's the only thing I can call my own, I'll hold on to it. To one and all I've been known for years as *Godhelpus*. Sometimes when children mock me they leave out the nice part of the name and call me something like *Helpus*, or worse.

I have only a hazy memory of my father … if I can give him that title. He was a drunken lout who terrorised my mother and all of us. I have a memory blackout on my accident. My mother would never talk about it. All I know is that he tossed over a table and that pinned me to the wall and left me crippled like this. That was the day he left us and we never saw him again. Nor wanted to.

I could have got on in life, inspite of my handicap, if I had got half a chance. I know I am intelligent because I can read and write even though I never went to school. I wasn't allowed go to school. And I'm not respectable enough to go to church.

Still, I'm luckier than some. I get enough food from the scraps at Mister Million's house. The servants are kind and the man himself has never turned me away.

I know that respectable people might turn up their noses at eating the bread used for wiping plates and fingers. But it is still the best of bread and beggars can't be choosers.

It's the same with my running ulcers. How could I afford any apothecary's bill? Dogs are friendly creatures. Their tongues are soothing and people say that their saliva can heal. I haven't had much luck so far, but I live in hope. In fact, my life is full of hope. I read the Holy Book and the stories give me great calm and strength. You mightn't believe me, but I feel that God is on my side. I have changed a lot over the years, I suppose. I was not always so calm.

There was a time when I was very angry at the whole set-up. I was angry with the system, with my father, with everybody. Most of all, with God. For a while I was planning my own perverted revenge. I would set fire to Mister Million's mansion during one of his parties and burn the lot of them to death. Crazy, wasn't it, for it wasn't his fault.

But that was ages ago and my anger has long since abated. I came to realise that the only person I was truly angry with was myself. Bit by bit I talked myself out of anger. I've grown more helpless with the passing years. I know I will always be poor. But strange to say, I enjoy deep peace and contentment. I don't wish an ounce of evil on Mister Millions. He's not the worst. In fact, I don't envy him at all. He doesn't look too happy to me. I think all these parties are only to escape from his thoughts. He looks bloated and unwell. I know that I haven't too long more to spend at his gate. I suspect that he won't be around very long either.

I wonder will we meet on the other side. There's such a great gulf between us.

Twenty-Seventh Sunday of the Year

Luke 17:5-10
The apostles said to the Lord, 'Increase our faith'. The Lord replied, 'were your faith the size of a mustard seed you could say to this mulberry tree, "Be uprooted and planted in the sea," and it would obey you. Which of you, with a servant ploughing or minding sheep, would say to him when he returned from the fields, "Come and have your meal immediately"? Would he not be more likely to say, "Get my supper laid; make yourself tidy and wait on me while I eat and drink. You can eat and drink yourself afterwards"? Must he be grateful to the servant for doing what he was told? So with you: when you have done all you have been told to do, say, "We are merely servants: we have done no more than our duty."'

First Reflection
Faithfulness
This is the first of four Sundays on which the gospel touches on aspects of faith and its expression in prayer. The background to today's reading is the teaching of Jesus on forgiving others again and again, as often as they come and say 'I am sorry'. Obviously this is a tall order, so the apostles ask the Lord, 'Increase our faith.' All this forms the lead-in to the point that what matters is not a faith associated with sensational signs but the faith that perseveres in humdrum duty. Not by accident is such quiet perseverance called faithfulness.

The mustard seed is tiny, not much bigger than a grain of dust you could blow off your hand. But, elsewhere in the gospel, we are told that it grows into a sizeable shrub which is a favourite shelter for birds. Remember that the context is about finding continuing forgiveness in the heart. It is only faith which can achieve the impossible in human relationships. Tiny faith will grow like the little seed through the ongoing challenge of responding with the shelter of forgiveness to the one who offends us. It will uproot any negative tendencies. Planting a tree in the sea is an image of the impossible and, in the context here, it refers to uprooting the barriers to forgiveness. This sentence is not to be applied to attempting sensational stunts in the name of faith.

The challenges of life form the atmosphere in which faith will grow in strength. What matters is the faith that perseveres. Such stamina is developed only under challenges, just as an athlete increases potential by pushing back the limits of endurance. When one perseveres in the face of adversity or challenge, then one has proved faithful.

The model of faithfulness is the humble, dutiful servant. The atmosphere of the parable is humdrum duty. The servant does his daily chores with no expectation of reward or affirmation beyond his usual upkeep. He is faithful to duty.

To be faithful is to persevere, to stay the course, to keep going, especially when the going is rough and there are no great signs of affirmation. Today's first reading from the prophet, Habakkuk, links up with the message of perseverance in faith. He writes in a time of oppression, injustice, tyranny, outrage and violence. Into this situation the prophet announces the vision or message of God, but he warns his readers to be patient and to persevere. 'If it comes slowly, wait, for come it will, without fail. See how he flags, he whose soul is not at rights, but the upright man will live by his faithfulness.'

'God's gift was not a spirit of timidity, but the Spirit of power, and love, and self-control' (Second Reading). In the power of the Holy Spirit, what is humanly impossible is totally changed under the light of divine power and love. The impossible barriers to forgiving are uprooted. What seems to be an impenetrable hardness of heart will be melted away in the warmth of God's love if we persevere in handing over the problems to God's grace. Persevere in the prayer that God's will, not ours, may be done. And God's will is always towards what is most loving and life-enhancing.

Second Reflection
The Unadorned Table

There are many tables in Luke's gospel but none as lonely and unadorned as this one. Here is a small farmer who has only the one servant for field and table. One hopes that between field and table he managed to wash his hands. There is no womanly warmth or attention to detail here. Drab, bachelor bareness. The place could do with a coat of paint ... and curtains. Last week's newspaper on the table, and a crazy pattern of brown tea rings. The food is unexciting, but functional. No idle talk interrupts this serious business of replenishing an empty stomach. Each one knows his place and keeps to it. There is mutual agreement that 'good fences make good neighbours.' The master offers not so much as a grunt of gratitude: the servant expects none. Duty is done, another day is lived and life goes on. Unexciting: humdrum: ordinary.

Luke's tables are paintings of life. One table supports a baron of succulent beef at the centre of a great family reconciliation. Around another table people in their foolish pride vie for position and prestige. We see a table where people relax together on the Sabbath, because the creator rested from work on the seventh day.

There is another picture with a sinner on her knees weeping tears of gratitude while the cold eyes at the head of the table pass disdainful judgment. Sometimes the courses are salted with lively repartee. Or there is an air of solemn quietness as one listens, like Mary of Bethany. Here is a purely functional table without the adornments of celebration or conviviality, relaxation or conversation.

The life of prayer brings one to sit at every one of Luke's tables. Prayer may be for long periods at this unadorned, humdrum table. One faithfully goes through the motions, but there is no excitement, no inner enlightenment, no answers coming through. There are the same psalms as before, the same words at Mass and no change in the Rosary. The most necessary functions of life are repetitious – breathing, eating, washing, sleeping, working … praying.

At the unadorned table one learns to see light in the greyness of humdrum, routine religious exercises and in the sameness of faces and occupations. Routine repetition need not spell boredom but can lead to calmness and a deeper appreciation of God in ordinary things. Living with the same people need not lead to indifference but challenges me to accept the others in the totality of their strengths and weaknesses. Hitting the wall in prayer or reaching the nights of darkness need not mean the death of prayer in me but rather the death of me in prayer. In today's first reading Habakkuk advises: 'If it comes slowly, wait for come it will, without fail. See how he flags, he whose soul is not at rights, but the upright man will live by his faithfulness.'

There is nothing glamourous about this unadorned faithfulness. One perseveres quietly and faithfully because one knows with certainty that God is faithful. And that is enough. God reaches out to me 365 days of the year in his unwavering, faithful love. The very least I owe to God is to respond in prayer 365 days of the year. 'We are merely servants: we have done no more than our duty.'

Twenty-Eighth Sunday of the Year

Luke 17:11-19

Now on the way to Jerusalem Jesus travelled along the border between Samaria and Galilee. As he entered one of the villages, ten lepers came to meet him. They stood some way off and called to him, 'Jesus! Master! Take pity on us.' When he saw them he said, 'Go and show yourselves to the priests.' Now as they were going away they were cleansed. Finding himself cured, one of them turned back praising God at the top of his voice and threw himself at the feet of Jesus and thanked him. The man was a Samaritan.

This made Jesus say, 'Were not all ten made clean? The other nine, where are they? It seems that no one has come back to give praise to God, except this foreigner.' And he said to the man, 'Stand up and go on your way. Your faith has saved you.'

First Reflection

Gratefulness

Luke is the evangelist of prayer, and this is the second of four Sundays when the gospel touches on some aspect of prayer. The story of the ten lepers offers great lessons on asking and thanking.

'Jesus! Master! Take pity on us.' The pleading lepers did not give detailed instructions as if the Lord were ignorant of their plight. They simply opened up their needs to his compassion. The purpose of petition is not to fill up any gaps in God's awareness of our situation. Petition is a way of acknowledging our poverty and of deepening our sense of dependence on God. In the return of the healed leper, Luke pictures the double movement of blessing prayer. Blessing is first of all a movement down from God to us. Then, going along the road this man 'found himself cured'. Luke's phrase captures the exhilaration of discovering the outpouring of God's healing love.

The second movement of blessing is in returning to God. Luke tells us that the man turned back on the road. He praised

God at the top of his voice and when he came to Jesus, he threw himself at his feet to thank him.

Is there a difference between praise and thanks? Sometimes one sees a young child who receives a gift going immediately to the giver to return a big hug and kiss, more delighted in praise of the giver than in the gift. But the older child, perhaps more schooled and less spontaneous, is likely to offer the perfunctory thanks and then concentrate on opening the package. Praise is concerned with the giver while thanks is more about the gift.

I think it is wonderful how Luke describes how the man found himself cured. Going along the road in the story represents the journey of life. The man found himself cured. Finding the blessings of God in our lives is the key to praise. If the man had never known leprosy it is doubtful that he would ever have known the same joyous appreciation of health. The fact that this man was an outsider, a Samaritan, probably added to his appreciation and gratitude. Familiarity usually dulls the edge of our appreciation. The greatest gifts in our lives are probably the ones we have not yet found because we simply take them for granted. Especially the people we take for granted in our day to day living. People who have been through a life-threatening crisis of health speak of how they now appreciate the wonder of each day they wake up and can get out of bed.

Some people get great help by keeping a journal. I would suggest that the most important items to note in life are one's blessings. Recognition of these will be a source of light and energy in life, far more than introspective analysis of feelings and motives. Also I would suggest that in approaching the Sacrament of Reconciliation, it helps to set the right atmosphere when one first recalls the blessings of God in life before confessing one's failures.

Part of the wonder of gratitude is the realisation that the gift is unmerited. Gratitude comes from the Latin, *gratis*, meaning the free nature of the gift. One of the great fruits of the virtue of poverty is the appreciation of the giftedness of things. Nowhere is this more clearly seen than in Francis of Assisi, the little poor man, who was at times deliriously drunk with the delights of creation. His biographers make the point that the more he delighted in the beauty of the world, all the more eager was he to return to the One who is Beauty. In all the works of art in nature he saw the Artist and his prayer was rich in the praise of God.

This movement back to the source of the gift draws the mind

to the Blessed Trinity. The Son is the Word who is ever expressing the fullness of the Father. He is 'the image of the unseen God' (Col 1:15), 'the radiant light of God's glory and the perfect copy of his nature' (Heb 1:3). The Son receives the glory of the Father and reflects that glory back in unending praise.

It is the awesome privilege of all who participate in the Eucharist to be participants in this divine worship. Through his incarnation the Son embraced all who accept him in faith, and through his death and resurrection he lifts them up in the perfect praise of the Father. The meaning of Eucharist is to give praise and thanks to God, through Jesus, with him and in him. And in keeping with the phrase 'grace in return for grace', after returning praise in the Eucharistic Prayer, we are further enriched in grace by receiving the Lord as our bread of life.

'The other nine, where are they?' Let us not point fingers at others but examine our own lives for the other nine gifts or blessings that God has given but we have not yet found. Why not take pen and paper to list nine favours you have not sufficiently appreciated.

Finding and returning form the heart of gratefulness. And gratefulness is the heart of prayer.

Second Reflection
The Other Nine

'The other nine, where are they?' There is a note of disappointment in the voice of Jesus. Maybe they praised God in their own way, but they should also have thanked Jesus, the agent of their healing. Perhaps their excuses were good. The story allows us room to imagine where they went.

Avi and Ben were Jews and they followed out the instruction of Jesus to go and show themselves to the priests. It was necessary before their return to society to have their cleanliness registered: and it was a long way from the borders of Samaria and Galilee to Jerusalem. Furthermore, now that they were clean again they should not associate with those Samaritans. What one did under pressure was best forgotten. So, in the name of religious observance they left Jesus behind.

Clopus also was a Jew but he felt that the registration with the priest could wait. His first call must be to his family from whose company he had painfully parted. He had moved far into Samaritan country, where he would not be recognised, to save them from embarrassment. Every day away was a day too long, so he made off for home with haste.

Then there was Demas, who went virtually berserk with excitement. He ran about, jumped in the air, rolled on the ground and shouted quite madly. He no longer cared what people thought. He was clean.

Elim, however, had a problem. Elim always had some problem. He had reluctantly joined the others in calling out to the prophet. Now that he saw himself cleansed, he said it was all imagination. It would wear off. The more he saw Demas dance, the more Elim doubted. This was but another cruel trick of fate. So he went off on his own with an ominous sense that the morrow would see the cure undone.

Two of them, Fabel and Gered, asked one another was it all a dream. They had to verify it. Cautiously they made their way for the nearest town, at every moment fearful of hearing that dreaded cry, 'Unclean! Unclean!' No cries came. Still they felt every eye turning towards them, piercing their composure. But no cries came. And their courage mounted. Into the crowded marketplace they went. Pushed, heaved and jostled by the press of people... such a lovely feeling! And the delicious stab of pain when somebody stepped on toes that were once again alive! Did people ever know that pain could be so sweet! They handled the hardness of wares and fingered the softness of cloth and felt the weight of things. No shouts of warning. Only the trader's soapy 'You like it, Sir?' Yes, indeed, they liked it very much, thank you.

And then there were Henoch and Itam who said that they would certainly go back to Jesus ... but not for a wee moment. Just one little celebration of their own first. Who would blame them? Long thirsty years, barred from every inn. Years when dreams of that drink shimmered like a mirage on the desert sands. Just one drink ... and then they'd go. The prophet would understand.

Jesus did understand. But he was a little sad nonetheless. Disappointed. The excuses were good. But then, excuses usually are. One out of ten. Ten percent. Is that a representative picture of our performance?

A word of appreciation or gratitude will never be in vain. Mark Twain said that he could live on a compliment for a month. Many people have to survive even longer between tokens of affirmation. When houses of affirmation are necessary and the ministry of affirmation needs to be highlighted, surely it indicates how remiss we are in offering praise and thanks to people. For every one whose ego is inflated by praise, there are a hundred whose beauty is withering because of lack of affirmation. 'The other nine, where are they?'

Twenty-Ninth Sunday of the Year

Luke 18:1-8

Jesus told his disciples a parable about the need to pray continually and never lose heart. 'There was a judge in a certain town,' he said, 'who had neither fear of God nor respect for man. In the same town there was a widow who kept on coming to him and saying, "I want justice from you against my enemy!" For a long time he refused, but at last he said to himself, "Maybe I have neither fear of God nor respect for man, but since she keeps pestering me I must give this widow her just rights, or she will persist in coming and worry me to death."

And the Lord said, 'You notice what the unjust judge has to say? Now will not God see justice done to his chosen who cry to him day and night even when he delays to help them? I promise you, he will see justice done to them, and done speedily. But when the Son of Man comes, will he find any faith on earth?'

First Reflection

Persevering in Prayer

The dominant theme of today's readings is that prayer is more than a matter of short sprints. It takes stamina and perseverance. The story of Moses in the first reading gives a great picture. As long as he can hold his arms raised, the battle is being won, but as soon as his arms fall the fortunes of war swing the other way.

The parable of the persistent widow is one of the how-much-more stories. If the judge, who was so unjust and heartless, was moved by her persistence, how much more will God, so loving and caring, take every cry to heart The one area open to question is the strength of our perseverance. Hence the final question: 'When the Son of Man comes, will he find any faith on earth?' Perhaps Luke intended this as a warning to the community of his time, some of whom were defecting under persecution from unjust judges.

Waiting patiently is not a virtue that comes easily to people who live in a society where technology had increased our expectation of instant answers. We are accustomed to instant coffee or soup, water on tap, heating and light at the flick of a switch, the music of our choice, or tablets for quick relief of pain.

One is impressed by the patience of people in the third world and the absence of complaining. They have never been accustomed to the instant answer and never had the experience of being able to take supply of food for granted.

God allows us to experience delays before the answer to our petitions and the working out of justice. There must be reasons of divine love and care behind these delays. From observing patterns of growth in nature and in relationships, we can venture a guess at some of God's reasons.

Growth is a process that takes time. Jesus told many stories about things growing. The plants which are destined for long life are usually slow starters. The oak tree, which will stand for hundreds of years, takes fully two years to advance from acorn to tiny fingerling. The builders of a certain great hall in Oxford, as they used oaken beams for the rafters, planted oak trees nearby, estimating that the rafters would last six centuries and the mature trees would be on hand to provide replacements. Plants which peep from the earth a few weeks after planting will not last more than a few months. Nature teaches us to wait, for lasting growth takes time to harden.

Our experience of life also shows how relationships can be bonded through the test of suffering. A group of people who have been through hardship together are drawn into a deeper relationship than if it had been easy and superficial.

Persistence in prayer is not to be understood as an effort to change God, as if God were not already well disposed towards us. It's we who need to change, by growing towards unselfishness in faith, and by coming into a deeper relationship with God.

Waiting on God affords the time needed for the growth of our dependence on Him. We are called to grow in patient calmness to pacify the fretting and anxiety which otherwise tears us apart. As faith matures and deepens, an unfaltering trust in God replaces the cries of panic and frenzy which make us tell God, 'My will be done ... and as soon as you can, please.'

The instruction of the Lord is to pray 'Thy will be done.' This is not a statement of abject resignation, but a calm and confident handing over to God's loving care, trusting that God's will is surely what is best for us.

At the great shrines of petition and grace, the most impressive answer to prayer is the deep sense of joyous resignation that God's love is very near, even if the curing of the ailment is far away.

This calmness is inherent in the words of the Lord to the fourteenth century mystic, Dame Julian of Norwich: 'I will make all things well. I shall make all things well. I may make all things well, and I can make all things well; and thou shalt see thyself that all things shall be well.' (*A Shewing of God's Love*, XV).

Persistence in prayer is the confidence to wait from Good Friday until the Sunday when all is made well, however long it takes. The day in between is the Sabbath, day of rest and calmness. It may seem long in our calendars, but to God a thousand years a like a single day. Perseverance in prayer brings us to grow into God's way of thinking.

Second Reflection
Beggars before God

The heavy arms of Moses were raised to heaven, propped up by a stone and supported by his friends. He is the picture of the soul that has learnt the depth of his dependence upon God and others. He has stayed long in prayer for he has now travelled far from the delusion of self-sufficiency and accepted his dependence. Moses knew that he was a beggar.

The prayer of child-faith looks for instant answers, bargains with God in an attempt to bring His will around to our point of view, and is prone to wavering in confidence.

The prayer of adolescent-faith cajoles with a friend in a relationship between equals. Since a limitation in adolescent-faith is the tendency to reject what has not been personally experienced or verified, there will be little allowance for mystery and little patience with divine delays. As faith matures, one realises that the relationship is not between equals. We have to learn our distance from God. And although God is closer to us than can be imagined, in another sense He is infinitely distant. There is more to God than the-friend-down-the-road who can be used when we need help or companionship. We gradually realise that we are not God's equal as we increasingly recognise our own inadequacy. And this shatters one of the common delusions of life … thinking we are self-sufficient. We are dependents. We are beggars before God. The persistent widow knew she was a beggar, and that was her strength.

Oriental beggars are extraordinarily persistent because they have a fundamental belief that they have a divine right to protection and to a share in God's gifts to the world. The calculating, shrewd steward of another parable acted unjustly because he was ashamed to beg. He was ashamed of exercising his divine right to beg. Knowing how much we depend upon God is no reason to feel ashamed. In fact it ought to bring a great sense of relief because the burden of having to do it all ourselves now slips from our shoulders. What a relief to know that we can depend on God ... and that we must depend upon him!

Remember Simon Peter. On the morning of the great catch of fish he discovered the power of Jesus and sensed his own distance, 'Leave me, Lord; I am a sinful man.' (Lk 5:8) Remember Paul, this intense, driving character with the brilliant mind, but humiliated in his inability to cope with the weakness that he called the thorn in his flesh. Paul pleaded with God to remove the thorn. But God would not. And through accepting his weakness, Paul found a new space for God's power within him: 'My grace is enough for you: my power is at its best in weakness.' (2 Cor 12:9) Remember the centurion who knew that he was not worthy to host Jesus in his house. Through a sense of sinfulness, weakness and unworthiness, these three souls advanced in faith. It can be a great answer to prayer when we learn our distance from God, our own weakness and insufficiency, and our unworthiness. Then we come to rejoice in the fact that we are beggars before him.

Thirtieth Sunday of the Year

Luke 18:9-14

Jesus spoke the following parable to some people who prided themselves on being virtuous and despised everyone else. 'Two men went
up the Temple to pray, one a Pharisee, the other a tax collector.

The Pharisee stood there and said this prayer to himself, "I thank
you, God that I am not grasping, unjust, adulterous like the rest of
mankind, and particularly that I am not like this tax collector here. I fast
twice a week; I pay tithes on all I get." The tax collector stood some distance away, not daring even to raise his eyes to heaven; but he beat his
breast and said, "God, be merciful to me, a sinner." This man, I tell you,
went home again at rights with God; the other did not. For everyone
who exalts himself will be humbled, but the man who humbles himself
will be exalted.'

First Reflection

A humbled, contrite heart

The parable of the two men in the temple gives us the fourth
instruction on prayer: pride gets in the way of true prayer
whereas humble contrition forms a prayer that goes straight to
the heart of God. The story is directed at those who prided themselves on their virtue and despised everyone else. The boastful
words of the proud are but a form of self-worship, whereas the
prayer of the humble person pierces the clouds.

The Pharisees have suffered from a bad press in the Christian
tradition, which has presented them as the embodiment of
hypocrisy and blinkered legalism. Their name means The
Separated, originating in their desire to keep the holy Jewish
heritage free from contamination by the pagan Greek culture
which was being imposed on them. They believed that the law
of God covered every facet of life. Perfection, therefore, would
be found in the meticulous observance of every detail. Some of
them, like the man in this story, not only kept all the laws but
added extra obligations. He did extra fasting and paid tithes on

all he got, not satisfied that they had already been deducted at the source of production, which is what the law required.

His fault obviously did not lie in his zeal for the law, but it was in the pride he drew from it, a mentality which claimed the right to judge others in the less favourable light of comparison. One small detail in the story is very significant. We are told that he said that prayer to himself. His fine words seemed to be addressed to God, but, in reality, they did not get beyond the clouds of his self-deception. In contrast, the prayer of the tax collector pierced the clouds and went straight to the compassion of God. 'God, be merciful to me, a sinner.' Jesus assures us that he went home at rights with God.

The simplicity of this prayer is exemplary. It cuts out all complications in his startling awareness of meeting with God. At basics, prayer is very simple. It involves God and me, and the meeting that happens between us. The essence of prayer is in our attention to God's presence. At times, it will be in awareness of God's glory, leading the soul to praise. At other times the soul is drawn to intimacy in the awareness of God's love. And there are times when the experience of God overcomes a person with a deep sense of sinfulness and unworthiness. This was the feeling of the tax collector in the Temple. 'God, be merciful to me a sinner.' The name of God did not need any further words of adornment, such was the directness of his contact with God. Similarly, his plea for mercy is utterly uncomplicated. All he can say of himself is that he is a sinner.

His experience is similar to that of Simon Peter after the miracle of the catch of fish, when Peter is suddenly aware of the infinite distance between himself and the holiness of Jesus. 'Depart from me for I am a sinful man, O Lord.'

Francis of Assisi was another who was caught up in this prayer of humble contrition. He would spend hours at length in the single prayer: 'Who art thou, my Lord, and what am I?'

Saint Augustine, unlike Francis as a man of multiple words, expanded on the sinner's unworthiness in his soliloquy which begins:

O Lord Jesus, let me know myself, let me know you
and desire nothing else but only you.
Let me hate myself and love you
and do all things for sake of you.

Those who raise themselves up will be humbled, but those

who humble themselves before God will be raised up. The prayer of the humble sinner pierced the clouds. The healing mercy of God poured down on him and he went home at rights with God.

A humbled, contrite heart you will not spurn, O Lord.

Second Reflection
A shocking story

In telling this story Jesus must have been like an actor, taking on the appropriate tones of voice and accompanying actions. The parable is a reversal story, one in which an accepted value or manner of behaviour is radically confronted and found to be lacking. A reversal story depends for effect on its power to shock. It must startle the audience into tearing aside the veils of familiarity which obscure the truth. To appreciate this story we must realise how it would have jolted the sensibilities of the dutiful Pharisees to hear Jesus suggest that a sinful tax collector was more righteous in God's eyes than one of their own kind.

The wisdom of the story belongs to all ages. The give-away signs of self-deception and bogus religion are the same today as in the days of Jesus. What is very interesting in the story is the way the Pharisee 'said this prayer to himself'. The habit of talking to oneself is a sign of pressure. There is a little boss in the mind who is calling all the shots and asking an explanation of every step one is taking. The Pharisee was under pressure to do extra fasting, extra good works to keep this boss off his back. Whenever you see zeal for superhuman perfection, watch out for what is being repressed or not admitted. When ordinary laws are not sufficient but extra obligations are invented, then you are dealing with somebody who wants to be his or her own redeemer: trying to earn God's favour through personal perfection. The genuinely holy person shows the minimum of fuss about laws and the maximum desire for spirit. Excessive piety is usually a cop-out or an attempt to wriggle out of the demands of charity, truth and justice.

The Pharisee was just too good to be true. Jeckell and Hyde is as true a story as was ever written. In each of us there is the opposite character locked away. If we are out of touch with the possibilities of our dark opposite, then beware! For those who regard themselves as angels quickly tumble like devils.

In recent times many have availed of courses like the Enneagram to grow in self-understanding. They have discovered that what they are good at may also be a trap that will prove to be their undoing. For instance, if you are interested in sport, you will have noticed that it is the muscular guys who have trouble with pulled muscles. Or that the thoroughbred is much more prone to infection than the animal which already has a touch of everything that is going.

The Pharisee was very good at the external works of religion. But therein lay the trap that caught him. He was so good that he thought that it was his own doing rather than the grace of God. He was ripe picking for the temptation of pride. He felt superior to the rest of humankind. And worse again, he felt entitled to pass judgement on the poor wretch at the back.

If the virtues of the Pharisee were the makings of his trap, then the burdened conscience of the sinner became the source of his meeting with God in humble prayer. As Shakespeare put it, 'sweet are the uses of adversity'. God can use even our sinfulness towards a good purpose. God can write straight on crooked lines. Our frailty and falls can be used to break our pride, shatter our delusions and smash the shell of mechanical prayer. Consciousness of our own sinfulness will make us slow to pass judgement on others, and it will develop our capacity for compassion.

The parable told by Jesus was meant to be a shocking story, startling complacency and reversing the expected order of affairs. Of all the forms of pride to which we are susceptible, religious self-righteousness is surely the most despicable.

Thirty-First Sunday of the Year

Luke 19:1-10

Jesus entered Jericho and was going through the town when a man whose name was Zacchaeus made his appearance; he was one of the senior tax collectors and a wealthy man. He was anxious to see what kind of man Jesus was, but he was too short and could not see for the crowd; so he ran ahead and climbed a sycamore tree to catch a glimpse of Jesus who was to pass that way. When Jesus reached the spot he looked up and spoke to him: 'Zacchaeus, come down. Hurry, because I must stay at your house today.' And he hurried down and welcomed him joyfully. They all complained when they saw what was happening. 'He has gone to stay at a sinner's house,' they said. But Zacchaeus stood his ground and said to the Lord, 'Look, sir, I am going to give half my property to the poor, and if I have cheated anybody I will pay him back four times the amount.' And Jesus said to him, 'Today salvation has come to this house, because this man too is a son of Abraham; for the Son of Man has come to seek out and save what was lost.'

First Reflection

The Inner Journey

Jericho was a wealthy town, set in a green, fertile oasis between the Jordan river and a brown, barren wilderness. Zacchaeus was representative of the town. As superintendent of taxes he was probably very rich, because there were many sources of taxation there: and yet for all his wealth he was not far from barren wilderness of the soul. But something was at work within him, exposing his inner poverty. Luke gives a perspicacious account of the inner movements in his conversion.

First of all we pick up the note of energy in the way he 'made his appearance.' There was something driving Zacchaeus – his inner emptiness, surely. He was short and could not see Jesus because of the crowd. Perhaps this is more than a statement about his physical stature. He was also short of self-esteem, because the popular estimation of tax collectors left him with little hope of God's favour. His anxiety to see Jesus drove him to throw caution to the winds in an action quite infradig for a man of his position: he ran on ahead and climbed a tree to gain a glimpse of Jesus through the leaves. Again we note what energy there is in his actions.

Zacchaeus had made his move. The next act belonged to Jesus. The sinner had recognised his need and shown his desire to do something about it. Then came the moment of unexpected grace, 'the point of intersection of the timeless with time,' (T.S. Eliot).

Here is one of those wonderful moments when Jesus looked at somebody. He reached out in an invitation which disarmed every opposition.

'Zacchaeus, come down from your tree of hiding. Open your door, let me in. I must sit at your table tonight.'

Long years of self-deception and unnecessary hiding behind barriers can melt away in one moment of grace. The sinner has imagined all sorts of complications and problems in the way of conversion.

But God's intersection is often lighthearted and always gentle. 'Little by little, therefore, you correct those who offend, you admonish and remind them of how they have sinned, so that they may abstain from evil and trust in you, Lord.' (Wis 12:2, in today's first reading) The approach of Jesus shows how God does not coerce the sinner but issues an invitation.

After the invitation of Jesus the action swung back to Zacchaeus. He hurried down and gave a joyful welcome to Jesus. But a conversion has to prove itself under testing. The social begrudgers were on hand to raise the objections and utter the complaints. But Zacchaeus was firm and he 'stood his ground.' Testing only strengthened his determination and clarified his resolution. The new life of the kingdom, which he had glimpsed in Jesus, would be very demanding. But his resolution was equal to the demand. He there and then gave half his property to the poor and promised restitution to anybody he had cheated, far beyond the demands of legal justice.

From the desert of a soul in pain Zacchaeus had journeyed to the oasis of new life and the wellsprings of resolution. And by the grace of God, the decisive step in the journey of conversion took only that brief moment when a look of gentleness and compassion was accepted with joy. It was a day of salvation... 'for the Son of Man has come to seek out and save what was lost.'

Second Reflection

The Witness of Zacchaeus

My name is Zacchaeus. And if it sounds like success I don't mind, because for years that was how I wanted to be known. Today it doesn't matter so much, ever since I met Jesus. But if you've been born into poverty, the need to succeed can be a tyrant inside you. You have to haul yourself so far out of that gutter to ensure that you, and the generations that carry on your name, will never fall back. You can't afford to be too choosey about the means nor about working in shady areas. And when you're small in life you get to be aggressive and make your presence felt. They might criticise you for working for the Romans. But taxes have to be collected. Otherwise there would be no roads, no aqueducts, no armies to maintain law and order. When you're poor you cannot afford to live in the past. The flags of the past don't put bread on the table. And if I had not taken the job, somebody else would. So what! I worked hard, very hard. But it's no skin off your knuckles when you are driven from the inside. I made contacts and made it my business to nurture them. After all, it's people who make the appointments. You don't get to be supervisor unless you show that you can manage people and organise them. The Romans are a practical people and that's to their credit. They respect hard work and they recognise talent.

Our own folk are too stuck in the past and all that business of what's-your-family-background . I was in a position to make a handsome penny and I availed of it. It wasn't the money itself that mattered. Money was never the god of my life, strange though that may sound. It was what the money could do. I bought up property, I cultivated the arts, I splashed out lavishly. I had to have the best and show that I was number one. I took enjoyment out of embarrassing people with costly gifts. But all the linen and silk in the world could not cover up a lonely heart. And all the forced friendships and exchange of flattery had not given me anybody I could really trust, anybody I could share the pains of my soul with. I was becoming morose and solitary. I was starting to drink myself into stupidity. It had to stop. And then came Jesus.

I had first heard of him from some of Levi's friends. Some were very impressed with him: others thought that he was a bit of a harmless idealist. He was said to be uncompromising with the rich. Poets, artists, dreamers – very impractical people. But I knew from experience how quickly they would change their tune for a generous benefactor. It is easy to curse what you haven't got.

I was surprised to hear of Levi's move. Admiring the preacher was one thing, but following him was another. Levi was a good tax collector. He was methodical. We liked the way he kept his book. And he could splash out on a party as good as the rest, all good for contacts. He could have gone a long way. But Levi had given us back his book and gone with the preacher. One mighty party and off with him. The thought became an obsession. I simply had to see the preacher at the very least. Looking back now, I have to laugh at myself. A man of my status in town hiding up a tree! And that's amazing really, because I was always very touchy about what others might be saying about me.

When Jesus stopped and the crowd halted too, my heart missed a beat. I was afraid even to breathe. But when he looked up, and I saw the gentleness in his eyes, I was no longer afraid. I knew immediately that he understood me. Then, what he said … I could hardly believe my ears! 'Zacchaeus', only later did I wonder how he knew my name. 'Zacchaeus, come down. Hurry, because I want to stay at your house today.'

It was all joy … joy and light … joy and welcome. I had never known anything so deep. That someone should understand you from the inside, could care enough to reach out to you, could love you as if you were the only one there on the face of the earth! That's how I felt. Everything else now is rubbish. Rubbish to me. Not to those who need it. Sharing out to the poor was a new sort of joy.

People said I was crazy. But love has the right to be a bit crazy. And what they say about me doesn't matter any more.

Thirty-Second Sunday of the Year

Luke 20:27-38

Some Sadducees – those who say that there is no resurrection – approached him and they put this question to him, 'Master, we have it from Moses in writing, that if a man's married brother dies childless, the man must marry the widow to raise up children for his brother. Well then, there were seven brothers. The first, having married a wife, died childless. The second and then the third married the widow. And the same with all seven, they died leaving no children. Finally the woman herself died. Now, at the resurrection, to which of them will she be wife since she had been married to all seven?'

Jesus replied, 'The children of this world take wives and husbands, but those who are judged worthy of a place in the other world and in the resurrection from the dead do not marry because they can no longer die, for they are the same as the angels, and being children of the resurrection they are sons of God. And Moses himself implies that the dead rise again, in the passage about the bush where he calls the Lord the God of Abraham, the God of Isaac and the God of Jacob. Now, he is God, not of the dead, but of the living: for to him all men are in fact alive.'

First Reflection
Journey's End

The dark November days of our northern latitudes lend a sympathetic setting for contemplating the end of life. It is journey's end for Jesus too, for his long pilgrimage has reached Jerusalem at last. A bitter reception awaited him there as the various factions of power, one after another, confronted him with hostile questions.

It was the turn of the Sadducees, a small but very wealthy faction in the city. In matters of theology, they were the arch-conservatives who would not accept any change or development from the five books attributed to Moses, the Torah. They did not accept the later doctrines about angels and life after death.

They set a trap for Jesus with their familiar ploy about the seven brothers married to the one wife. The basis for their case was the levirate law which sought to provide a legal heir for a man who died childless, by obliging the next brother to take the wife. They fancied that their case made the hypothesis of the after-life appear absurd. One can hear the certainty of their tone: 'We have it in writing from Moses.'

Jesus replied that a law pertaining to marriage would have no relevance in the resurrected state when there would be no further need to propagate life. The children of the resurrection are 'the same as angels,' he said, and 'they are sons of God.' Jesus, furthermore, swept away the foundation of their argument with a counter-appeal to Moses. 'If you rely on Moses, well then so can I.' Belief in the after-life was implied by Moses in calling the Lord the God of Abraham, Isaac and Jacob, who were long dead at this time. It is because God is a God of the living that we are alive to him. God did not create us to disappear into extinction.

The Sadducess represented a minority view-point. The vast majority of Jesus' audience already accepted the doctrine of life after death. The third chapter of the Book of Wisdom clearly expressed this belief in words of consolation for the virtuous and of warning for the unfaithful. 'But the souls of the virtuous are in the hands of God, no torment shall ever touch them ... those who are faithful will live with him in love ... but the godless will be duly punished for their reasoning, for neglecting the virtuous man and deserting the Lord.'

In the synoptic gospels, the teaching of Jesus presents appealing, homely images of heaven and rather terrifying pictures of hell. The most frequent image of heaven is the great banquet, like a wedding feast or the celebration of a victory. Sometimes what is emphasised is the idea of reward for fidelity or for using one's talents with profit.

Two particular images appeal to the race-memory of the people: the idea of being united with all our forebearers and the notion of returning to the lost paradise. The poor man, Lazarus, is pictured as being taken up into Abraham's bosom. And on Calvary, the repentant thief is promised that he will be with Jesus that very day in paradise.

Hell is the opposite of all these homely pictures of heaven. It means being refused admission to the banquet, or being cast out into the cold and dark where there will be weeping and the gnashing of teeth. The most terrifying image is of fire, greatly ex-

panded upon by preachers, artists and writers. Hell is the rub-
bish-dump of wasted life and talent, where 'their worm does not
die nor their fire go out.' (Mk 9:47)

In contrast to the homely images of the synoptics, the evangelist John uses philosophical language, mainly about life. The
believer will enter into the fullness of life. Eternal life means
knowing the Father and Jesus Christ whom he has sent.

To know Jesus Christ is to realise that all is made new
through his resurrection. In death, life is changed, not ended;
changed in the power of Christ's resurrection. He has taken the
sting out of death. Journey's end means arriving home at the
fullness of our calling. 'Dying you destroyed our death. Rising
you restored our life. Lord Jesus, come in glory.'

Second Reflection
Children of the Resurrection

This November morning is perfectly calm and not a breath of
wind is stirring. Yet, even without a breeze, the yellow leaves
are losing their hold on the parent stem and glide languidly to
the earth. It is only half a year since their fresh, green promise
uplifted their hearts in Spring joy. During the week we will be
out with rake and barrow to gather up these leaves for spreading in the garden so that their decomposition will enrich the soil
for next year's vegetables.

While the body is busy at these chores, the mind understands
how somebody without the light of revelation would tend to
translate our intimations of immortality into a theory of reincar-
nation.

But the revealed word teaches that we do not come back, but
we will be called forward to a higher form of life, being 'the
same as angels … children of the resurrection … sons of God.'

St John expands upon this call to be children of God, though
he makes no attempt to describe the future condition, except as a
reflection of God who will then be seen.

'My dear people, we are already the children of God but
what we are to be in the future has not yet been revealed; all we
know is, that when it is revealed we shall be like him because we
shall see him as he really is.' (1 Jn 3:2)

St Paul was faced with the question, 'How are dead people
raised, and what sort of body do they have when they come
back?'

He suggests that just as the seed which is sown in the earth differs from the plant it produces, so is life on earth different to the resurrected state. He indicates four ways in which the resurrected state is of a superior order. 'The thing that is sown is perishable but what is raised is imperishable; the thing that is sown is contemptible but what is raised is glorious; the thing that is sown is weak but what is raised is powerful; when it is sown it embodies the soul, when it is raised it embodies the spirit.' (Cor 15: 42-44) The last quality there refers to the superiority of sharing in the divine life through the gift of the Holy Spirit over the natural life of our earthly existence.

Death, which is the end of one journey, is the beginning of another . Just as Jerusalem marked the end of the walked journey of Jesus but would be the place for his return to the Father.

Death is the only doorway into the higher form of life.

It is the great step forward into that imperishable, glorious and powerful fullness of life in the Spirit.

Life is changed, not ended. And the change is to a new life in which we are to become 'the same as the angels ... children of the resurrection ... sons of God.'

Thirty-Third Sunday of the Year

Luke 21:5-19

When some were talking about the Temple, remarking how it was adorned with fine stonework and votive offerings, Jesus said, 'All these things you are staring at now – the time will come when not a single stone will be left on another: everything will be destroyed.' And they put to him this question: 'Master,' they said, 'when will this happen, then, and what sign will there be that this is about to take place?'

'Take care not to be deceived,' he said 'because many will come using my name and saying, "I am he" and, "The time is near at hand." Refuse to join them. And when you hear of wars and revolutions, do not be frightened, for this is something that must happen but the end is not so soon.' Then he said to them, 'Nation will fight against nation, and kingdom against kingdom. There will be great earthquakes and plagues and famines here and there: there will be fearful sights and great signs from heaven.

But before all this happens, men will seize you and persecute you; they will hand you over to the synagogues and to imprisonment, and bring you before kings and governors because of my name – and that will be your opportunity to bear witness. Keep this carefully in mind: you are not to prepare your defence, because I myself shall give you an eloquence and a wisdom that none of your opponents will be able to resist or contradict. You will be betrayed even by parents and brothers, relations and friends; and some of you will be put to death. You will be hated by all men on account of my name, but not a hair of your head will be lost. Your endurance will win you your lives.'

First Reflection
Problems and Possibilities

November, a sombre and grey month of shortening days in the northern hemisphere, is a suitable setting for this gospel. We can see the passage developing in three stages.

Firstly, there is the message that all material things pass away. The Temple in Jerusalem, by any standard, was a most impressive construction. One can imagine how the disciples, coming from rural Galilee, must have been overawed at this splendid building. The sheer size of the structure with its various courtyards, and the massive stones especially, impressed them. Practical workmen would have wondered how they got these mighty stones into place. Talk about the Titanic being unsinkable! To their minds this building was destined to last the ages. But Jesus warned them that it would not be so. And by the time Luke was writing, his readers already knew that, after the siege of Jerusalem, the Roman troops wrought vengeance on the very stones of the holy structure. The message is that all things on this earth have their sell-by date.

The second stage picks up the alarm felt at this astounding news about the seemingly indestructible Temple. 'Master, when will it happen? Will there be any warning signs?' On another occasion Jesus was asked when would the end of the world happen. He replied that in his human knowledge he did not know, nor do the angels know. Yet the world is never short of cult leaders and self-appointed prophets who do not hesitate to interpret natural catastrophes as divine punishment and who confidently predict a certain date as doomsday.

Writing the original version of this book some twelve years ago, I said that we could expect a rash of self-appointed prophets, quoting apocalyptic texts, in the time coming up to the new millennium. Millenarianism, the doctrine which marks off God's working in neat, thousand year blocks, has always been attractive to those fundamentalists who take scriptural texts out of context and read into them an application to contemporary happenings. Writing now some three months into the new century, I must admit that, although there were some doomsday alarmists, they were fewer than I had anticipated. Perhaps they were pushed out of the news by the prophets of technological chaos in the anticipation of a computer super-bug beyond control. The only scared people I met, apart from the followers of dubious visionaries, were addicts of Star Wars and X Files who feared an invasion by alien, evil forces.

The third stage of this passage is an encouragement to calm confidence in the difficult days ahead for the disciples. Again we remind ourselves that the people for whom Luke was writing knew at first hand the price they had paid for following Jesus. Many of them had been ejected from their Jewish background. Yet they were regarded as a Jewish sect by the Romans and subjected to persecution. Some of them had experienced the cruel fate of being cut off from their own kith and kin because of their belief.

In our own day, family mockery of religious practice is not unknown. Persecution comes through anti-church prejudice, slanting of news and selective recall of the past. Jesus has a marvellous answer for the hard times: 'That will be your opportunity to bear witness.' He has promised his disciple his presence and his power, his eloquence and his wisdom. With his presence our problems become possibilities. For with him, all things are possible. Our part is to stay, to stand firm in hope. 'Your endurance will win you your lives.' And this power to stand firm will bear eloquent testimony to the help of God.

Depressing social factors like drug abuse, violent crimes, suicides and family instability feed the neurotic anxiety of the prophets of doom. But the message of Christ is to repent, to endure in faith and to believe that God is in charge and loves his world.

Julian of Norwich, living in the dreadful days after the plague called the Black Death, got the message of God's maternal care for the world. She would stay in prayer with this belief: God is my maker, my lover and my keeper.

Second Reflection
I shall give you ...

One of the seven great gifts of the Holy Spirit is fortitude. It is only when the natural resources of our courage are exhausted that we recognise the source of the new strength which is greater than the trial. It comes from God. It is the Spirit's gift of fortitude.

Jesus did not remove his followers to some state of life removed from the sins and injustices, the tribulations and betrayals of the world. But by enduring in faith they would learn how the presence and power of the Holy Spirit operates within suffering.

The followers of Jesus found out by experience that persecution afforded them the greatest opportunity to bear witness. Their natural resources did not supply their eloquence and courage. These were God-given, a special gift. The promise of the Lord had said as much, 'I myself shall give you an eloquence and a wisdom that none of your opponents will be able to resist or contradict.'

The witness of faith given by those who were persecuted was so important to the early church that martyrs, meaning those who gave witness in the shedding of their blood, were venerated as the perfect Christians. The accounts of many of these early martyrs show how the church recognised that their courage and eloquence were nothing less than a special gift from God.

The strengthening gift of the Holy Spirit can be recognised also in the extraordinary fortitude that people show in the harrowing experiences of life such as illness, bereavement, severe handicap or the collapse of a life-project.

There were people in the concentration camps whose experiences there helped to make saints of them, and some have been canonised. Viktor Frankl observed that the pains of Auschwitz were like a wind which quenched the weak spark of faith but fanned the stronger spark into a roaring fire.

The gifts of the Holy Spirit are most clearly recognised in adverse conditions because these show up that whatever is accomplished could not have been done without divine aid.

One is drawn back to the theological insight of St Paul regarding his own experience of weakness. He repeatedly besought God to remove the 'thorn in the flesh' which humiliated him. The answer he received was not the removal of the problem but the assurance of God's sustaining help. 'My grace is enough for you: my power is at its best in weakness.' In the strength of God's gift he was able to go on and say: 'So I shall be very happy to make my weakness my special boast so that the power of Christ may stay over me, and that is why I am quite content with my weaknesses, and with insults, hardships, persecutions, and the agonies I go through for Christ's sake. For it is when I am weak that I am strong.'(2 Cor 12:7ff)

That is the effect of the gift of fortitude. And adversity only served to show up God's power all the more. It is the fulfilment of the Lord's promise, 'I shall give you...'

Last Sunday of the Year
Our Lord Jesus Christ, Universal King

Luke 23:35-43

The people stayed there before the cross watching Jesus. As for the leaders, they jeered at him, 'He saved others,' they said 'let him save himself if he is the Christ of God, the Chosen One.' The soldiers mocked him too, and when they approached to offer him vinegar they said, 'If you are the king of the Jews, save yourself.' Above him there was an inscription: 'This is the King of the Jews.'

One of the criminals hanging there abused him, 'Are you not the Christ?' he said, 'Save yourself and us as well.' But the other spoke up and rebuked him. 'Have you no fear of God at all?' he said. 'You got the same sentence as he did, but in our case we deserved it: we are paying for what we did. But this man has done nothing wrong. Jesus,' he said, 'remember me when you come into your kingdom.' 'Indeed, I promise you,' he replied, 'today you will be with me in paradise.'

First Reflection
King of the Universe

At the end of his journey, over his head they wrote the words, Jesus of Nazareth, King of the Jews. It was a neat bit of politics, a ploy to get rid of him, a way to silence his challenging voice. Jesus of Nazareth, King of the Jews, indeed!

How many took the charge seriously? Did anybody of sane senses really think that he was a threat to Caesar or to public order? The irony of that day was that he was a king, though not in a way that the worldly mind could understand.

Jesus as king was the reversal of the ways usually followed by the royalty of this world. He did not sit on an elevated throne to symbolise his power: but he hung from a cross, too weak to save himself from death. He did not wear a bejewelled crown as a dazzling display of triumph and wealth: but, capped by a crown of thorns, he was an appalling sight, without beauty, without majesty, a thing despised and rejected by men. He had no armies at his command nor servants in attendance: instead, he came to serve and to offer his life as a ransom for many. Earthly kings are removed from commoners and are not expected to associate with them as equals: he came unto his own, he lived among them and now he was dying between two of the lowliest of them, condemned criminals.

His redeeming work was for millions of people: yet his immediate focus was on the individual, the one. That one, a repentant thief, was promised paradise that very day.

The kingships of this world show an immense love of power: but the kingship of Jesus was built on the immense power of love. And the characteristics of his kingdom are justice, peace and joy in the Holy Spirit.

A sense of the divine irony is needed to understand how the one who was mocked as the King of the Jews is in fact the King of the Universe: how the apparent weakness of this dying man is in fact the power of God giving new life to the world: how the foolishness of the man from the country, who is gobbled up by the connivings of the city, is in fact the wisdom of God, which sees beyond the petty plottings of today with the eyes of eternity.

Honouring Jesus as king is not an affair of waving banners and chanting his name. It means a commitment to working for a world of justice for all, as family equality demands: a world where might and violence no longer give the right to dominate: where there is a fair sharing of the resources of field and factory: where there are opportunities for all to grow in body, mind and spirit. Only in that just society may one write the slogan: God's Rule OK Here !

The first fruit of justice is the mood of reconciliation which enables peace to flourish: peace between people, peace with the environment, peace within lives and peace with God.

When peace flourishes, then faces will be bright with joy. And joy is a sure anticipation of heaven.

At the end of his journey, over his head they wrote, Jesus of Nazareth, King of the Jews.

We are called that the journey of our lives will write the words justice, peace and joy all over the world. Then we can sincerely say: Jesus of Nazareth, King of the Universe.

Second Reflection
The Prayer of the Kingdom
We will reflect on the Our Father as the prayer of the Kingdom. Jesus came to establish the Kingdom or Reign of God

on earth. To that end, he taught people, cast out demons, and healed people in soul and body. When his disciples asked him to teach them a prayer which would express their identity, what he taught them was the Our Father. Not so much as a prayer-formula to be recited by rote as the model of what our prayer should express.

We have already reflected on this prayer on the Seventeenth Sunday, but here we will concentrate on it as the prayer of the Kingdom.

The two key words of the prayer are 'Father' and 'Kingdom'. The title 'Father'. more than any other, expresses the relationship of God with us, set up in Jesus Christ. On God's side the relationship is born out of his love which creates us, wants us and provides for us. On our part, we are to recognise with gratitude what God has done for us and go forward in total confidence that he will continue to care and provide for us.

God is as near as Father, as intimate as the life-blood and genes that we have drawn from our earthly parents. And yet, in a divine contrast, God is mysterious, beyond our knowing, infinite and transcendent. So we say, 'Father ... who art in heaven.' God is as near as Father but as distant as heaven. Our minds must be lifted up beyond the things of this life, our hearts must expand in the glory of his blessed name ... 'hallowed be thy name.'

The second key word is 'Kingdom'. If 'Father' expresses the relationship of God with Jesus, 'Kingdom' expresses the work of Jesus. At the start of his mission, he announced that he had come to establish the reign, or Kingdom, of God on earth. To this end, he taught the people, cast out demons, and healed people in body and soul. His disciples would be Kingdom-people rather than followers of worldly values.

Just as God is at once both near and distant, so too the Kingdom belongs to the here and now, but its heavenly perfection is of the distant future. The Kingdom has been established by Jesus like a seed that is planted. In the power of the Spirit, it is alive and ever-growing; yet its perfection is not yet seen in the ugliness of sin that we witness every day. The great sigh of our soul at prayer is ... 'Come ... thy Kingdom come.'

The mass media of communication are avid for the sensational and are fascinated by evil. The good things that happen receive very little publicity. Too many people are unaware of the amount of goodness around us. They do not catch the breath of the Spirit nor do they see the stirrings of growth.

The people of the Kingdom rejoice in all that they see of the Kingdom every day, yet they are painfully aware of the extent of evil in the world. They long and sigh for the speedy growth of the seeds of goodness ... that the perfection of justice, peace and joy will hasten back to our world from the distant future. Their prayer is a constant sigh and invitation: 'Come ... come, Lord Jesus ... come, O Holy Spirit of growth ... come, may thy Kingdom come.'

The remainder of the Our Father is an expansion of this prayer. 'Thy will be done' interiorises the longing for the Kingdom. The social state of justice, peace and goodness must first be born in the hearts and souls of people. World peace begins in soul peace. Social justice must begin with personal repentance. The conversion of the world begins in my own life.

Two great dreams for hope in the world are then expressed: bread for everybody today, and total forgiveness.

We pray in total trust to our provident Father who already knows all that we need. Our petitions must not be self-seeking but expressions of our loving concern for all of God's people. The great messianic banquet is one of the favourite images of heaven. In our prayer we earnestly desire that this heavenly fullness will hurry back to our world and that everybody today will have adequate food and resources.

We pray that the happenings of the past, which have divided people and torn us apart interiorly, will be healed in perfect reconciliation. The key to healing is forgiveness – the love of God which continues to give in spite of previous rejection. And in the manner of God's forgiveness, may we too have that great love which will forgive those who have offended us.

The final petition is for perseverance in the way of the Kingdom. There will be temptations and obstacles set by the evil one. We humbly acknowledge our constant need of the Father's protection to lead us and deliver us.

Jesus Christ is our king. The Kingdom he established is our very life. We live amidst the struggles of life and with our own many imperfections. We hope to see the paradise promised to the repentant thief. Our pilgrimage towards the heavenly perfection of paradise comes together in one great prayer: 'Father, may your Kingdom come.'